Globalization and Third World Trade Unions:

The Challenge of Rapid Economic Change

Edited by **Henk Thomas**

u Ottawa
Bibliothèque de Droit
Brian Dickson
Law Library

Zed Books
LONDON AND NEW JERSEY

Globalization and Third World Trade Unions: The Challenge of Rapid Economic Change was first published by Zed Books Ltd, 7 Cynthia Street, London N1 9JF, UK, and 165 First Avenue, Atlantic Highlands, New Jersey 07716, USA, in 1995.

Copyright © Henk Thomas and individual contributors, 1995

Cover designed by Andrew Corbett
Set by Idiom, Plymouth
Printed and bound in the United Kingdom by Biddles Ltd, Guildford and King's Lynn

The rights of the editor and individual contributors of this work have been asserted by them in accordance with the Copyright, Designs and Patents Act, 1988.

A catalogue record for this book is available from the British Library.

US CIP data is available from the Library of Congress.

ISBN 1 85649 345 8 hb
ISBN 1 85649 346 6 pb

Contents

List of Tables

Preface

Although trade unionism continues to have a strong appeal as an instrument and symbol in the search for industrial and economic democracy, there is ample reason to ask whether trade unions will survive into the next century. For large parts of the world, particularly in Asia and Africa but also in South and Central America, this is no longer a question leading to an unequivocally affirmative answer.

The trade union movement in these continents is hardly equipped for the totally new challenges posed by phenomena like structural adjustment packages, the exclusion of labour national politics, the informalization and feminization of industry, flexibility in labour relations and the casualization of work. The earlier strength that was based on a long-standing record of achievement through collective bargaining, struggles for democracy and campaigns for international solidarity no longer exists.

Trade unions themselves are highly concerned about these developments, and such concerns are reflected particularly in the international institutions and networks around programmes of cooperation for training, education, research and local institution building.

This book originated in an extensive evaluation of one such programme, the Trade Union (international) Co-financing Programme of the two national labour federations in the Netherlands, Federatie Nederlandse Vakverenigingen (FNV) and Christelijk Nationaal Vakverbond (CNV). The programme is largely funded through development cooperation resources. The study was undertaken by an international team associated with the Institute of Social Studies (ISS), The Hague, which reported to Jan Pronk, Minister for Development Cooperation and through him to The Netherlands parliament.

The study dealt with projects, programmes, facts and trends from 1985 onwards. The reports that examined involvements in more than 50 countries in three continents resulted in 17 monographs – desk studies, field studies, background documents and policy recommendations.

The background documents became key inputs for the preparation of this book. Much attention was given to themes that have generally been dealt with inadequately in trade union studies: regional (that is, sub-continental or continental) labour-market developments, patterns of industrial reorganization and aspects of labour and work in the informal sector. These studies included continental overviews and country studies.

The first were multidisciplinary analyses of crucial factors which in essence define the space and relevance of the trade union movement in Asia, Latin America and Africa. The six country case studies then focused explicitly on an understanding of the strengths and weaknesses of trade unions in specific countries.

For Africa and Latin America it has been possible to adopt a continental approach; in Asia, at least three different sub-regions are to be distinguished. Only two country studies could be undertaken for each continent, due mainly to budgetary constraints.

In Asia, the cases of Malaysia and Pakistan represent the huge contrast between the highly impressive take-off stage of Southeast Asia and the relative stagnation that is still so widespread in South Asia. In both regions, but for different reasons, the outlook for the trade union movement appears to be gloomy. In Latin America, the Chilean and Venezuelan cases provide strong illustrations of development towards and away from democratization; these reflect the tenuous nature of the political situation in that continent and the difficulties which labour organization encounters. The overwhelming odds against the trade union movement, whether in the political, social or economic domains, form the basis for the selection of Zambia and Zimbabwe in Africa, the first with an historically strong labour movement, the latter with one that is just emerging as an independent organization.

The study owes thanks to many colleagues who ensured that great expertise on themes and countries mentioned above could be mobilized. First, I am extremely grateful for the great efforts made by Syed Hussein Ali, Charles Amjad-Ali, Paschal Mihyo, Patricio Frías, Domingo Mendez, Jaime Ruiz Tagle, Amrita Chhacchi, Freek Schiphorst, Dirk Kruijt, Kees Konings, E.A. Ramaswamy, and Frits Wils. They accepted the challenge to return to earlier drafts, rewrite and add new insights. I owe them an apology for imposing very tight limits on length in which to contribute their broad knowledge as close observers of trade union developments.

Many thanks go to colleagues in the Employment and Labour Studies programme at ISS who *de facto* converted my agenda of work into an informal sabbatical for six long months.

Robert Molteno, chief editor of ZED Books, London, was most encouraging and expressed once again a commitment to publish a book on the predicaments faced by working people in so many parts of the world. Wim Zoet, of the Netherlands Directorate General for Development Cooperation, made special efforts to ensure support from several departments. Karamat Ali, of the Pakistan Institute for Labour Education and Research, was available where possible with support and insights.

Many thanks go to Michel Hendriks for the skilful manner in which instruments of modern communication were applied to keep in touch with all authors. The way in which he prepared the manuscript for final editing was just superb. Gerry Schipperijn pitched in most professionally whenever there was a need for extra assistance.

Amin Kassam performed linguistic magic by wielding his (electronic) pen with precision during the final editing. My thanks to him for his comments on the content and for carrying out the difficult tasks of correcting grammar, ensuring conformity with the publisher's stylistic rules and rewriting as necessary, all while retaining the flavour of the original.

Lastly, instead of the usual thanks to people who have suffered during the preparation of this book, I would like to mention an informal support group. During a period which in the Netherlands coincided with the closest to a tropical summer since 1718 when statistics on weather conditions began to be collected and reported, Geertje, Ram, Dirk, Freek, Frits, Abbas, and Paschal left a lasting impact.

Henk Thomas

Institute of Social Studies, The Hague

Introduction

1. The Erosion of Trade Unions

Henk Thomas

Given the current global problems regarding employment, working conditions and labour organization, one would expect that the concept of trade unionism, in essence embodying a search for economic democracy, would still be as widely accepted as it has been for the past century; also, that the trade union movement would have more tasks at hand and therefore be as legitimate an institution as in the past.

Current trends however point in a different direction. Confusion and lack of clarity with respect to roles and possibilities are apparent. While for more than a century the trade union movement has been an important actor in defending the interests of workers and in struggling for independence and democracy, it now faces in large parts of the world almost total elimination as a significant social institution.

Highly unfavourable trends have taken place, particularly in Asia, Africa and Latin America. In East Asia, for instance, unprecedented rapid industrialization has been achieved along with oppression of labour organization. In Africa overwhelming problems are being faced by the labour movement in the absence of feasible industrialization, whereas in Latin America the trade union movement has to define completely new roles due to adjustments in macro-economic policy making. To make matters worse, the impact of organized labour has been much reduced and seriously eroded in industrialized countries during the last two decades, first in the United States of America and later also in Western Europe. With the emergence of a global economy and world-wide capital markets, the international labour movement has been weakened significantly.

This book explores the depth of the current crisis in the labour movement by focusing on some strategic economic, social and political dimensions in a number of major regions of Asia, Africa and Latin America. This approach reveals in particular major predicaments faced in national labour markets by men and women in their search for employment and decent earnings. The deep crisis of identity faced by the trade union movement may well be related to a failure to address these labour-market problems. Probably equally important, however, is the current global acceptance of new forms of industrial organization and management practices which have no place for the traditional adversarial role of the trade union movement.

This chapter begins with two sections analysing these dominant trends which are currently eroding the role that trade unions can play at all: on the one hand, industrial reorganization and new management strategies and on the other hand the destabilization of labour markets. The next section briefly reviews past research on international and comparative Third World labour relations and trade union aspects. A concluding section lays out the format of the study.

The book is in three parts, each consisting of a continental study and two case studies. An attempt is made to analyse national labour movements in the context of the complexity of their own country, and to locate the analysis in the wider geographical region to which the country belongs. The hypothesis is that such an approach is more fruitful than a direct linking of local trade union developments to global structures. A concluding section highlights the main findings and suggests some policy implications.

Industrial reorganization and human resource management

The history of the trade union movement is deeply rooted in processes of industrialization that have developed very unevenly in countries around the world since the industrial revolution began in Great Britain.[1] A convenient method of analysing these unequal beginnings has been to distinguish between early starters, latecomers and late-latecomers. For instance, late-latecomers like the second tier of newly industrializing countries (NICs) in South East Asia may industrialize at higher speeds than latecomers due to lessons drawn from their experiences; but they still need to win new positions in a highly competitive market (Gerschenkron 1962; Kaplinsky 1984; Sutcliffe 1971; Weiss 1993).

As in advanced industrialized countries, national policies were of crucial importance in Third World countries for the promotion of industry and for the formation and control of labour through industrial relations legislation. A clear illustration of this close association between trade unions and modern economic sectors has been the history of the labour movement in India which, as Ramaswamy states, '... is intimately linked with the protectionist economic policies followed by the government for forty years' (Ramaswamy 1995). The specific characteristics of industrialization have to be taken into account for an understanding of the trade union situation in any particular country.

In the past the development of industry and the formation of labour in different countries usually passed through clearly defined phases. Mostly, the analysis of industrialization patterns concentrated on the advantages and disadvantages of, respectively, an import-substitution and an export-oriented strategy. Completely new issues are currently being raised due to the impact of the Japanese model of industrial organization and the introduction of new labour–management practices.

Import substitution and export orientation

In countries such as India, Brazil and Mexico, to mention some of the clearest examples, the labour movement could reap considerable benefits as long as an import substitution industrialization (ISI) strategy provided protection and predictability in domestic markets.

First, as industrialization proceeded under protective conditions gradual shifts from labour-intensive industries, such as textiles and leather, to capital-intensive ones, like engineering and capital goods, took place in numerous countries. The transformation was accompanied by changing patterns of work organization, employment creation, skill formation and international linkages (for example, through technology transfers).

Second, protection of workers was often much enhanced as, with import substitution, the state frequently became heavily involved in the economy as owner of strategic enterprises in the public sector. Its key motivation, for example in Turkey, India, Nigeria and Mexico, was to generate an industrial momentum in order to accelerate development. Mostly under such circumstances, the trade union movement was favourably placed to build powerful positions in collective bargaining processes in these parastatal enterprises. Regrettably, such positions were used also to put undue pressures on the management of such enterprises resulting in overemployment and in wage structures that diverged considerably from the ones that would have resulted from market functioning. Labour legislation, often shaped after the model of the colonial powers, was implemented to regulate industrial relations institutions and collective bargaining patterns.

The complete turnabout towards export oriented industrialization (EOI) came in the 1980s, with the failure of the ISI strategy. The process was also fostered by ideological, neoliberal preferences for free markets and the assumed *laissez-faire* character of the successful East Asian model. This change, of course, had a deep impact on systems of industrial relations that had developed for decades in close cooperation with the state. The availability of cheap labour, including child labour, and discriminatory treatment of women became crucial in the struggle to conquer international markets. Naturally, the oppression and control of labour organization formed an important part of this strategy of industrialization. Typically, the trade union movement in Latin America and South Asia that could earlier develop rather strongly under ISI found itself on the defensive. In East Asia, there was no emergence of a strong trade union movement at all.

It appears that these well-known strategies and concepts that have been so useful in analysing past developments and defining policy options are about to become obsolete. From the perspective of industrial organization – the organization of enterprises in larger systems and markets – and due to innovative management practices, hitherto unknown phenomena have begun in a major way to influence the potential for industrial development and the roles that trade unions can play.

Economic successes, for instance, nowadays presumably depend on characteristics such as dynamic comparative advantages, availability of entrepreneurial talent, quality of institutional infrastructure, size of domestic markets and access to technology. These typically belong to the field of industrial organization to which we will now turn.

Industrial reorganization

One may, in an historic perspective, distinguish three major stages, and thus three models, of industrial organization: a British variant of capitalism with emphasis on owner control, the American variant of capitalism laying all accent on the key role of management, and the Japanese model characterized by huge networks of firms, financial institutions, and close links with state institutions that play a crucial role in formulating and implementing legislative systems (Chandler 1977, 1990).

Lazonick, building on Chandler's work in an outstanding synthesizing study, has argued that the dynamic developments of capitalism can only be understood as the outcomes of major successive, and each time superior, innovations in organization rather than as the results of anonymous market forces. He distinguishes three models, of 'proprietary capitalism', 'managerial capitalism' and 'collective capitalism', which represent the successive stages of technological and innovative superiority (Lazonick 1991).[2]

The superiority of each model is expressed in the lowering of costs per unit of product and thus the conquering of national, international and ultimately global markets. Each of these models can be linked to specific characteristics of industrial relations patterns and thus trade union involvement.[3]

Proprietary capitalism has been implemented most consistently in Britain, the cradle of the industrial revolution during the 19th century (Lazonick 1991: 23–7). The growth of craft-based industries with close alliances between management and ownership of firms in specific geographical regions has been the hallmark of this model. These institutional features were ultimately instrumental in the decline of the British industrial hegemony. The organizational segmentation between top management and employees, the shopfloor control over production by a workforce organized along craft-based lines, and the underdeveloped nature of managerial coordination, created an environment which provided both employers and senior workers with strong incentives to ensure the survival of the firm by squeezing as much productivity as possible out of existing technologies. As international competition forced a lowering of unit costs of production and management did not innovate sufficiently, the squeezing of labour costs formed the key strategy to remain competitive. As a result, the trade union craft model typically belongs to the British model of industrial organization.

Managerial capitalism, because of superior management and separation of ownership structures from day-to-day management, succeeded in creating national and ultimately global enterprises (Lazonick 1991: 27–36). National and global markets could be captured by the lowering of unit costs of production. However, in contrast to the British model, the American variant allows for higher wages and, in spite of low union densities, permits active industrial and craft trade union postures, thereby providing incentives for management to innovate continuously. The state needs to play a crucial role through huge investments in education, whereas trade unions are fully incorporated and controlled in a package deal which includes rapidly rising wages as well as a worsening of human and participatory conditions under mass production. The prerogatives of management in essence do not allow for any participatory role of the labour leadership, and unions are confined to antagonistic bargaining for higher wages and better working conditions. It goes without saying that this model has found wide acceptance globally.

Collective capitalism is a recent description of the third model. The losing of markets to Japan and other East Asian countries was originally ascribed to their excessive exploitation of labour, and thus lower unit costs of production,[4] but with time different views began to emerge. The rapid growth of real earnings, the technological lead in many areas and the sustained force with which the East Asian industries conquered global markets called for a more sophisticated explanation. This new watershed in the history of industrial capitalist organization has gradually come to be accepted with new conceptualizations, such as

'The Second Industrial Divide' (Piore and Sabel 1984), 'The New Competition' (Best 1990), 'Toyotism' (Womack *et al.* 1990) and 'collective capitalism' (Lazonick 1991). These authors and many other observers point to the superior impact of enterprise networks along with other institutions, flexibilities through sub-contracting, and major organizational restructuring which in particular is characterized by continuous technological innovation. Dynamic industrial (and service) sectors are established, which are fed by inherent innovation as a powerful force in itself. Continuing human resource development in the context of human-resource management practices forms an integral part of this model (Dore 1989). The institutional basis for consultative and consensus-based decision making is permanent, or lifetime, employment. Workers need to become partners rather than adversaries of management for the system to function successfully. As for trade unions, their only role is one of critical but constructive cooperation.

Summing up, one may state that through highly sophisticated forms of institutional networking and human resources management, the Japanese model has overtaken previous models in lowering production unit costs, and is now being copied in other parts of the world. These days even traditional industrial strongholds, particularly in Germany and the United States of America, have begun to compete with Japanese firms on their own terms, namely the application of the new, superior methods. This approach towards industrial development matches well with the thoughts of classical economists, in particular those of Marx and Schumpeter, who took dynamic changes rather than market equilibria as the framework for their analyses.[5]

From a developmental perspective, this new pattern of industrial organization may be highly frustrating, particularly for late-latecomers and those countries where industries are struggling to overcome the setbacks of the 1980s mostly as a result of failed import substitution and forced adaptations under structural adjustment packages. As an increasing number of economic sub-branches is expected to be controlled by an ever smaller number of large conglomerates, each with its own dynamics and oligopolistic tendencies, it appears as if a continuing diminishing space will be available for the remaining countries.

Probably for medium, small-scale and micro-enterprises in a limited number of product lines, it will be possible to maintain positions of some stability in markets which will be increasingly conquered by the large international conglomerates, located mainly in the United States of America, some European countries and Japan. A number of large domestic markets, for example, Brazil, India, China, Mexico, Nigeria and South Africa, will also provide this possibility.

A likely outcome will be that large numbers of relatively small, if not very small, firms will engage in cut-throat competition instead of building cooperative networks. In other words, there exists a considerable risk that the less efficient British model of clustering of individual self-owned firms in local regions will be followed. Preference should be given to an array of effective policy interventions that form adaptations of the sophisticated Japanese model of networking of enterprises into coherent marketing strategies.[6]

The implications for the trade union movement are severe. In essence, the issue is whether an efficient and competitive economic base in Third World countries can be established at all. If not, then the labour force will remain highly fragmented in different segments of informal economies that are squeezed badly.

The threat to trade unions is not only that their very economic base will be extremely difficult to establish and maintain. Through new human-resource management practices, management will compete with the unions for the loyalty of workers, as the enterprise seems to hold out the best possibility of providing them with benefits.[7] The instruments used by management to secure such deepened loyalties are well known: lifetime employment, personal commitment to the enterprise, payment systems according to results achieved and, above all, promotion to higher ranks through internal recruitment.

This trend is the more threatening as medium and large enterprises will also introduce flexibilities in the workforce, and in so doing reduce the number of tenured workers. Whether trade unions can adjust to these major changes in the labour market remains to be seen.

Early transformations of organizational systems were largely related to similar, and high, levels of industrialization and development. These had undergone similar processes, first of political emancipation, then of social distribution, and finally of economic involvement and redistribution in the framework of macro-economic Keynesian management of national economies. Today, relatively small countries that have not acquired experience in this field face huge problems in designing adequate industrial strategies. Such designing includes both the more familiar issues of trade and industrialization policies, static and dynamic comparative advantages, and access to large markets, as well as completely new issues of policy making and institution building to confront the threats of international 'new competition'.

Supply versus demand; growth or equity?

A second fundamental issue concerns the question of whether trade unions hold sufficiently strong positions in labour markets to be involved at all in an effective manner in bargaining and consultative procedures.[8]

Since the trade union movement around the world had been heavily influenced by and is still closely linked with the much stronger trade union movement in the advanced industrialized countries, it is important to note that there, too, major setbacks have been faced during the past two decades. These setbacks relate particularly to changes in labour markets and are worth brief analysis from a comparative perspective.

At high levels of industrialization, the labour movement's central concern in recent decades, particularly in Western Europe, has been with the shaping and implementation of welfare states and the distribution of its benefits. A hidden assumption here for a long time has been that a fundamental condition for this, a high degree of employment, would be fulfilled. At times of downward movement of the business cycle and even structural weakening of national economies, the state is expected to ensure that the labour force continues to receive an adequate income.

In exchange for restraint in wage claims at the micro level in various economic branches, the workers obtained major benefits through the welfare-state mechanisms that formed an integral part of aggregate income and demand policies. Whether in a market form, as developed in the United States of America, or with corporatist variations, such as in Western Europe, the labour movement came to accept the societal inequalities in power structures.

This well-known Keynesian approach was pursued to its limits. In Eastern Europe the welfare state associated with a command economy broke down completely in the late 1980s. It simply could not cope any more with the requirements of a modern society. In Western Europe also, structural changes in the economy occurred so fast that massive unemployment resulted. This trend led to fiscal crises for states while oversized and ineffective bureaucracies were no longer able to manage the welfare-state programmes in a cost-effective manner.

An important indicator of the major changes in European labour markets is the demand for migrant labour. In contrast to the late 1950s and 1960s when immigration was encouraged all over Western Europe to reduce tensions in the labour market, since the 1970s the labour market has been characterized by disincentives and negative attitudes towards immigration.

The impact of this complete turnabout is undoubtedly a major factor in explaining the heavy drop in union membership and reduced bargaining effectiveness experienced by the labour movement. This adverse trend has had a deep impact also at the supranational level. It forms an important element in explaining the weak articulation of social policy issues in the emerging European Union.

The situation in Third World countries has been, for the most part, far worse. Here welfare-state mechanisms are largely absent while the preoccupation of policy makers with macro-economic balances has left little space to pay attention also to the creation of employment and labour-market issues.

Whereas till the late 1970s the absorption capacity of new industries and modern services might, admittedly with a high degree of unfounded optimism, be said to have displayed acceptable employment elasticities, the 1980s showed that deep imbalances had become a fundamental characteristic of the labour market in most of Asia, Africa and South and Central America. The emergence of large urban informal economies, massive rural underemployment and new migratory patterns are vivid symptoms of the seriousness of the labour-market situation.

Worse, due to the technological breakthroughs on the demand side and unfavourable demographic trends on the supply side, it appears that further weakening of labour-market situations is to be expected for at least another decade in large parts of the Third World.

A major factor of macro-economic management, whether in South Asia, most of Africa, or most of Latin America, has been a sustained adherence to structural adjustment packages. These policies have focused largely on deregulation of markets, on a *laissez-faire* policy towards industries to be exposed to international competition, with the risk, as Hans Singer observes sharply,'... that in a headlong rush for deregulation and flexibility of labour markets the baby of productive employment will be thrown out with the bathwater of rigidity' (Singer 1991: vi).

Standing and Tokman (1991) have produced a first comprehensive synthesis of recent research in which they argue for a search towards a new macro-economic framework. Such a framework should be supply-oriented, and thus conducive to growth, instead of Keynesian and demand-oriented; the latter has for too long been accepted as a guideline to ensure social focus in macro-economic policies.

Different forms of Keynesianism, such as Scandinavian, Austrian and an American market variation, all relate to circumstances which even under favourable circumstances have resulted in a situation where

> ... structural change, hindered through its focus on the preservation of stability, ... in the longer term leads to an erosion of technological competitiveness. (Standing and Tokman 1991: 12)

Given the much more unfavourable situation in developing countries, and with reference to a decade of structural adjustment practices, Standing states the need for a new theory eloquently:

> So we are faced with a questionable macro-economic model, and a micro-level analysis that is institutionally impoverished and misleading. It is time to rethink. (Standing and Tokman 1991: 45)

Clearly a new assessment of the labour-market situation in different parts of the world is a high priority. A major first step is the acquisition of knowledge regarding the functioning of local labour markets to obtain frameworks for policy options in fields such as vocational training, education programmes, wage policies and policy interventions in the informal sector.[9] These findings should then be related to national labour markets to ensure that issues of employment and working conditions will form an integral part of macro-economic policy formulation. The analysis should be integrated within a framework of international labour markets to understand the broader trends of development, industrialization, technological development and issues such as regional political formations and international migratory patterns.

Any search for a new framework of macro-economic management in Third World countries should thus take current developments in labour markets as its point of departure. Fortunately, extensive insights have been gained already on important categories of work.

First, the earlier relatively simplistic approach of considering the informal economy a part of dual urban structures has been improved upon. From an economic perspective, the differentiation between production in households, micro-enterprises and informal small-scale firms is nowadays taken as a point of departure for the analysis of the informal sector and the need for differentiation in policy designs and interventions. Such policy differentiation would depend upon, for example, whether the activities serve only to combat poverty as a survival strategy, or whether there exist some stable forms of productive organization which have a potential for growth and further development.[10]

From a social and labour-market perspective, the huge variations in labour segmentation (for example, according to ethnic, religious and gender characteristics) have been found to form deeply ingrained characteristics of urban labour markets (Scoville 1991).

Research on rural labour markets has shown that in large parts of South Asia local institutions still exercise excessive forms of control over rural workers, thereby hampering opportunities for skill formation and improvement of working conditions. The mirror image of this fossilized pattern of rural labour markets consists of forced, circular or external migration as the only outlet for those who no longer have access to them.

A second issue of strategic importance relates to the limited employment-generating capacity of medium- and large-scale industry. As the trade union movement is generally directly linked with these enterprises, it comes as no surprise to find that structural adjustment, with its emphasis on market performance, international competitiveness, efficiency and cost effectiveness, has rendered severe blows to the labour movement. Both privatization of public enterprises and the exposure of previously protected industries to international competition have posed huge threats to the survival of numerous firms; in the process, of course, the labour movement's very basis of existence has been deeply eroded without an alternative source of strength having been developed to replace it.

A third issue concerns the controversy regarding labour regulation and protection of work. Just as in the informal sector, categories of vulnerable workers exist which at higher levels of welfare would be a prime object for protective labour legislation. We refer here to a range of poverty-related phenomena such as child labour, excessive working hours, the absence of safety and health regulations, absence of legal protection in a contractual sense and, above all, to the casualization of work. Under these circumstances, trade unions have almost no option but to oppose structural adjustment policies which delete current systems of rights and justice in production without substituting them with any other social policy framework.

The impacts of these developments differ in the main regions of the Third World. For instance, labour-market research in Africa shows dramatic falls in real wages for a workforce which is shrinking rapidly due to the privatization of public enterprises as well as actual deindustrialization. Throughout Latin America, in almost all countries, a switch-over from import substitution to export orientation has taken place subsequent to the debt crisis. Where previously organized labour could obtain certain national-level benefits through negotiations with the state in exchange for ensuring peaceful labour relations at shopfloor level, with export orientation such trade-offs are no longer possible.[11]

Widely diverging patterns are found in Asia. For instance, in East Asia, a serious controversy exists regarding the role of gender discrimination and whether labour has paid an excessive price in terms of lower wages than would be warranted by the region's rapid growth. The precise way in which labour markets have functioned is particularly relevant for Southeast Asia, which till now has adopted a largely labour-intensive strategy of development and industrialization. Again, the question may be raised whether existing inequalities in income and wealth could not have been reduced to achieve the same growth and efficiency. South Asian labour markets, meanwhile, are facing enormous difficulties in almost all aspects, rural and urban as well as public and private. Deep segmentation and large un- and underemployment defy any search for short-term solutions. Probably a long-term human-resources development strategy forms one of the few realistic policy options with which the trade union movement could align itself.

The foregoing sketch explains why a considerable risk exists that organized labour may lose its historical national stature. Its traditional economic branches offer only very modest employment opportunities; new constituencies in informal urban and rural labour markets have hardly developed; and there has been insufficient awareness of the structural way in which fragmentation and segmentation of the labour force have become deeply ingrained in many countries.

Third World trade union studies

What are the consequences of these widely differing patterns of industrialization, of variations in macro-economic conditions and in labour-market situations for current analysis of Third World trade unionism?

In the past much attention has been given to political and social aspects of trade unionism, understandably so given the role of trade unions before and after decolonization.[12] Through close contacts with governments, often characterized as forms of corporatism, trade unions managed to play relatively strong political roles in eking out privileged positions for their members.

Today, the harsh new circumstances call for a higher priority to be given to the analysis of the economics of Third World trade unionism. There is a need for a well-defined multidisciplinary approach which would pay adequate attention from an economic perspective to industrial relations and labour-market developments.

Any future for 'industrial' relations?
In the past trades unions' structures and characteristics were defined largely in terms of national institutions and industrialization patterns (Regini 1992; Southall 1988a and b).[13] Elaborate national industrial-relations systems became established around the world. Significant benefits could be obtained, sizeable constituencies and respectable union densities were built up, and in many situations the trade union movement was respected as a national actor. Currently, negative developments are taking place on all counts.

An almost complete erosion of possible action strategies has occurred in Third World countries. With structural adjustment the state is no longer in a position to share benefits. The ceremonial side of collective bargaining, whether or not in the form of corporatist state controls, may still be there but any nominal wage increases are more than neutralized by subsequent inflationary pressures. Instead of benefits, trade unions receive messages of retrenchment, reductions in tenured employment and worsening contractual conditions. This of course means that even the trusted bonds with their own constituencies have suffered.

As noted above, the key sectors forming the traditional recruiting ground for trade unions have been mostly medium- and large-scale industry, mining, banking, insurance and transport sectors, often in parastatal organizations. In most of the Third World a number of factors has prevented trade unions from expanding in ways similar to those in industrialized countries. First, these traditional sectors have remained of modest importance in economies with a large rural base. Second, in a number of countries structural adjustments have decimated public-sector employment. Third, trade union organization is heavily constrained or forbidden in the dwindling public sector of many countries. Expansion of the trade union movement into other domains such as small-scale enterprises, the informal sector or household work, while theoretically possible, till now has hardly taken place on a large scale. In other words, the legitimization of the trade union movement has become an issue of concern.

Finally, traditional goodwill no longer exists in large parts of society. In East Asia, for instance, rapid industrialization took place with explicit trade union exclusion from policy involvement. In Africa especially, a relatively strong trade union movement was in no way prepared for the battering it received as a result of structural adjustment policies. Increasingly, trade unions that had been accustomed to being accepted as social partners in national policy making began to face an antagonistic climate as they resisted changes without formulating alternative strategies. From now on, particularly with the expansion of the Japanese model, there will be less and less scope for trade unions that do not have a sound base in firm- and sector-specific domains.

To summarize, a major risk exists that traditional trade union strategies of involvement primarily in national issues are no longer opportune. Industrialization reaches from the global and regional to micro-enterprises and household work in the informal economy.

Regional and local labour markets

Today and in the foreseeable future it appears that a new rationale needs to be defined in which key labour-market issues such as segmentation, un- and underemployment, household work and poverty are taken on as direct challenges. The trade union movement otherwise risks being reduced to a marginal societal phenomenon. Human resource development, in the sense of preparing people to be better equipped to function in labour markets, has become the slogan of the day and is probably the only feasible strategy to combat unemployment and mass poverty.

It goes without saying that the large and increasing proportion of workers who are engaged in various categories of informal work relations, and who are the victims of casualization of work in medium- and large-scale enterprises, represents a further problem to trade union recruitment. Union strength is also eroded by management successes in dividing the workforce. This observation is pertinent to most developing countries but currently applies also to large parts of the industrially advanced regions of the world.

It was shown above that in advanced industrialized countries trade unions derive their strength largely from tight labour markets. Only in the context of such markets has it been possible to engage effectively in national issues of distribution, training and education, and to defend the position of weak and well-defined segments, such as handicapped people and young recruits. Such conditions allow for careful monitoring and targeted action programmes.

In large parts of the world, however, national labour markets are not monitored and steered in such a manner; the administrative capacity is not available and the database at best very weak. Furthermore, labour markets are connected closely with wider geographical regions through migratory patterns. It is not unthinkable that with globalization of major markets, new and significant migratory flows will become a permanent labour-market characteristic. For instance, mobility and migration in and between countries has become a significant aspect of labour-market performance in Africa. Migratory patterns in Central America, such as those between Mexico and the USA, have a long history, but new flows, like those between Colombia and Venezuela, are noticeable. In East Asia and the Pacific, migration, whether temporary or permanent, forms a significant aspect of labour markets.

As larger trading blocs are likely to be formed in all continents, it goes without saying that it will become increasingly difficult for national trade unions to build effective strength in negotiations.

The seriousness of this situation in large parts of the Third World is the more alarming since major changes have also been noticed in traditionally tight labour markets. In the advanced industrialized countries as a result, much research focuses on exploration of future trends and the dilemmas which the trade union movement is facing.[14]

New approaches are called for in times 'of institutional upheaval and renewal, when traditional models of union growth lose much of their explanatory power' (Strauss *et al.*, 1991: 35).

In the absence of coherent national labour and employment policies in Third World countries, the characteristics of local, sub-national markets that are intimately connected with regional, supra-national ones, may well have greater impact on workers than their association with probably non-existing or very weakly defined national labour markets. If such is the case, it calls obviously for a deep transformation of the trade union movement that is mostly oriented towards national issues.

Nature of data and sources

A last methodological aspect concerns the shortage of reliable data which has generally hampered research efforts in Third World countries with a few exceptions such as India and Chile. We refer here to information on trade union membership patterns, strike behaviour (number of workers involved, duration), unemployment, inflation, wage trends and productivity as indicators to sketch the behaviour and impact of collective labour actions.[15] With the availability of such information over a number of years, a new development in comparative studies, namely the application of innovative quantitative methods to a field that hitherto has been highly qualitative in its methodological approaches, will be possible.[16]

Record of studies

The arguments for separate Third World analysis have not yet been generally accepted. For instance, in 1972, in a postscript to their classic *Industrialism and Industrial Man*, Kerr, Dunlop, Harbison and Myers expressed the view that:

> ... industrial systems, regardless of the cultural background out of which they emerge and the path they originally follow, tend to become more alike over an extended period of time; that systems, whether under middle-class or communist or dynastic leadership, move to-wards 'pluralistic industrialism' where the state, the enterprise or association, and the individual all share a substantial degree of power and influence over productive activities. (Kerr *et al.* 1972: 296)

They were convinced of a long-term global convergence of industrial systems embodying 'the general direction of change'.[17]

The impact of their approach and conceptualization, through project involvements in 35 countries in all continents, is a well-known case of cultural domination originating in the United States of America. The structure of the International Labour Organization (ILO) and the global respect for collective bargaining procedures, even if they are of a purely ceremonial character, are evidence of the strength with which these views were propagated.

A first attempt to recognize global differentiation was undertaken at the International Institute for Labour Studies (IILS) at the ILO in Geneva, where an ambitious research project had been started on 'future industrial relations with the objective of clarifying thinking about probable developments and *alternative* [emphasis added] futures for industrial relations in the mid-1980s' (Cox, Harrod *et al.* 1972: iii). A recognition of either a very long process towards convergence or even long-term divergence was thus implicit in this huge research effort in which industrial relations were defined

> as social relations of production which would thus include unorganized as well as formally organised systems, rural as well as urban labour, etc. (Cox, Harrod *et al.* 1972: iii)

Taking a theoretical framework developed by Cox as the point of departure, different patterns of social relations of production were identified for a dozen major regions in the world. A four-volume series by Cox and Harrod at a later stage was to provide the further deepening of theoretical reflection as well as a comprehensive analysis of different patterns of social relations. Different patterns could thus co-exist simultaneously in one country, whereas over time deep changes in the national mixture could take place. In their approach, trade unions only figure prominently in some modalities, such as tripartite and bipartite bargaining, or corporatist structures and may be completely absent from other forms, such as enterprise market and household systems. Due to the long gestation period of this ambitious attempt to redefine industrial relations as labour relations in a global sense, regrettably no conclusive assessment of the Cox–Harrod approach is possible till today.

NIDL and NILS
A direct focus on Third World labour in the context of global exploitative labour relations, in essence from a radical or Marxist origin, emerges in the late 1970s and 1980s. The work by Fröbel, Heinrichs and Kreye looks at the dynamic patterns of capital accumulation in a global perspective as the premise for a newly emerging global, highly unequal (when comparing centre to periphery) distribution of production systems. These in turn lead to a global formation of labour markets, to a 'world market for labour power' (Fröbel *et al.* 1981), to controlled migratory flows and to the generation of reserve armies of potential workers, to mention only a

few of the concepts that play a central role in this approach (ibid.; Wallerstein 1983).

In this approach much attention falls on issues such as the role of transnational corporations, often associated with so-called free production zones, and the impact of foreign direct investments and of technology transfers. The Third World, with the exception of a small group of newly industrializing countries (NICs) in East Asia, was doomed to play only a subordinate role. The analysis of reproductive work, of subsistence and household production and of the role which women's work plays in the global economy forms an integral part of this global theory at micro level (Mies 1982).[18]

This new international division of labour (NIDL) formed a stimulant for the 'new international labour studies' (NILS) which considered the formation, segmentation and articulation of labour and labour organization in the Third World as determined by the dominant forces of the NIDL, and devoted much attention to Third World trade unionism (Cohen 1980, 1991; Southall 1988a, 1988b; Waterman 1993).

The NILS undertook research on key labour themes in a number of countries in Africa, Latin America and Asia (Munck 1988; Southall 1988a, 1988b; Cohen 1991). For instance, labour protest, industrial democracy, labour and the state and, of course trade union patterns were analysed, with illustrations from a rather eclectic choice of available case study materials in order to obtain global insights.

In Latin American labour studies, for example, the concept of 'political unionism' was critically examined from a 'labour process' perspective. And in African labour studies a new debate was introduced on the old theme of the existence of a 'labour aristocracy' (Southall 1988a).

The colonial heritage figures prominently in this stage, and these studies often adopt a distinct national and historic orientation in the chosen methodology. The focus on other categories of work such as plantation work, agricultural labour, and of course colonial mining history, provided much information on which to build the studies; furthermore, labour relations in informal production became an innovative theme which was obvious given the rapidly increasing popularity of the informal-sector conceptualization.

Clearly this approach, in testing so many concepts in different non- or less industrialized situations, has shown that any restriction of labour relations to industrial relations in these countries would be misplaced. One may state somewhat cynically that the NILS approach has yielded an interesting mixture of radical concepts and new case studies that serve to develop new hypotheses and questions for subsequent research efforts.[19]

An interesting new direction recently has been explored through an institutional approach towards Third World labour studies. A group of researchers, mainly associated with European institutions, was brought together by Rodgers under the sponsorship of the same IILS that 20 years earlier had initiated the project on future industrial relations systems. This approach wishes to identify with great precision the complexity of labour issues and work through a focus on institutions (and actors). Rodgers argues for five categories as adequate analytical tools for labour, employment and development analysis: '1) organizations, 2) formal labour market institutions, 3) informal labour market institutions, 4) underlying formal social rules, and 5) underlying informal social rules' (Rodgers *et al.* forthcoming: 3).

A research programme, associated with both the IILS and the European Association of Development Research and Training Institutes, has begun to yield a first harvest of case studies; these studies refer mainly to an institutional analysis of segments of labour markets in Asian countries, particularly India (Rodgers *et al.* forthcoming).[20]

Interestingly enough, the new field of institutional economics with its emphasis on transaction costs, actors and agents has induced this new direction. Rodgers and others seek to explore the identity of institutions by referring to the 'neo-institutionalist' school as well as the French regulationist school (Aglietta 1987).[21] An extension of this literature from a labour, gender and work perspective could be valuable, because it provides a lead for a stronger focus on inequalities in power that originate in labour-market fragmentation.

Recent research by Konings on labour protest in Cameroon, by Hashim on the relationships between state and trade unions in a corporatist framework, and by Schiphorst on workers' participation in Zimbabwean factories are examples of a new methodology that applies both quantitative and qualitative data with rigorous adherence to disciplinary methods.[22] This approach may well indicate that Third World labour and trade union studies need no longer be defended as a separate field of inquiry. Rather, the study of trade unions in various continents, just like that of other issues of labour, work and employment, begins to form an important chapter of global and comparative labour, and thus trade union, studies. In our view Deyo's approach to studying labour issues in a region which includes a number of countries provides an important example for further research as it examines the labour situation from different disciplinary perspectives in a wide geographical territory.[23] This approach avoids the pitfalls of narrow descriptive studies of labour issues that become biased through a national focus; on the other hand, it does not reach out towards all-encompassing global concepts that derive from ideological preferences and biases rather than rigorous research.

Conclusions

In this chapter it has been argued that changing patterns of industrial organization as well as changing labour-market conditions currently pose fundamental dilemmas for labour organization.

In the greater part of the Third World these trends pose such challenges that no smooth transition will be possible from a largely political and social orientation towards a trade union strategy which addresses socio-economic problems at macro, meso and micro levels.

An argument has been presented for a new methodology towards the study of trade unions that is based on a balanced input from various social sciences; however, the dramatic changes in organizational and economic realities call for extra attention to be given to the aspects of industrial organization and labour-market analysis.

This book attempts, through its composition and presentation of new realities in Asia, Latin America and Africa, to provide an adequate framework for the investigation of current dilemmas which trade unions are facing particularly in the Third World. It attempts to identity significant trends, whether of a political, economic or social nature, in continental or sub-continental regions.

For each continent two case studies have been selected in order to allow both for comparisons between continents as well as between countries in these regions, The selection has been made according to regional differences in Asia, reflecting different societal involvements in Latin America, and corresponding to political differences in Africa. Malaysia and Pakistan have been studied as illustrations of the huge differences in development found in Asia. The Latin America study contains an analysis of the labour movements in Chile and Venezuela, the first facing growth with reduction of poverty, and the latter, in spite of its rich natural resources, particularly oil, experiencing the worst urban poverty and political instability. Given the prominent political role played by trade unions in Africa in the past, the Zambia and Zimbabwe case studies stand for other experiences as well. In Zambia, a traditionally strong trade union movement, particularly in articulating political demands, has completely lost its economic base, whereas in Zimbabwe a young labour movement is attempting to free itself from corporatist state controls.

In this way an attempt is made to test whether, through a focus on large geographical regions which display commonalities in terms of economic characteristics, insights can be gained that otherwise would be given inadequate attention. Comparative and comprehensive information on three categories of indicators – basic information, labour indicators and social indicators – for each of the three continents is given in the Statistical Appendix (see pp. 249–52).

Trends that currently are given much attention in specific regions have been highlighted in the various chapters, in particular the continental overviews. In the case of Asia, for example, issues of ethnicity, militarism and feminization of industrialization are addressed as separate themes. For Latin America, the changing roles of trade unions and the state (that is, corporatist relationships) have received special focus, while in the case of Africa, the major disturbances in labour markets, as reflected in migratory patterns and growth of informal-sector activities, have been singled out for special attention. In all three continents, the dwindling formal sector plays a role, along with rapid expansion of informal labour relations both in formal sectors and in informal economic relationships.

Third World trade unions cannot be compared in a simple manner under conditions where there is no welfare state and stable dynamic patterns of industrialization are lacking. The diversity of conditioning factors, whether of an economic, political, or social nature, is so large that 'divergent labour systems' (Deyo 1989) rather than convergence are to be expected in the foreseeable future.[24] Naturally, such a finding would be enormously important for assessing the role that trade unions can, in fairness, be asked to play in developmental processes.

Notes

1. 'Industrialization' also refers to modern organization in the services sectors, that is, banking and insurance, transport and public services.

2. From within a wide range of literature, we draw in particular on Lazonick (1991) as he views the role of labour to be one of the central elements in capitalist development; for the most part, the labour factor hardly figures in other studies as more than an abundant production factor, or an abstract element of human capital formation and skill development (for example, Chandler 1990).

3. The following sections attempt to summarize and paraphrase some of the key arguments that play a central role in Lazonick's study (1991).

4. This interpretation typically fitted into the 'ISI versus EOI' approach. In this view the Japanese successes were caused by extreme labour exploitation, illegal copying of technologies, and dumping of products in international markets.

5. Lazonick in particular takes issue with Williamson who, as Lazonick argues, in essence takes neoclassical equilibrium analysis as the framework for this theory (Lazonick 1991: 206–27).

6. See, for example, Schmitz and Musyck (1994); this argument is also elaborated upon by Thomas and Hendriks (1994).

7. See Ramaswamy (1994) on this issue of the loyalty of workers.

8. For Third World labour-market developments, we refer particularly to the three continental chapters: Chapter 2 on Asia, Chapter 5 on Latin America and Chapter 8 on Africa. On labour-market segmentations due to caste, gender and

customs, see in particular Scoville (1991); for a global comparative study on structural adjustment and labour markets, see Standing and Tokman (1991). Relationships between poverty and labour-market characteristics are adequately analysed in Rodgers (1989).

9. For a statement on a research agenda, see House (1992).

10. See, for example, Baud and de Bruijne (1993); Helmsing and Kolstee (1993); and Thomas *et al.* (1991).

11. The debate on the merits and disadvantages of import substitution and export orientation, and their implications for labour and work in the other continents, is either overshadowed by more serious problems (as in Africa) or has largely been settled (as in Asia). For an in-depth analysis of the ISI versus EOI controversies, see Kaplinsky (1984) and Weiss (1993).

12. The reasons lay with the crucial role played by institutional dimensions such as the role of the state and political linkages, legal frameworks, cultural dimensions and economic institutions. The national domain then conveniently forms a common denominator with which the trade union domain can be linked methodologically.

13. See Poole (1986) for a good introduction to the theory of trade unions. He provides numerous arguments based on cultural, political and sociological insights for a distinction according to national patterns. Studies of aspects of trade union behaviour generally place the analysis in a national framework in order to show how the institutional characteristics of, for example, 'working-class culture' in Britain (Hobsbawm 1984) or wage formation, strike behaviour and employment patterns in the United States (Rees 1977) have been patterned.

14. Many observers foresee completely new practices of industrial and labour relations emerging towards the end of this century in the industrialized countries. See, for example, Brody (1991), Krop *et al.* (1993), Mortimer (1988) and Regini (1992).

15. For problems with data on industrialization in sub-Saharan Africa, see Riddell (1990: 10).

16. Methodologically, because comparative labour research has admittedly benefited somewhat belatedly from the technological breakthroughs in quantitative handling of huge masses of statistical information. For examples of how excellent databases lead to excellent studies and insights, see Visser (1990, 1992).

17. See also Doeringer (1981).

18. In addition, the highly diverging patterns of industrialization within the Third World, the challenges posed by new industrializing regions to the older areas in Western Europe and the United States of America, and the macro-economic implications of structural adjustment raised numerous questions which could not be answered by referring to theories based on a highly deterministic and abstract approach towards the global economy (Cohen 1991: 123–49; see also Kaplinksy 1984; Peet 1991; Weiss 1993).

19. With the fading relevance of the NIDL approach, NILS also appears to have reached certain limits. Cohen and Waterman place a heavier importance on the new social movements area (Cohen 1991; Munck 1988). We will not elaborate further on the theme since this approach extends far beyond production relations into the political realm; it thus begins to form part of a rapidly expanding literature

on social movements rather than a deepening of labour organization theory. The modest impact of this approach can be assessed in a statement by Waterman who mentions 'an informal and partly unpublished debate taking place around the concept of "social-movement unionism"' (Waterman 1993: 245).

20. An interesting characteristic of labour studies has been the simultaneous existence of this approach, along with the neoclassical, and radical/Marxist methodologies (see, for example, Mangum and Philips 1988).

21. In our discussion of industrial reorganization above, the institutional approach, referring to the work of Chandler and Lazonick, figured prominently. For classic studies, see North 1990 and Williamson 1985.

22. Konings's study is an excellent example of empirical research that is guided by strict adherence to existing literature on plantation labour and state involvement coupled with extensive fieldwork (Konings 1993); Hashim addresses a wide variety in patterns of African state–union relations by applying a synthesizing theoretical framework, for example, macro-corporatism. Subsequently, a testing of the model on a case study, Nigeria, has been undertaken (Hashim 1994). Schiphorst has undertaken a study of worker perceptions in Zimbabwean factories as an industrial-anthropologist; again, an emerging theoretical framework will provide a base for further comparative analysis in other parts of the world (Schiphorst, forthcoming).

23. Deyo has introduced new concepts of labour exclusion and inclusion which allow for a multidisciplinary implementation and can be applied to wider geographical regions (Deyo 1989).

24. Deyo's own work provides a pioneering contribution to multidisciplinary research through a careful blending of political, economic, social and cultural arguments.

References

Aglietta, M. (1987) *A Theory of Capitalist Regulation. The US Experience.* Verso, London.

Baud, I.S.A. and G.A. de Bruijne (eds) (1993) *Gender, Small-scale Industry and Development Policy*. IT Publications, London.

Best, M. (1990) *The New Competition. Institutions of Industrial Restructuring.* Polity Press, Cambridge.

Brody, D. (1991) 'Labour's Crisis in Historical Perspective', in G. Strauss, D.G. Gallagher and J. Fiorito (eds) *The State of the Unions*, pp. 277–311. Industrial Relations Research Association Series, IRRA, Wisconsin.

Chandler, A.D. (1977) *The Visible Hand*. The Belknap Press of Harvard University Press, Cambridge, MA.

——— (1990) *Scale and Scope. The Dynamics of Industrial Capitalism*. The Belknap Press of Harvard University Press, Cambridge, MA.

Cohen, R. (1980) 'The "New" International Labour Studies', Working Paper 27. Centre for Developing Area Studies, McGill University, Montreal.

——— (1991) *Contested Domains. Debates in International Labour Studies*. ZED Books, London.

Cox, R., J. Harrod and others (1972) *Future Industrial Relations*. An Interim Report. IILS, Geneva.

Deyo, F.C. (1989) *Beneath the Miracle. Labor Subordination in the New Asian Industrialism*. University of California Press, Berkeley.

Doeringer, P.B. (ed.) (1981) *Industrial Relations in International Perspective*. MacMillan, London.

Dore, R. (1989) 'Where we are Now: Musings of an Evolutionist', *Work, Employment and Society* Vol. 3, No. 4: 425–46.

Flanders, A. (1968) *Trade Unions*. Hutchinson University Library, London.

Fröbel, F., J. Heinrichs and O. Kreye (1981) *The New International Division of Labour*. Cambridge University Press, Cambridge.

Gerschenkron, A. (1986, reprint of 1962) *Economic Backwardness in Historical Perspective*. The Belknap Press of Harvard University Press, Cambridge, MA.

Golden, M. (1988) *Labour Divided – Austerity and Working-Class Politics in Contemporary Italy*. Cornell University Press, Ithaca and London.

Hashim, Y. (1994) 'The State and Trade Unions in Africa: A Study in Macro-corporatism', Ph.D. Thesis. ISS, The Hague.

Helmsing, A.H.J. and Th. Kolstee (eds) (1993) *Small Enterprises and Changing Policies*. IT Publications, London.

Hobsbawm, E.J. (1984) *Worlds of Labour*. Weidenfeld and Nicholson, London.

House, William J. (1992) 'Priorities for Urban Labor Market Research in Anglophone–Africa', *The Journal of Developing Areas* 27 (October): 49-68.

Kaplinsky, R. (ed.) (1984) *Third World Industrialisation in the 1980s: Open Economies in a Closing World*. Frank Cass, London.

Kerr, C., J.T. Dunlop, F. Harbison and C.A. Myers (1972) *Industrialism and Industrial Man*. Penguin Books, Harmondsworth.

Konings, P. (1993) *Labour Resistance in Cameroon*. Africa Study Centre, Leiden, in association with James Currey, London.

Krop, M., M. Ros, S. Stuiveling and B. Tromp (eds) (1993) *De toekomst van de vakbeweging*. Arbeiderspers, Amsterdam.

Lazonick, W. (1991) *Business Organization and the Myth of the Market Economy*. Cambridge University Press, Cambridge.

Mangum, G. and P. Philips (eds) (1988) *Three Worlds of Labour Economics*. M.E. Sharpe, New York.

Mies, M. (1982) *The Lace Makers of Narsapur: Indian Housewives Produce for the World-market*. Zed Books, London.

Mortimer, J.E. (1988) 'Problems Facing the Trade Union Movement', review article, *Work, Employment and Society* Vol. 2, No. 4: 535–48.

Munck, R. (1988) *The New International Labour Studies. An Introduction*. ZED Books, London.

North, D.C. (1990) *Institutions, Institutional Change and Economic Performance*. Cambridge University Press, Cambridge.

Olson Jr., M. (1971) *The Logic of Collective Action*. Schocken Books, New York.

Peet, R. (1991) *Global Capitalism (Theories of Societal Development)*. Routledge, London.

Piore, M. and C.F. Sabel (1984) *The Second Industrial Divide*. Basic Books, New York.

Poole, M. (1986) *Industrial Relations: Origins and Patterns of National Diversity*. Routledge & Kegan Paul, London.

Ramaswamy, E.A. (1994) *The Rayon Spinners: The Strategic Management of Industrial Relations*. Oxford University Press, Delhi.

—— (1995) 'The Power of Organized Labour', in *India Briefing 1995*. The Asia Society, New York.

Rees, A. (1977) *The Economics of Trade Unions*. The University of Chicago Press, Chicago.

Regini, M. (ed.) (1992) *The Future of Labour Movements*. Sage Publications, London.

Riddell, Roger C. (1990) *Manufacturing Africa: Performance and Prospects of Seven Countries in Sub-Saharan Africa*. James Currey, London.

Rodgers, G. (ed.) (1989) *Urban Poverty and the Labour Market*. International Labour Office, Geneva.

Rodgers, G., K. Fóti and L. Lauridsen (eds) (forthcoming) *The Institutional Approach to Labour and Development*. EADI Working Group on Labour, Employment and Development, Geneva.

Schiphorst, F. (forthcoming) 'Worker Representation in Zimbabwe', Ph.D. Thesis. University of Leiden.

Schmitz, H. and B. Musyck (1994) 'Industrial Districts in Europe: Policy Lessons for Developing Countries', *World Development* Vol. 22, No. 6: 889–910.

Scoville, J.G. (ed.) (1991) *Status Influences in Third World Labor Markets. Caste, Gender and Custom*. Walter de Gruyter, Berlin and New York.

Singer, Ho. (1991) in G. Standing and V. Tokman (eds) *Towards Social Adjustments (Labour market issues in structural adjustment)*: iv. ILO, Geneva.

Southall, R. (ed.) (1988a) *Trade Unions and the New Industrialization of the Third World*. ZED Books, London.

—— (1988b) *Labour Unions in Asia and Africa*. Macmillan, Basingstoke.

Standing, G. and V. Tokman (1991) *Towards Social Adjustment. Labour Market Issues in Structural Adjustment*. International Labour Office, Geneva.

Strauss, G., D.G. Gallagher and J. Fiorito (eds) (1991) *The State of the Unions*. Industrial Relations Research Association Series, IRRA, Wisconsin.

Sutcliffe, R.B. (1971) *Industry and Underdevelopment*. Addison-Wesley, London.

Thomas, H., F. Uribe-Echevarría and H. Romijn (eds) (1991) *Small-scale Production. Strategies for Industrial Restructuring*. IT Publications, London.

Thomas, H. and M. Hendriks (1994) 'Competitive Development and the Role of Small Firms: The Feasibility of a Clustering Strategy', Mimeograph. ISS, The Hague.

UNDP (1994) *Human Development Report 1994*. Oxford University Press, Oxford.

Visser, J. (1990) *In Search of Inclusive Unionism*. Kluwer Law and Taxation, Deventer and Boston.

—— (1992) 'The Strength of Union Movements in Advanced Capitalist Democracies: Social and Organizational Variations', in M. Regini (ed.) *The Future of Labour Movements*: 17–52. Sage Publications, London.

Wallerstein, I. (1979) *The Capitalist World-Economy*. Cambridge University Press, Cambridge.

———— (ed.) (1983) *Labour in the World Social Structure*. Sage, Beverly Hills.

Waterman, P. (1993) 'Social–movement Unionism: A New Union Model for a New World Order?', *Review* No. 16: 245–78.

Weiss, J. (1993) *Industry in Developing Countries (Theory, Policy and Evidence)*. Routledge, London.

Williamson, O. (1985) *The Economic Institutions of Capitalism*. Free Press, New York.

Womack, J., D. Jones and D. Roos (1990) *The Machine That Changed the World*. Rawson Associates, New York.

World Bank (1992, 1994) *World Development Report*. Oxford University Press, Oxford.

Part One: Asia

2. Three Highly Differentiated Trajectories

Henk Thomas
E.A. Ramaswamy
Amrita Chhacchi
Michel Hendriks

The sheer size of Asia and the profound differences between its various regions undermine the accuracy of any aggregated study at the continental level. Therefore, the main trends that have an impact on labour, employment and earnings must be analysed separately for the major regions of the continent.

This chapter will concentrate on the East, Southeast and South Asian regions. East Asia and the countries comprising the Association of Southeast Asian Nations (ASEAN) are characterized by impressive sustained economic performance and rapid industrialization; both regions, however, have characteristics of their own. South Asia, on the other hand, presents a contrast to these two regions in the political, economic and social fields. Labour conflicts are here at their most acute, and so the chapter will particularly emphasize the problems confronting labour and trade unions in South Asia.

The first question to be analysed will be the political differences and their effect on developmental processes. The economic record will be presented only briefly since information about it is easily accessible. Subsequently, the labour-market situation will be introduced along with a number of key themes relevant to any analysis of the labour situation in these regions. Lastly, the characteristics of trade unions and their limited room for action will be spelt out.

State intervention

East Asia

The success of the Newly Industrializing Countries (NICs) was often credited in the 1980s to their export orientation and presented as proof of the soundness of a neo-liberal approach towards industrial development. A typical policy consequence of this view has been the pressure exerted by international institutions on governments in other parts of the world to end artificial pricing by similarly removing distortions in capital and labour markets.

It was gradually recognized, however, that strong state involvement in almost all markets was one of the main factors underpinning the spectacular performance of the NICs. Comparative studies, particularly in Latin American countries, reveal the sophisticated nature of state involvement as an independent actor in the NICs, steering the economy into the required deep structural changes (see, for example, Jenkins 1991).

Cultural factors may partly explain the NICs' special social and political fabric, but the key explanation probably lies in more mundane factors. Early land reforms, an initially weak industrial bourgeoisie and a controlled labour supply to the industrializing urban economy constitute elements that are often absent in other countries. International capital inflows and military alliances, closely associated with the communist threats of the 1960s and 1970s, have been additional factors.

The critical element, however, is that the import-substitution industrialization (ISI) strategy during the initial stages of structural change was superseded in time by an orientation towards international markets. The successful implementation of this change can be traced back to coherent industrial and macro-economic policies that ensured the high levels of domestic savings needed for investment and a strong state, and to indicative planning methods that allocated investment among the different economic sectors.

In the literature, one observes major shifts over time in the analysis of the 'East Asian Miracle' (World Bank 1993). In the wake of the early excessive focus on the opening up of economies to international markets, sometimes in combination with a touch of Confucianism to explain the hard-working labour force and national coherence, a political-economy approach has gradually won the day. Policy makers in the NICs have clearly not refrained from extensive interventions, but these were mostly implemented with great caution and a readiness immediately to change course when this was necessitated by unexpected external shocks or when the expected results did not emerge (Chowdury and Islam 1993).

The autonomy of the state is particularly reflected in the identity of its bureaucracies. Compared to countries elsewhere, the bureaucracy is less politicized and the decision-making and steering mechanisms are highly centralized. The state has developed instruments to ensure adequate control over capital markets and financial flows as well as the functioning of labour markets. State controls have been equally important in ensuring that wage increases do not jeopardize the labour-intensive strategy of industrialization, which has constituted the core of a unique chapter in the history of global industrialization (Chowdury and Islam 1993; World Bank 1993).

The results of these policies have been a record of sustained growth, with impressive gains in total factor productivity, as well as high levels of investment and an expansion of employment along with a gradual upgrading of workers' capabilities.

The state has generally been authoritarian, ranging from the soft approach in Japan to the hard one in South Korea and Taiwan. In the Japanese model, maximum commitment and productivity are achieved through a labour-relations system characterized by tenured employment and wages linked to individual seniority. The mobilization of labour by means of trade unions is curtailed through sophisticated forms of social engineering, by forbidding strikes and by restricting labour organization to the firm through the concept of the 'enterprise union'. Another dimension of this soft-option model, as for instance found in Singapore, can be the state's willingness to allow trade unions to play a role in the distribution of welfare-state benefits.

The hard-option model forbids strikes and exercises strong control over the trade union movement, allowing no deviations from the free functioning of the labour market. Typically one observes sweatshop working conditions in small-scale enterprises, which also co-determine the contractual outcomes in medium- and large-scale industry. Lifetime employment guarantees, which interfere with free-market forces, are not allowed (for example, Deyo 1987, 1989).

Deyo has characterized the East Asian model as one of both labour exclusion and labour inclusion. Exclusion to the extent that labour is only allowed to play a passive role as an actor in the developmental process. Inclusion in the sense that a high degree of income equality ensures wide distribution of the benefits of development among the workforce through the authority of the state. Most recent evidence strongly supports the view that both favourable initial policies, such as land reform, as well as continued public attention to social questions, particularly access to primary and secondary education and the reduction of gender gaps, constitute strategic explanatory elements for the impressive East Asian developments over the past decades.[1]

Southeast Asia

Indonesia, Thailand, the Philippines and Malaysia form a second tier of rapidly industrializing countries. They constitute a substantial region of Asia that has achieved sustained economic growth, but initially at rates lower than those of the NICs. Since the ASEAN countries are significantly better endowed with natural resources, there is an obvious need for comprehensive multi-disciplinary analysis to explain their relatively less impressive performance in comparison with the East Asian countries.

Mackie (1988) lists five reasons: the ASEAN countries have much larger rural sectors, with lower growth rates than those of industry, as compared with the NICs; the removal of colonial legacies has been more costly; the ASEAN region displays a more ambivalent attitude towards foreign capital as compared with that of the NICs; this socio-psychological aspect is further complicated by ethnic factors, in which political measures against the dominant role of the Chinese segments of the population is a central issue; finally, the levels of domestic saving in the ASEAN countries compares unfavourably with that in the NICs.

While governments in the ASEAN countries have played strong roles, they are less autonomous than in the NICs. Coalitions of interest groups have had a considerable impact on the entire political framework. In such a situation, the extent to which elite groups reach a consensus that places national interests above their own immediate class interests becomes important in determining development. The specific characteristics of the emerging middle classes will probably be important in ultimately understanding economic developments in these countries.

It is remarkable, and in sharp contrast to the situation in South Asia, that the existing deep differences in ethnic, religious and cultural values and systems have not led to military confrontation and mutual alienation. Instead, one observes a determination to form regional linkages, which, at least in the economic domain, could give the region considerable clout internationally. It is interesting to note that, in spite of their differences, it was observed in the late 1980s that these countries 'have established the most successful regional grouping in the entire Third World' (James, Naya and Meier 1989: 13)

Labour relations in Southeast Asia range from the extreme form of dependence on the state in Indonesia to a relatively liberal attitude in the Philippines. Two key elements in this region's development have been wages lower than in the NICs, and quiet and docile labour, valued highly by foreign investors, which helps to guarantee stability. The widespread use of child labour, as in Thailand, for example, is only one articulation of the deep segmentations that are deliberately created in the labour market. The successful exploitation of ideological and ethnic dimensions is another illustration of the profound problems faced by the labour movement. Consequently, a wider socio-political analysis is necessary for a fuller understanding of the labour situation in these countries.

Lastly, it should be noted that trends in income distribution as measured by Gini-coefficients in each of these countries have moved significantly towards less inequality (see Figure 3, World Bank 1993: 4). It appears that these countries, starting their development well after that of the NICs and from different initial conditions, nevertheless pursue a similar strategy.

South Asia

In contrast to the other regions, economic growth in South Asia has been insufficient to allow for significant increases in per capita incomes between 1965 and 1990. One main reason for this undoubtedly has been that the necessary switch from an inward-looking development model to an outside-oriented one has begun only recently. As a result, economies like those of Pakistan and India, which around the mid-1960s experienced the successes of the 'Green Revolution' and served as models for development, have lost their relatively advantageous position in less than a generation.

The five factors that have been put forward as a partial explanation for the lower growth performance of the ASEAN countries in comparison to the NICs play an even more pronounced role in South Asia. This can be observed particularly in India, where the enormous size of the rural economy indicates that, more than anything else, rural development is a precondition for wider economic development.

India's colonial heritage is still an important factor in explaining the state's involvement in the economy and its impact on class formation. A strong state along with weak social classes has, for centuries, been the dominant political form in the sub-continent. Since Marx first wrote about the fate of artisanal industry in India, the phenomenon of de-industrialization during the nineteenth century as a result of colonialism has been well-documented. One effect of this was that no strong urban middle class had emerged by Independence in 1947. However, an urban proletariat had grown since the last century because of the establishment of large-scale textile and jute industries (Sen 1982).

At Independence the state was suddenly charged with new developmental tasks. Its socialist ideology led to the pursuit of an ideal state model of long-term economic planning and development, but without fundamentally altering the underlying forces of the inherited state mechanisms. Thus, the bureaucracy, originally established to serve the colonial power, assumed a highly independent role but stifled the growth of private capitalist development.

In contrast to East Asia, the Indian bureaucracy neither fostered private capitalist development nor could it design macro-economic policy frameworks that would be conducive to sustained structural transformation and industrialization. At the same time, the emergence of a strong middle class was hampered, while the labour force was encapsulated in some form of corporatism dominated by the state bureaucracies.

The professed admiration for Russian achievements under a central command economy resulted in a capital-intensive industrialization strategy with heavy state involvement. Public ownership, or very extensive administrative regulation, of major enterprises as well as nationalization of banks consolidated the power of the Indian state. Only recently have important steps been taken towards reorienting the economy to an outward-looking strategy. Privatization of public enterprises, involving workers being laid off on a massive scale, is presently on the political agenda, and the expanding middle class is starting to assert itself. In the absence of a broad consensus on these new developmental strategies, however (to which, for example, trade unions are totally opposed), and lacking clarity on the strength of the emerging class formations, it is difficult to predict whether the measures will endure.

The differences between the various countries of South Asia are huge; yet, in terms of economic growth, social impact and political characteristics, their common heritage still makes itself felt in many spheres, such as the behaviour of key actors like state bureaucracies and the labour leadership.

Economic performance

Extensive analyses have been produced of the comparative economic performance of the regions as well as of individual countries, and these are readily accessible.[2] The discussion here will, therefore, be brief. The starkly contrasting experiences in Asia are best illustrated by a comparison of some key indicators.[3] Table 1 (A) of the Statistical Appendix (pp. 249–52) provides statistical information on some key trends in the three regions under examination.

The differences in GNP per capita growth rates – around or less than three per cent for South Asian countries, roughly averaging four per cent for Southeast Asia and above five per cent for the NICs – underscore the arguments presented above. The outcome after 25 years is telling: none of the South Asian countries has a GNP per capita above US$540 in 1992, less than one-tenth of the minimum NIC figure of US$6,790.

The implications of these figures and the challenges to be overcome are brought home vividly by the statistics on populations, their growth rates and the expected rates of urbanization (and, for many people, urban poverty) till the year 2000. More than a billion people live in the region with the lowest per capita income, with every country except Sri Lanka facing the most rapid population growth rates as well. South Asian countries are all beginning to experience lower population growth, yet their urban growth rates for the coming decade will remain alarmingly high. The NICs, in contrast, have achieved a stage of increasing stability, and display even growing signs of tightness in labour markets, with modest rates of population and urban growth.

The depth of the structural transformation that has occurred in the past decades is well illustrated by the data on sectoral composition in Table 1(B). Most significantly, in South Asia agriculture still accounts for about 30 per cent of Gross Domestic Product (GDP) compared to about 20 per cent in Southeast Asia, where industrialization rates already approximate the levels in East Asian countries.

While the timely switch to an outward-looking strategy was a vitally important element in the success of East Asian economies, particularly given their limited natural resource base, the East Asian model does not equate with an exclusive reliance on market forces. The state, as stressed above, has played a key role, in close collaboration and interaction with the existing entrepreneurial class. Similarly, qualitative dimensions such as the role of technological advance through learning-by-doing in production processes, human resource development and the high priority accorded to R&D are now recognized as indispensable components of this developmental model.

The Southeast Asian countries occupy a middle position between East and South Asia. In spite of their enormous differences, they share a number of similarities from a developmental perspective, particularly their abundant supply of raw materials and rapid incorporation into the global economic system through multinational capital. The region has been made attractive to foreign capital by 'authoritative, corporatist regimes and complex bureaucratic structures' (Dixon 1991: 4). Since the 1970s this has resulted in deep structural changes taking place within a process of rapid industrialization. The enormous potential of their internal markets and their plentiful natural resources hold a long-term promise of continued dynamic development. A heavy price is being paid by labour; for instance, low wages and docility of the workers are used to attract foreign direct investment.

Southeast Asia's middle position probably will be sustained for two reasons. First, the existing internal coalitions of interest groups accept the exclusion of large segments of their societies. Second, given the strong impact of foreign capital, national interests are unlikely to be fully realized for a long time.

Social development

With the well-known exception of Sri Lanka, which for decades has made relatively high investments in its social development, the regional differences in life expectancy show some significant features. Table 1(C) summarizes the impact of poverty on men and women. In South Asia female mortality is close to or equal to male mortality because women are at a disadvantage in benefiting from the still modest advances in economic growth. Elsewhere, their relative position concurs with global trends at higher levels of development.

The statistics on adult literacy – to the extent that literacy at different levels of development can be compared using current data collection methods – underscore even more the enormous achievements in East and Southeast Asia.

Lastly, the Human Development Index (HDI), a composite of three basic components: longevity, knowledge and standard of living,[4] indicates that major differences had emerged between countries and regions as early as 1960. Already at that time, Sri Lanka's egalitarian and social policies had resulted in a high level of human development considering its GNP per capita, whereas the Southeast Asian countries were lagging in human development despite their higher levels of GNP per capita.

In 1992, substantial differences could still be noted even though the HDI had improved for all countries. For instance, the extent and depth of poverty in Bangladesh and India was reflected in the limited progress achieved there while substantial progress was made in Southeast Asia (with the exception of the Philippines). The same was true of East Asia where high levels were further consolidated, the South Korean performance being particularly impressive, surpassing that of Singapore which it had trailed in 1960.

The foregoing comparative analysis of political, economic and social trends in East, Southeast and South Asia, succinct as it is, owes much to recent in-depth research on the unprecedented changes that have occurred in East Asia within only a few decades. The political-economy approach accords importance to the role played by labour, whether through labour-intensive production, enhanced skill formation or the acceptance of strict wage policies.

It remains to be seen whether past formulas will be equally effective in the near future. Some analysts argue that signs of looming decay can already be discerned in countries like South Korea, Taiwan and Singapore (for example, Bello and Rosenfeld 1992). Others argue that this need not happen provided policy makers ensure a timely switch to innovative and capital-intensive production methods. This would call for deep institutional and political changes, implying democratization and labour participation (Chowdury and Islam 1993). While the latter consider such far-reaching adaptations a feasible proposition, the former point to policies and traditions of labour exclusion as well as rapidly growing trade union protest to support their case.

Labour and labour markets

National labour markets – in a narrow sense, referring only to trends in employment, unemployment, wages and wage structures – show highly distinct regional patterns in Asia. In East Asia, and in parts of Southeast Asia, labour markets have lost their abundance and have gradually become tighter due to labour-intensive industrialization. This phenomenon is evidenced by the decline in unemployment and substantial increments in real wages. Above all, a reversal in migratory flows is observed. In countries such as Japan, Singapore and Hong Kong, which till recently exported workers because of insufficient domestic employment opportunities, immigrant labour is reducing labour-market pressures.

The opposite is found in South Asia, particularly where import substitution industrialization strategies have been adopted. High population growth rates have ensured rapid expansion of the labour supply while employment elasticity, to the extent that industrialization has been achieved, has been very low. Rapidly growing urban labour markets are the most clearly visible symptom of this extremely unfavourable development for labour. Urgently needed modernization of large-scale (often public) enterprises may induce a further deterioration in the employment situation. Rural (circular) migration, temporary international migration and low-productivity off-farm employment are indicative of the poor outlook in rural labour markets. In South Asia one thus observes stagnation if not a decline in real wages as a visible sign of the predicaments faced in national labour markets.

Southeast Asia typically finds itself between these two extremes. Labour supply pressures, which make themselves strongly felt in the urban labour markets, are still high but are likely to lessen in the near future. On the one hand, wage structures are conditioned by international competitive forces, resulting in lower wages than in the NICs, in order to attract investment and strengthen new industrialization. On the other hand, the upward pressures cannot be withstood for too long as skill levels need to be improved if labour is to remain competitive in international markets.

These differing macro-scenarios have deep impacts on the profiles of the labour markets. In East Asia, and to some extent Southeast Asia, rapid and labour-intensive growth in manufacturing has raised the earning potential of large numbers of workers. In South Asia, capital-intensive industrialization along with stagnating productivity has generated low earnings for a limited number of workers.

Precise knowledge within a specific national context is required for in-depth understanding of a particular labour-market development. For instance, an impact on aggregate levels of employment, unemployment and wage trends can be achieved by completely different patterns of labour-market segmentation and thus also of policies, as in Latin America.

East Asia

A major transformation of employment structures in agriculture, industry and services has resulted from changes in East Asian economies. Due to the labour-intensive nature of the industrialization process, it was possible for much labour to move from low-productivity agriculture into high-productivity industry and services.

Necessary changes in occupational structures and educational profiles rapidly followed (for example, Galenson 1992). The demand for labour was so high that by the end of the 1980s unemployment had declined to less than two per cent (Chowdury and Islam 1993).

The degree of state involvement in steering labour markets can be seen clearly in the working week, which has been continuously long, with South Korea's 50.5 hours in 1989 and Taiwan's 47.2 hours in 1989 providing peaks (Chowdury and Islam 1993; Galenson 1992). The huge increases in labour productivity are reflected in major rises in real wages for several decades. South Korea and Taiwan stand out in this respect, whereas increments in Singapore and Hong Kong have been more modest (Deyo 1989). It should be noted that these increments have been monitored and controlled to ensure that the level of national savings, and thus the basis for accumulation, would never be jeopardized.

With the increasing tightness in labour markets, new issues of labour policy, in addition to wage restraints and control of labour organizations, needed to be taken up. Policies to steer and monitor immigration were required to replace the stimulation of workers to take up temporary employment abroad. This issue is of particular relevance as industrial competitiveness calls for considerable enhancement in skill levels to allow for major shifts towards capital-intensive production systems. Athukorala argues that both Japan and Singapore used immigrant workers only at times of temporary shortage in the labour market and thus forced entrepreneurs to shift to robotized industrialization. Hong Kong, in contrast, freely allowed the inflow of foreign unskilled workers, which sustained its 'comparative advantage in labour-intensive products much longer than warranted by the size of its national workforce' (Athukorala 1993: 50).

Two major views are presented in the analyses of labour in East Asia. One approach emphasizes the efficient adjustment of labour markets to the continuously changing demands of economic restructuring and export markets. This view typically stresses the flexibility of labour markets in response to competition (Galenson 1992; World Bank 1993). The other approach points at strong state interventions controlling labour organization, wage increases and wage structures in order to create a docile workforce prepared to accept long working hours, sweatshop conditions and an oppressive environment instead of struggling to obtain greater benefits from national development (for example, Deyo 1987, 1989).

Chowdury and Islam provide an excellent synthesis of these polar positions on the basis of access to a range of indicators. In addition to the usual indicators of employment, wages and educational level of workers, a set of data referring to 'human resource management' (for example, labour–management relations, strike-days lost and absenteeism) and to 'human resource development' (for example, training, skill levels and flexibility patterns) could be utilized.

They tentatively conclude that there is insufficient evidence to show that labour is an oppressed victim of development. On the contrary, the trends in total factor productivity 'could have been and probably have been affected by the cumulative effects of human capital formation' (Chowdury and Islam 1993: 158). This, in turn, implies that efficient labour markets rather than oppressed labour are a key characteristic of the NIC model of development. The one major exception to this view is the well-documented and significant wage discrimination against women. As for gender relations, systematic labour-market segmentation has been noted for many years (Chowdury and Islam 1993; Galenson 1992).

Southeast Asia
In Southeast Asia, a second tier of rapidly industrializing countries has emerged with such force that in its widely publicized report, *The East Asian Miracle*, the World Bank has merged Indonesia, Malaysia and Thailand with the NICs in one category of High-Performing Asian Economies (Amsden 1994; World Bank 1993). Given their competition against the NICs, it is no surprise that heavy burdens have

fallen on the labour market in these countries. Unions are even more controlled than in the NICs with the labour market needing to be very flexible and wages having to adjust rapidly to falls in demand.

Regrettably both the quality of data and the comparative research undertaken on labour-market performance in this second tier of rapidly industrializing countries lag far behind those for East Asia. Yet some important characteristics can be noted that are deeply rooted in these societies. We refer here to the segmentation in labour markets by ethnicity and the influence of the military on the functioning of the economy and labour markets.

Gender segmentation and discrimination are also more deeply rooted than in the NICs where increasing efforts are made to overcome labour market shortages by paying more attention to the position of women through human-resource development policies. Again, migration flows are an important indicator of the state of labour markets. Huge flows of skilled and unskilled workers are observed both within this region and elsewhere, showing the weak position of labour.

Whether the labour situation will move in the direction of that in the NICs or result in a further weakening of bargaining power along with deepening of segmentation is hard to predict. According to recent findings, the latter outcome cannot be ruled out (Muqtada and Hildeman 1993). In Thailand one now observes huge mismatches in demand and supply for young workers, reminiscent of the problems spotted by the well-known ILO mission to Sri Lanka in the early 1970s. The outlook in the Philippines is gloomy, with the labour market being characterized by a new 'general trend towards labour casualization via job subcontracting, service agency hiring and other casualization measures' (Ofreneo 1993: 266).

South Asia

In most of South Asia the labour situation offers a depressing picture. Inward-oriented industrialization strategies have mostly resulted in low employment creation, whereas the recent moves towards far-reaching structural adjustments have eroded earnings patterns.

Deep-seated patterns of labour segmentation persist, demarcated along lines of gender, ethnic and communal identities. Furthermore, exceptionally exploitative conditions can be found in both rural and urban labour markets. Work on plantations and bonded labour form elements of rural markets. In his case study on Bangladesh, for instance, Datta (1991) found that 76 per cent of workers were socio-politically dependent on their employers and had effectively lost their right to leave the job before completion of the contracted period, while from the employers' side a contract could be terminated immediately without compensation. For plantation workers, earlier forms of indentured labour with obligations to work (for example, five years for the same employer in the same line of work) have been abolished. Yet new systems of 'free' wage labour, recruited through intermediaries, retain almost as complete control over workers (for example, through different forms of indebtedness) as did earlier forms of bondage.

Dire conditions prevail in much of the informal urban economy. Many people act as members of a household engaged in strategies of survival rather than as participants in the labour force attempting to gain access to decent income levels. In Jakarta, for instance, household strategies of creating multiple jobs through combinations of some wage work, informally earned incomes and subsistence labour are a key characteristic of the urban labour market (Evers 1989). The informalization of economic activities is taken up below (pp. 49–53) as an issue of special concern to the labour movement.

All these varied aspects of the labour-market situation must be reflected in policies towards labour if these are to stand any chance of success. While human resource development aimed at enhancement of skills and training is important in East Asia, and policies in Southeast Asia are focused on special categories such as youth or migrants, improvements in monitoring labour-market trends are the best that can presently be expected in South Asian countries. For instance, recent case studies exploring policy options for employment planning and human resource development in India and Pakistan consider the worsening macro labour-market situation adequate justification for first improving labour-market monitoring before formulating any specific advice (Kemal 1993; Papola 1993).

Prospects may improve considerably in the long run. In the near future, however, it can be expected that due to privatization of public enterprises and the need to introduce greater flexibility in labour markets, market forces will further worsen conditions of work. Symptoms of this trend are the high incidence of child labour in various sectors as well as the rapid casualization of work in even medium- and large-scale enterprises.

It therefore comes as no surprise that in their assessment of policy options, Amjad and Edgren (1991) argue that the most fundamental aspects should be given priority: access to primary education and improvement of the quality of secondary education and vocational training. In short, there appears to be no substitute for a re-orientation of national development strategies towards human capital formation as a precondition for a turn for the better.

Key labour themes

Ethnic conflict and militarization

Most Asian societies are multi-ethnic in character. The ethnic identification can be based on racial, religious, linguistic or regional sentiments. This multi-ethnicity is the result of historical processes, both internal to these societies as well as induced by colonial rule; for instance, large-scale migration and the settlement of labour from other regions in the plantation economies.

Such forced multi-ethnicity has almost without exception resulted in a marked polarization, often leading to active conflict within these societies. Colonial rulers not only manipulated this polarization to strengthen and perpetuate their rule, but also institutionalized further divisions through the selective and differential incorporation of various ethnic groups into the colonial economy and state structures. Communities were thus set against each other on an almost permanent basis.

Conflicts acquired an added dimension in the post-colonial period when the arbitrary demarcation of boundaries of newly-independent states by disengaging colonial powers led to violent conflicts between neighbouring countries. These conflicts were related to territorial claims and/or the alleged maltreatment of ethnic minorities. Regional conflicts and internal ethnic conflicts, in turn, interacted and gave rise to both secessionist and autonomist political movements in a number of countries.

These particular developments, in tandem with a host of socio-economic and political problems, have greatly contributed to the excessive militarization of Asian societies during the post-colonial era and the creation of repressive, 'national-security' states. The most striking examples of such debilitating developments are found in Southeast and South Asian countries.[5] Most have been affected by internal ethnic strife and/or are engaged in long-standing conflicts with one or more neighbours. In many instances these frictions have resulted in armed confrontations.

Ethnic conflicts have had significant long-term impacts on the social, political and economic development of these societies. The high degree of militarization not only created an enormous drain on scarce resources but also induced a further strengthening of already over-centralized bureaucratic states. Thus, the badly needed participation of aggrieved ethnic groups was impeded, which otherwise could have been pursued through decentralization and democratization of the state and societal institutions. In many cases, conflicts have led to the direct involvement of the military in politics and the establishment of military dictatorships. This has, in turn, further complicated existing ethnic problems.

Ethnic conflicts have a direct impact on labour markets and industrial relations as well. Unresolved conflicts tend to consolidate a certain division of labour that invariably corresponds to the ethnic hierarchy prevailing at the wider societal level. The upward occupational mobility of workers belonging to disadvantaged ethnic groups is effectively blocked. This increases the frustration and alienation among these workers and pushes them further towards narrow ethnic politics. Employers often use such divisions to achieve short-term objectives: to block the formation of trade unions, break strikes and, above all, to reduce wages.

In many countries the armed forces have entered directly into the production and labour sphere, either through army officers managing the state-owned defence production units or the placing of strategic public-sector units under the control of serving (or retired) senior army officers. In some cases, 'armed forces foundations' have been established which own a number of industries. In all such cases, workers have either been deprived of their basic rights or have had severe restrictions imposed on them. Defence and related production units are generally declared to be 'essential services' in which workers are denied their right to organize and/or bargain collectively.

Southeast Asia

The armed forces in most countries are heavily dominated by a single or a few dominant ethnic groups. Fortunately the twin menace of ethnic conflict and militarization has been brought under control by the ASEAN countries. During their annual meeting in July 1994, for instance, it was decided to confer ASEAN membership on long-standing adversary Vietnam within the coming two years. Border disputes and ethnic irritants have been resolved through mutual consultation among member countries and by the creation of more space for the participation of all ethnic groups through decentralization and democratization within countries.[6] This has also led to the reduction of wasteful defence expenditures.

At the same time, these countries have been able to develop mutually beneficial economic ties with a relatively free mobility of labour and capital. Labour-market developments, such as the increasing tightness experienced in Singapore and Malaysia, pose, as Suhrke states sharply, 'a major domestic challenge for the successful ASEAN states. The perceived problem is no longer how to keep people out…but how to bring in the "right" kind' (1992: 20).

South Asia

Despite the creation of the South Asian Association for Regional Cooperation (SAARC) in 1984, the situation in South Asia has not improved much since. The four largest countries of this region, (with a total population of about 1.2 billion India, Pakistan, Bangladesh and Sri Lanka), not only remain internally locked into ethnic confrontations of varying intensity but also live in permanent fear of each other. India and Pakistan have had four major confrontations in the past four decades.

These countries are among the highest spenders on armaments and the military among Asian developing countries. According to official figures, defence expenditures constituted 15.0, 27.9, 10.1 and 8.5 per cent of the total central government expenditures of India, Pakistan, Bangladesh and Sri Lanka respectively in 1992.[7] Their expenditure on health and education amounted only to 3.7, 2.6, 16.0 and 14.9 per cent respectively (World Bank 1992, 1994).

The ruling elites in South Asia have adopted different strategies to deal with internal and/or cross-border ethnic conflicts. The responses range from accommodation of some of the demands for autonomy (for example, India till the 1960s), enforced integration (Pakistan to date) and violent suppression (Sri Lanka during the 1980s and, to some extent, Bangladesh recently). Meanwhile, they have invariably sought to manipulate their neighbours' ethnic problems to their own advantage.

Internally, the manipulation of contending ethnic groups is most disquieting when carried out by military regimes. Of all South Asian countries, Pakistan is perhaps most deeply caught up within the vicious circle created by the menace of ethnic conflict and militarization. However, similar problems, and their dangers, can be found throughout the region: the repression of (the descendants of) Nepali immigrants in Bhutan; the continuous turmoil in Assam, India, between Kuki and Naga tribes or Bodo tribals and Muslim refugees from Bangladesh; the protracted struggle of the Shan, Karen and Kachin against the Burmese state. All are examples of conflicts with ethnic under- or overtones.

The internal conflicts and external disputes between the countries of South Asia are in many ways similar to those among the ASEAN nations. There is an urgent need for the South Asian countries to more seriously learn some lessons from ASEAN experiences in addressing and resolving these issues. In his in-depth analysis of these phenomena in five South Asian countries, S. Mahmud Ali (1993: 255) summarizes succinctly a strategy that transcends ethnic divisions and reliance on military strength:

> Any restructuring of political and economic relations within and between states would depend on and, at the same time, encourage

negotiation, accommodation, democracy, devolution, pluralism and, perhaps, social peace. That could permit the community to devise means to fight its real adversaries – mass poverty, disease, distributive injustice, ignorance and low productivity.

Gender and labour

Recent studies have shown an increase in women's employment in manufacturing in many developing countries. In Asia, women constitute about 29 per cent of the industrial labour force, as compared to 18 to 26.5 per cent worldwide. However, considerable regional variations exist. In South Asia, women constitute 53 per cent of all industrial workers in Sri Lanka, less than 10 per cent in India and 14 per cent in Pakistan. In Southeast Asia, women constitute a much larger part of the industrial labour force: 45 per cent in Thailand, 46 per cent in the Philippines and 48 and 45 per cent respectively in Malaysia and Indonesia. For East Asia the corresponding figures are almost as high: 42, 40, 44 and 39 per cent for Korea, Hong Kong, Singapore and Japan (ILO 1992). The exceptionally high female manufacturing employment in Sri Lanka may be explained by the sizeable demand for labour in its Free Production Zones (FPZs).

Significantly, the trend of increasing female employment in manufacturing is not only a reversal of earlier declining tendencies, but also demonstrates an increase in women's share of employment, relative to that of men, in a context where total industrial employment is expanding only slowly (Shah *et al.* 1994). This increase, however, is not spread evenly. It tends to be concentrated in newly set up export-oriented factories, and usually in only three industrial sectors: textiles, food processing, and electronics and other consumer goods.

As mentioned before, one of the main trends in the 1980s and probably 1990s is the process of flexibilization of labour. New technologies have enabled the decentralization of production, whereby the corresponding new management and production techniques include subcontracting, just-in-time delivery and home-based production. Their combination with the implementation of structural adjustment programmes in several countries, programmes which have prompted labour-market deregulation and a transfer of jobs from the formal to the informal sector, has undermined the position of labour as a factor of production, a position that will deteriorate even more. This is reflected in a weakening of both legislative and customary job security, a shift to contract-based employment, retrenchments and lower wages. Women workers are often hardest hit by these measures because they often already occupy the weakest positions. Any decrease in security or wages is therefore detrimental to them (Standing 1989).

Thus, although women's employment is generally expanding, most of the growth is in the least desirable and lowest-paying jobs. Recent industrial trends may have created the conditions for women to gain economic independence and thereby increase their bargaining power within and outside the household, but the nature of employment available to them and the structure of trade unions perpetuate female industrial workers' subordinate position in the labour market, the home and society.

Free Production Zones[8]

The FPZ concept originated in East Asia where it attained its image of rapid outward-oriented growth through foreign investments. FPZs are most often characterized by their massive employment of young women, usually below the age of 25 years, presumably because they are unorganized, docile and easily controlled.

The impact of FPZs on working conditions and labour relations has been considerable, in the sense that the harsh conditions that were previously characteristic of work in FPZs have now spread throughout entire economies. Some recent evidence indicates that even with respect to labour relations and working conditions, work in FPZs no longer compares unfavourably with the national labour markets of which they used to form an isolated segment.

Trade unions and alternative organizations

The overall membership of mainstream trade unions is low in Asia, often not crossing 10 per cent of the total labour force. Women's participation in trade unions also remains extremely low. In Pakistan a survey conducted by the Pakistan Institute for Labour Education and Research (PILER) reveals that women constitute only around 10 per cent of the total unionized workforce in the multinational sector in electronics, pharmaceuticals and cosmetics.

In certain sectors and countries, trade unions have been able to take up issues of wages and working conditions and ensure some level of job security. Nonetheless, the trade union movement has developed as a male-dominated movement. Even where it has fought for women's rights, it has done so from a masculine point of view: equal pay for the same work, but not for work of equal value; the reservation of 20 per cent of jobs in all industries for women (called for by the women's wing of central trade unions), but not for an equal opportunities policy. This has resulted in protection and benefits for women, but based on the assumption of a rigid domestic division of labour.

Most crucially, trade unions have been unable to reach out to workers in the informal sector where women workers predominate. In some cases unions have worked with management to retrench women workers from formal industry by forcing them to accept voluntary retirement and take up home-based subcontracting work in the same industry. Such actions reinforce the dominant assumption underlying most trade union bargaining strategies: the 'male breadwinner/women dependant' model. Traditional trade unions have serious limitations, given their patriarchal orientation, methods of functioning and neglect of non-factory life and unwaged labour, which exclude women as well as an increasing cross-section of casual labour (Chhachhi and Pittin, forthcoming).

These limitations have led to questions as to whether unions are the most effective form of organization for women workers. It is interesting that especially in South and Southeast Asia a number of innovative alternative organizations have emerged which have addressed the needs of women workers, particularly in the informal sector. The most well known is the Indian Self-Employed Women's Association (SEWA), which developed a trade union-cum-cooperative structure which has been the key to its success. The innovative organizational structure of SEWA and of the Working Women's Forum (Madras, India) has conferred legality on masses of unrecognized workers and has allowed these organizations to link their mobilizing activities with income-generating projects for casualized workers. It is significant that both are women's organizations, independent of the mainstream trade union bodies in India. A very important aspect of the activities of such new 'unions' is their emphasis on lobbying at a national level and the initiation of central legislation which would have implications at a national level (SEWA 1989; Rose 1992).

A further initiative has been the setting up of community and labour centres to provide assistance to women in wage bargaining and social support. The centres have proved useful in mobilizing workers where unionization is difficult, as in the Sri Lankan FPZs and the garment industry in Pakistan. In the Philippines, where the number of home-based workers is estimated at seven to nine million, the National Association of Home-Based Workers (PATAMBA) was initiated in 1991, its objectives being the provision of a platform for home-based (female) workers, initiation of market research, provision of credit support and intervention at the level of government policy (Honculada, forthcoming).

Labour and the informal sector

Despite family-planning successes in parts of Asia, the population growth rates in some of the region's countries are among the highest in the world. Annual projections for 1995–2000 are 1.68 per cent for Asia, with East, Southeast and South Asia experiencing 1.14 per cent,

1.76 per cent and 2.11 per cent growth respectively.[9] The average annual world growth rate is estimated at 1.63 per cent (UN 1991). The limited availability of additional cultivable land compels most new entrants to the labour market to look for incomes outside agriculture, and their ranks are further swelled by the outflow of rural labour due to the modernization of production. Since employment creation in the formal economy has rarely matched the growing labour supply, most entrants, of necessity, have to find work in the small-scale and informal sector.

Most small-scale and informal activities are located in urban areas due to their close links with the urban economy on the demand and/or supply side. Activities more closely linked to agriculture, and many of the traditional cottage industries, are still located in rural areas. The expectation of more ample employment opportunities in cities contributes significantly to rural–urban migration flows. Thus population growth, reinforced by rural–urban migration and lack of formal employment opportunities, has created a large informal and small-scale sector in urban areas.

Comprehensive continent-wide data on the size and composition of the sector are virtually non-existent. Statistics are available mostly on a country or sectoral basis and comparative analyses are impeded by, among other things, diverging definitions. A seven-country survey by the Asian Development Bank (ADB) contains the following aggregates: firms with fewer than 50 employees account for only 14 per cent of value-added but provide 57 per cent of employment; for firms with fewer than 10 employees the respective figures are five per cent and 46 per cent (ADB 1990: 9). Even such limited statistics indicate clearly the informal sector's importance as a source of employment and income. Its dynamics and development, therefore, cannot be ignored in a labour analysis. Despite the existing data constraints, some analysis is possible on regional differences regarding the informal sector's experiences, policy approaches towards it and its prospects.

East Asia
In East Asia, the size of the informal sector is declining. The small-scale sector is incorporated into the formal economy through subcontracting relationships. Due to the initial reforms (for example, of land), the early reduction of population growth rates, and fast economic growth resulting from the economic policies implemented, the formal labour market has increasingly been able to absorb the sections of the labour force previously employed in the informal sector. Policies have been growth oriented (that is, concentrating on future

potential rather than past contributions), resulting at times in a thorough restructuring of activities within and between sectors.

Though the policies have mostly favoured large-scale industries, the problems, potential and contribution of small-scale and informal activities have in different ways formed an essential dimension within the development strategies pursued in the region. In South Korea, for instance, all emphasis fell on large-scale industrial development along with severe exploitation of cheap labour in small enterprises (sweatshops), whereas Taiwanese policies strongly promoted small-scale, decentralized and regionally dispersed industrialization (Cheng and Gereffi 1994).

While these countries explicitly pursued a differentiation in the exploitation of labour, an entirely new model was introduced in Japan in which small and large enterprises interact on the basis of a well-understood mutual interest.[10] This close interaction benefits both parties, as well as the economy as a whole. Contracting enterprises, and the state, assist and stimulate subcontractors to invest, for example, in R&D and new innovative techniques, and to receive higher quality (or lower-priced) inputs in return. Subcontractors can rely on orders and are able to invest on the basis of these future prospects, increasing the stability of their firms. Japan has recently experienced shortages of skilled or specialized labour, creating a powerful incentive for both parties to continue to cooperate in this manner.

Within such a system of industrial organization, small enterprises and their workers share the benefits of increasing sectoral profitability, although there is a time-lag before workers receive the benefits. This contrasts sharply with the position of informal workers in the rest of Asia where they are characterized by vulnerability and static poverty.

Southeast Asia

It remains to be seen whether Southeast Asia can equally successfully incorporate the small-scale and informal sector into the formal system. Many studies indicate that the majority of subcontracting relationships that have developed in these countries, as in South Asia, are of a more exploitative nature. Due to fierce competition within the small-scale and informal sector, contracting firms can often choose from a wide range of alternative suppliers. They are in a position to change suppliers without notice, squeeze the profits of subcontracting firms and exert economic power in other ways at the expense of their subcontractors. Unlike in East Asia, they are not inclined to invest in the development of their subcontractors, and short-term gains and advantages often prevail over long-term considerations. There is evidence to indicate that the present favourable growth performance (and competitive position) of these countries is based, and indeed highly dependent, on the continued existence of this dual production system.

A major proportion of the risks, hardships and uncertainties of small entrepreneurs is, in turn, transferred to the workers. The labour surplus in these regions prevents the development of stable, growth-conducive subcontracting relations and, at the same time, maintains or even aggravates the disadvantaged position of workers in small-scale and informal enterprises.

Again, one can observe major intra-regional differences. For instance, in the Philippines and Indonesia, the pressures in urban labour markets are such that there is yet little perspective for rapid improvement in earnings and working conditions (Ofreneo 1993; Tambunan 1994). However, recent research in Thailand has revealed high dynamism within the small-scale sector as a result of which a sizeable number of small-scale firms gradually succeed in 'formalizing' (Romijn 1993).

South Asia

South Asia, especially India, has a long-standing tradition of protecting small-scale enterprises through the outright reservation of certain industries, elaborate institutional support structures and other mechanisms. This protective approach is closely tied to India's ISI model of development and also follows on from a political preoccupation with the protection of existing employment opportunities for certain disadvantaged groups. Prolonged insulation from foreign competition and direct competition by large-scale units [11] has resulted in a relatively stagnant, undynamic small-scale sector. Though India's economic policy orientation has changed dramatically since the installation of Narasimha Rao's cabinet in 1991, it will be many years before existing structures and imbalances are overcome. In fact, the present liberalization will most likely affect small and informal-sector undertakings negatively in the short and medium term.

While the other South Asian countries have not adhered to the ISI model as rigidly as India, similar policies have been pursued, leading to comparable problems. In combination with South Asia's still worrisome demography, this has resulted in a vast small-scale and informal sector of which only a minor section can be considered growth oriented, the majority consisting of survival activities.

Whether in Pakistan, India or Bangladesh, the greater part of the informal sector is linked to the rural economy where it is highly unlikely that demand and supply conditions will allow the generally low-productivity cottage industries to achieve progress. Even with macro-economic policies becoming less biased against rural development, it is doubtful that a sustainable path of expansion can emerge (Islam 1987). For instance, recent evidence in Pakistan, which has performed more strongly than India, shows that growth rates of small-scale and micro-enterprises and of their employment do not represent dynamic growth because the increases in value-added have been very modest. Thus the result may have been an impoverishment of those involved rather than success in overcoming poverty (Mahmood 1994).

The position of labour
The position of workers within the small-scale and informal sector is very weak. The over-supply of labour ensures fierce competition for available jobs. The bargaining strength of individual job-seekers, or even groups, is extremely limited, and this may partly explain the often-found preference for self-employment even when less remunerative.

Formal-sector enterprises also exploit the existing sharp differentials in job security, wage levels and safety standards between the sectors: labour is increasingly casualized by formal enterprises; work is subcontracted to small units and home workers or activities are permanently moved to firms in the small-scale and informal sector. In this way, larger enterprises further reduce labour costs and evade existing regulations such as those on health standards, retrenchment and social security contributions.

Thus, the unregulated small-scale and informal sector is not only expanding at the expense of the formal sector. Its existence is being used as leverage against trade union demands in the formal sector. Confronted with such developments, the unions have tended to concern themselves only with protecting the rights and position of their existing constituencies in the formal sector rather than attempting to extend their aims and constituencies and addressing the problems and needs of labourers in both sectors.

Trade unions and industrial relations

The Asian experience of the past decades poses enormous dilemmas to the labour movement. Instead of rapid industrialization creating a well-organized labour force, a unique socio-economic development along with marginalization and suppression of labour organization can be observed in East Asia. Similar trends are found in Southeast Asia, together with fragmentation along ethnic lines. In South Asia the threat of privatization of public enterprises and the likelihood of a further weakening of labour's position in labour markets provide ominous signals to the trade union movement.

A relatively strong tradition of trade union organization has been established in South Asia. However, labour was not allowed to develop any organizational strength in East Asia, a divergence from the history of industrialization in other parts of the world (Deyo 1989). The well-known and much praised flexibility of labour markets in East Asia may be related to this weak organization of trade unions. Labour organization has also been suppressed to contain wages and ensure an uninterrupted supply of cheap, docile labour.

It is interesting that analyses of the labour situation in East Asia generally agree on the weak structure of industrial relations, the strict controls on collective bargaining and the determination to prevent and preempt the emergence of strong trade unions. These are generally explained in terms of an ideological base rooted in Confucianism (thus transcending class analysis); a labour force consisting mostly of young and unskilled workers; the employment of women with a very high turnover; and the speed with which the fruits of development were made available to society at large. Deyo argues for a more comprehensive approach that not only includes these factors but also pays attention to the specific national 'economic and social structural context within which these variables operate' (Deyo 1989: 7). In such an analysis the country-specific articulation of phenomena such as paternalistic traditions and the precise nature of elite interventions determines the space that remains 'to sustain autonomous class politics, oppositional ideologies and organized resistance to elite controls' (Deyo 1989: 9).

Some view the current situation as highly unstable and point to the violent outburst of strikes and work stoppages in Korea in 1987 when controls were loosened slightly (Bello and Rosenfeld 1992). Others believe that the higher levels of welfare and the need for upgrading of the labour force provide the necessary incentives to promote democratic tendencies, and will thus also provide more space for the organization of workers. However, the challenges posed to trade unions by innovative management–labour practices of the type implemented in Japanese industrial relations make such a turn for the better unlikely.

The foregoing analysis which suggests that the specific national context determines the space for labour organization probably applies even more strongly to Southeast Asia. Its intermediate economic position in Asia creates a demand for cheap and docile labour to attract direct foreign investment. Attempts to control and fragment labour organizations in spite of the lower degree of regimentation of these societies characterize trade union development. The Malaysian case study (as well as, in South Asia, the Pakistan case study) illustrates both the larger space as well as the weaknesses and dependence of the trade union movement.

The remaining sections of this chapter will elaborate on aspects of trade union organization in South Asia. Whereas in East and Southeast Asia the trade union movement was excluded, in South Asia it became an important actor, especially in countries with a strong public-sector profile. Three aspects of the current South Asian experience appear to be highly relevant to an assessment of the dilemmas facing the international union movement: in its tripartite involvement the government has failed to bridge conflicts between management and labour (Ramaswamy 1984); the labour movement has developed into a dual structure in which the national leadership institutions have lost contact with the union movement at the grassroots level (Ramaswamy 1988); and management is engaged in the introduction of new labour–management practices which form a direct challenge to the roles that trade unions have played traditionally (Ramaswamy 1994).

Government

South Asian countries display fundamental similarities in the way labour is organized and relations between labour, management and the state are ordered. The countries of the sub-continent share a tradition of a strong state presence between labour and management. In some ways this is a legacy of British colonial rule, the countries having found it convenient to continue the system after the British left. Simply stated, the government provides conciliation services when an industrial dispute occurs or is expected, and where conciliation fails, the parties can be asked to go before a court or tribunal. The rationale is that state intervention is necessary to prevent unbridled conflict, although all the evidence shows that this aim has never been achieved.

In the early years of Independence, few unions could have taken on the employers on their own and the fledgling labour movement was happy to have the state oversee labour–management relations. In return for this, the labour movement has had to pay a stiff price. The employer is not required to recognize a union for the obvious reason that labour places its demands not before the employer but before a government official, nor is labour accorded the right to bargain because the basic system is one of conciliation and adjudication, not of collective bargaining. Even now there is no statutory support of collective bargaining in India, although the case of Pakistan is different.

This does not imply that no collective bargaining occurs. It does, but under the shadow of state regulation. The government can forbid strikes and lockouts, forcibly refer the dispute to a court or refuse to ratify a bargained settlement, making it legally invalid. Far more serious is the damage caused to the fabric of the labour movement. Any union can raise an industrial dispute, even without the support of workers. With the right political contacts, a union can extract benefits even if it has few members. Thus trade union unity is not a compelling necessity, and fragmentation has become a common feature of the labour movement.

Although it is widely conceded today that the tripartism which places the state between labour and management has failed on almost every count, the arrangement continues. All three partners have to agree before systemic change can be brought about, and reaching such agreement has proved extremely difficult.

Trade unions

Although trade unionism has existed in South Asia for well over a century, the labour movement is in the throes of a serious crisis. In many ways, the most fundamental problem is its seemingly endless fragmentation. Party politics is the primary axis of this division, but internal affiliation, personal ambitions and the politicization of industrial relations have also contributed.

The level of unionization is extremely patchy, with well under five per cent of the total working population in the South Asian countries being union members. Even if agricultural labour (which is unorganized for the most part) were to be excluded, the extent of unionization would still be quite modest. The labour market in every country is segmented into a formal and informal sector. Medium- and large-scale firms in the manufacturing and service sectors, large plantations and government, which comprise the formal sector, offer by far the best wages and employment security. Small and tiny enterprises of all kinds, which make up the informal sector, are often sweatshops. Trade unions have a better presence in the formal sector, but are almost totally absent in the informal.

There is also a dual labour movement, with national and regional trade union federations dominating the macro scene and a growing number of enterprise-level unions operating at the grassroots. The characteristics of the two levels are easily spelt out. The macro federations recruit their leadership from outside the body of employees, generally from professionals such as lawyers, doctors, social workers and politicians. They have strong links with political parties, though some non-political ones also exist, under whose overall control they function, and they affiliate themselves to international labour bodies such as the International Confederation of Free Trade Unions (ICFTU) and in earlier times the World Federation of Trade Unions (WFTU). The macro organizations of course do have a presence at the enterprise level, but this is increasingly limited to older industries such as coal, steel, textiles and plantations. Even where they do have a presence, their membership is generally low. The federations often speak of a following that can be mustered during a crisis rather than a steady dues-paying membership.

Enterprise-level unions are built on two major planks: their leadership is drawn substantially from the ranks of workers and they shun any contact with the macro federations, let alone international affiliation. The very word 'affiliation' brings the fragmentation of the labour movement to their mind. This is not surprising considering that the first division in the sub-continent occurred over the question of international affiliation, a conflict which few workers understood, let alone empathized with. The micro unions, as we might call this segment, are strongly represented in newer industries such as chemicals, pharmaceuticals, fertilizers and power generation. They are able to achieve high membership levels, on occasion more than 90 per cent of the workforce. Despite an atmosphere dominated by the oppressive presence of the state, political parties, the judiciary and every conceivable external force, many micro unions manage to break out of the shackles of state regulation to build a more imaginative agenda which questions managerial prerogative and extends trade unionism into new areas. It is increasingly the case that dynamic trade unionism, to the extent that it exists at all in South Asia, is to be found within this layer of the labour movement and not at the level of the federations. The problem, however, is that because the micro unions lack any coordination or apex organization, governments rarely consult them on issues affecting labour.

It is useful to consider another important characteristic of trade unions in South Asia. The labour movement is quite substantially caught up in the culture of adversity. Most trade unions do not know what else they can be if not anti-management. Fragmentation adds further fuel to this tendency, and the unions vie with one another to flaunt their radical credentials. With most unions taking the view that it is the management's job to manage and their job to challenge, a participatory culture is singularly lacking. There are exceptions, but they are once again to be found at the level of enterprise unions. The employers are not interested in participation either, while the state, with an eye on its own power, has not done much to persuade labour and management to move towards a more constructive relationship.

Management

To understand management strategies, it is necessary to bear in mind the duality of the labour market. Because labour is so much cheaper in the informal sector, large enterprises are sub-contracting an ever increasing part of their production. This is probably happening everywhere, but the additional problem in the sub-continent is that there is a growing duality within the formal sector itself. All large firms use substantial numbers of workers who are not employees. Supplied by labour contractors, these workers work alongside regular employees but at a fraction of their pay. Employers are by and large willing to engage in wage negotiations with the trade unions if they limit their claims to permanent workers. The unions have, for their part, been content to ignore contract workers, whether because of legal restrictions, as in Pakistan, or because of indifference, as in India. Either way, it suits the management to have this class of workers, and work is being transferred not only from the large to the small firms but also from regular workers to contract labour within the large firm. As a result, trade unions are representing an ever-shrinking pool of workers.

There is also a growing interest amongst employers in modern human–resource management (HRM) strategies. The object of adulation is increasingly the Japanese model, the essence of which is to deal with the individual, whether in tandem with the conventional union–management relationship or over the union's head. Communication exercises, education programmes and quality circles are among the chosen methods deployed to build bridges between the firm and the individual employee. This poses a direct threat to trade unionism in South Asia, even if not so intended, because the conventional union is built simply on worker alienation from the enterprise. A non-alienated labour force will probably feel the need for more intelligent forms of trade unionism, but these can hardly be found in South Asia. The stark question facing trade unions is whether they have anything to offer which an intelligent management adopting HRM strategies does not. Few unions have a convincing answer.

All in all, the labour movement faces stiff challenges. The countries of the region are heterogeneous and polyglot. There is a broad acceptance that there are and always will be conflicts of interest between workers and employers. Trade unions have lost much of their popular support, but the disenchantment is more with the role played so far by the unions than with unionism as an ideology.

The analysis of the political, economic and social context in these major Asian regions has once again demonstrated that an in-depth study of labour organization and trade unionism is impossible without reference to such wider frameworks. A thorough analysis of labour-market developments needs to be an integral part of any such study. If the latter key dimensions are ignored, the outcome will be a biased study.

Labour-market performance and policies have been of central importance in determining the current outcomes, achievements and failures at national and even regional levels. The impressive achievements in East Asia were realized as a result of a sophisticated macro-economic management in which precise steering of labour-market elements such as wages, strikes, organization, migratory patterns, training and education was a core strategy.

Especially in the past decade, Southeast Asia has also progressed rapidly, but less sophisticated patterns of labour control have been implemented here. The results have been that low wages and oppression of trade unions have become selling points to attract foreign investments; major dualities in labour markets have emerged; and both rural and urban poverty are expected to persist and have a deep impact on vulnerable working groups. However, the impressive economic and political performance of this ASEAN region appears to hold the possibility that the exclusion of labour and labour organization will be reduced.

South Asia provides an even more complex situation for the labour movement. Its labour markets are characterized by permanent dualities along with multi-faceted segmentation mainly along ethnic, communal and gender lines. The trade union movement here needs to undergo a comprehensive restructuring if it is to remain a key actor in industrial and labour relations. The undoing of historic patterns has to be a high priority. The role of the state in collective bargaining procedures needs to be changed, trade unions need to build new constituencies as public enterprises are privatized and the challenge of new labour–management practices in medium- and large-scale enterprises has to be met.

It is hard to envisage how trade unions will be able to perform a respected role unless key issues such as categories of work in the informal sector, the position of women, regional patterns of development and industrialization become the core of trade union strategies.

Notes

1. See, for example, Figure 1.3, p. 31 in World Bank (1993) for a comparison over the period 1960–89. It indicates a strong positive association between high rates of growth in GDP per capita and low inequalities in income distribution.

2. For example, the annual *Asian Development Outlook* by the Asian Development Bank, World Bank reports and the UNDP's *Human Development Report*.

3. See Wignaraja *et al.* (1991) for a more extensive comparison.

4. See Box 5.1 in UNDP (1994: 91) for a succinct explanation of the HDI.

5. The military also played a prominent role in Taiwan and Korea, prompted by distinct external causes. However, militarization has not negatively influenced the economic development of these countries.

6. See, for example, Brown (1994) for case studies on the diverse patterns of interaction between ethnicity and state Policies in Southeast Asia.

7. Figures for Bangladesh refer to 1990.

8. Alternatively named Free Trading Zones or Export Processing Zones.

9. The East Asian figure includes China.

10. See Iwaki (1992) for a concise analysis of the Japanese system.

11. Large firms also indirectly invaded the territory of small-scale firms through the administrative break-up of units in order to qualify as small producers.

References

ADB (1990) *The Role of Small- and Medium-scale Manufacturing Industries in Industrial Development. The Experience of Selected Asian Countries.* Asian Development Bank, Manila.

Amjad, R. and G. Edgren (1991) 'The Role of Labour Markets in Employment Generation and Human Resource Development in Asian Countries', in G. Standing and V. Tokman (eds) *Towards Social Adjustment. Labour Market Issues in Structural Adjustment*, pp. 293–308. ILO, Geneva.

Amsden, A.H. (ed.) (1994) 'The World Bank's *The East Asian Miracle: Economic Growth and Public Policy*', *World Development* (Special Section) Vol. 22, No. 4: 615–70.

Athukorala, P. (1993) 'International Labour Migration in the Asian–Pacific Region: Patterns, Policies and Economic Implications', *Asian-Pacific Economic Literature* Vol. 7, No. 2: 28–57.

Bello, W. and S. Rosenfeld (1992) *Dragons in Distress: Asia's Miracle Economies in Crisis.* Institute for Food and Development Policy, San Francisco.

Brown, D. (1994) *The State and Ethnic Politics in Southeast Asia.* Routledge, London.

Cheng, L.-L. and G. Gereffi (1994) 'The Informal Economy in East Asian Development', *International Journal of Urban and Regional Research* Vol. 18, No. 2: 194–219.

Chhachhi, A. and R. Pittin (forthcoming) 'Introduction', in A. Chhachhi and R. Pittin (eds) *Confronting State, Capital and Patriarchy: Women Organising in the Process of Industrialisation.* MacMillan, London.

Chowdury, A. and I. Islam (1993) *The Newly Industrialising Economies of East Asia.* Routledge, London.

Datta, A.K. (1991) 'Control, Conflict and Alliance. An Analysis of Land and Labour Relations in Two Bangladesh Villages', Ph.D. Thesis. Institute of Social Studies, The Hague.

Deyo, F.C. (ed.) (1987) *The Political Economy of the New Asian Industrialism.* Cornell University Press, Ithaca.

―――― (1989) *Beneath the Miracle. Labor Subordination in the New Asian Industrialism*. University of California Press, Berkeley.

Dixon, C. (1991) *South East Asia in the World Economy*. Cambridge University Press, Cambridge.

Evers, H.-D. (1989) 'Urban Poverty and Labour Supply Strategies in Jakarta', in G. Rodgers (ed.) *Urban Poverty and the Labour Market. Access to Jobs and Incomes in Asian and Latin American Cities*, pp. 145–72. ILO, Geneva.

Galenson, W. (1992) *Labor and Economic Growth in Five Asian Countries: South Korea, Malaysia, Taiwan, Thailand, and the Philippines*. Praeger, New York.

Honculada, J.A. (forthcoming) 'Philippine Trade Unions and the Challenge of Gender', in A. Chhachhi and R. Pittin (eds) *Confronting State, Capital and Patriarchy: Women Organising in the Process of Industrialisation*. MacMillan, London.

ILO (1992) *Yearbook of Labour Statistics*. International Labour Office, Geneva.

Islam, R. (ed.) (1987) *Rural Industrialisation and Employment in Asia*. ILO-ARTEP, New Delhi.

Iwaki, G. (1992) 'SMI Development and the Sub-contracting System in Japan', in K.S. Jin and S. Jang-Won (eds) *Co-operation in Small- and Medium-scale Industries in ASEAN*, pp. 309–51. Asian and Pacific Development Centre, Kuala Lumpur.

James, W.E., S. Naya and G.M. Meier (1989) *Asian Development. Economic Success and Policy Lessons*. University of Wisconsin Press, Madison.

Jenkins, R. (1991) 'The Political Economy of Industrialization: A Comparison of Latin American and East Asian Newly Industrializing Countries', *Development and Change*, Vol. 22, No. 2: 197–231.

Kemal, A.R. (1993) 'Monitoring of Labour Markets in Pakistan', in M. Muqtada and A. Hildeman (eds) (1993) *Labour Markets and Human Resource Planning in Asia: Perspectives and Evidence*, pp. 169–90. UNDP/ILO-ARTEP, New Delhi.

Mackie, J.A.C. (1988) 'Economic Growth in the ASEAN Region: the Political Underpinnings', in H. Hughes (ed.) *Achieving Industrialization in East Asia*, pp. 283–326. Cambridge University Press, Cambridge.

Mahmood, M. (1994) 'Assessment Study of the Small-scale and Micro-enterprise Sector in Pakistan', Mimeograph.

Mahmud Ali, S. (1993) *The Fearful State. Power, People and Internal War in South Asia*. Zed Books, London.

Muqtada, M. and A. Hildeman (eds) (1993) *Labour Markets and Human Resource Planning in Asia: Perspectives and Evidence*. UNDP/ILO-ARTEP, New Delhi.

Ofreneo, R.E. (1993) 'Structural Adjustment and Labour Market Responses in the Philippines', in M. Muqtada and A. Hildeman (eds) (1993) *Labour Markets and Human Resource Planning in Asia: Perspectives and Evidence*, pp. 243–68. UNDP/ILO-ARTEP, New Delhi.

Papola, T.S. (1993) 'Labour Market Monitoring for Employment Planning: A Framework Illustrated with the Indian Experience', in M. Muqtada and A. Hildeman (eds) (1993) *Labour Markets and Human Resource Planning in Asia: Perspectives and Evidence*, pp. 127–39. UNDP/ILO–ARTEP, New Delhi.

Ramaswamy, E.A. (1984) *Power and Justice: The State in Industrial Relations*. Oxford University Press, New Delhi.

—— (1988) *Worker Consciousness and Trade Union Response*. Oxford University Press, New Delhi.

—— (1994) *The Rayon Spinners*. Oxford University Press, New Delhi.

Romijn, H.A. (1993) 'Dynamism in the Informal Sector in a Fast Growing Economy: The Case of Bangkok', Working Paper (Dec.). ILO–ARTEP, New Delhi.

Rose, K. (1992) *Where Women Are Leaders. The SEWA Movement in India*. Zed Books, London.

Sen, A. (1982) *The State, Industrialization and Class Formations in India*. Routledge & Kegan Paul, London.

SEWA (1989) *Shramshakti. A Summary of the Report of the National Commission on Self-employed Women and Women in the Informal Sector*. SEWA, Ahmedabad.

Shah, N., S. Gothoskar, N. Gandhi and A. Chhachhi (1994) 'Structural Adjustment, Feminisation of the Labour Force and Organisational Strategies', *Economic and Political Weekly* Vol. 29, No. 18: WS39–48.

Standing, G. (1989) 'Global Feminisation through Flexible Labour', *World Development* Vol. 17, No. 7: 1077–95.

Suhrke, A. (1992) 'Migration, State and Civil Society in Southeast Asia', Working Paper No. M4. Chr. Michelsen Institute, Bergen (Norway).

Tambunan, T. (1994) 'The Role of Small-scale Industries in Rural Economic Development', PhD Thesis. Erasmus University, Rotterdam.

UN (1991) *World Population Prospects 1990*. United Nations, New York.

UNDP (1994) *Human Development Report 1994*. UNDP, Oxford University Press, Oxford.

Wignaraja, P., A. Hussain, H. Sethi and G. Wignaraja (eds) (1991) *Participatory Development. Learning from South Asia*, pp. 121–61. Oxford University Press, Karachi.

World Bank (1992, 1994) *World Development Report*. Oxford University Press, Oxford.

—— (1993) *The East Asian Miracle. Economic Growth and Public Policy*. Oxford University Press, New York.

3. Economic Take-off: Trade Unions in Malaysia

Syed Hussein Ali

Malaysia is a Federation consisting of eleven states in Peninsular or West Malaysia, two states in Borneo (East Malaysia) and a Federal Territory. It covers an area of about 330,000 km,^{2} of which about three-quarters is still uncultivated.

In 1992 Malaysia's population was close to 19 million. With a growth rate of 2.1 per cent, it is projected to cross 22 million by the year 2000. Its composition is skewed. Persons below the age of 20 make up 48.6 per cent of the population, while those between 20–40 years constitute 31.3 per cent.

The rural population is mainly Malay, predominantly in the northern and eastern part of the peninsula. The Chinese, a little less than one-third of the population, are concentrated in the western parts, dominating the larger towns. The third major group, Indians, make up one-tenth of the population. There are also other, small ethnic groups in the rural areas. The Malay share in the urban population is increasing rapidly as a result of the government policy of encouraging rural–urban migration.

Political, social and economic background

Political

Although Malaysia has undergone a series of political and cultural influences, it is British rule that has left the deepest imprint on all spheres. The British colonized the island of Penang in 1786. Subsequently, through conquest, diplomacy and other interventions, they were able to subjugate one Malay state and its ruler after another.

The initial seeds of anti-colonial struggle were sown before the Second World War. After the war the struggle intensified, led mainly by the Malay Nationalist Party and the Malayan Communist Party (Abdullah 1985; Stenson 1970). The state of emergency declared in June 1948 banned the two parties. Thousands of people were detained or confined in newly constructed villages. Many escaped to the jungle and the struggle escalated into guerrilla warfare.

At the same time, the United Malay National Organization (UMNO), formed in 1946 and encouraged by the British, began to monopolize the political arena. Around 1952 it formed an alliance with local Chinese and Indian political organizations. The alliance spearheaded the struggle for *Merdeka* (Independence) which was achieved in 1957. The transfer of political power occurred, however, without much fundamental change.

Singapore, Sabah and Sarawak achieved Independence from Britain in 1965 and joined with Malaya to form the Federation of Malaysia. Soon afterwards Singapore separated and the Indonesian Confrontation, launched by President Soekarno to oppose the formation of Malaysia, reached new heights. Once more an emergency was declared, followed by mass arrests, particularly of opposition party leaders, a large number of whom were from the Socialist Front (SF) and Muslim Party (PAS).

The government's pro-Malay policies created tense ethnic relations, especially between the Malays and Chinese. The campaigns for the 1969 election were highly charged with ethnic sentiments. A few days after the election, bloody ethnic conflicts, often referred to as the May 13 Incident, erupted in Kuala Lumpur.

An emergency was declared yet again, parliament was suspended and a National Operation Council was formed to govern the country. A National Consultative Council was also set up, consisting of representatives from various political and non-political organizations as well as of individuals. When parliament was reconvened nearly two years later, several opposition parties had joined the ruling alliance to form the National Front (NF).

In the 1974 election the NF won by a landslide. But trouble soon followed, involving the PAS, which was subsequently excluded from the NF and the government. An emergency was declared in the PAS-controlled state of Kelantan and a split was engineered in the party. When elections were held, UMNO (the main component of the NF) regained control of the state government.

Between 1982–85 the economy took a turn for the worse and a general uneasiness grew in the country and within UMNO. Before and after the 1986 elections, non-governmental organizations (NGOs) became more active and outspoken in their criticism of government leadership. Opposition parties also stepped up their criticism of the government and a major split occurred within UMNO.

In October 1987 the government detained 119 people from various political and social organizations under the Internal Security Act (ISA). Two dailies, the *Star* (English) and *Sin Chew Jit Poh* (Chinese), and the Malay-language weekly tabloid *Watan* were banned (CARPA 1988).

In the wake of all these events, the King suspended the lord president from his office as head of the judiciary, and in August 1988 his services were terminated. A few months later, two senior judges were sacked. The executive began to gain greater control over the judiciary. Protests from various quarters were ignored.

These and many other events became hot issues during the 1990 general elections. Despite a strong challenge from opposition parties, which united in a loose coalition under the leadership of Semangat 46, a new party formed by the breakaway group from UMNO, the NF won more than a two-thirds majority in parliament. However, it obtained only about 52 per cent of the votes.

Social

Two significant social developments resulted from changes under colonial rule and following *Merdeka*. First, Malaysia developed into a multi-ethnic society *par excellence*. The Malays, who, together with various indigenous groups in Sabah and Sarawak are called *Bumiputera* (sons of the soil), constitute the largest group. In 1990 they made up about 58 per cent of the population. The second largest group is Chinese (about 31 per cent), followed by Indian (about 10 per cent).

The ethnic groups are not homogeneous. There are many different sub-cultures among the *Bumiputera*, with many retaining their own languages and customs. Although most of these are Muslims, some groups in Sabah and Sarawak have different lifestyles from those of peninsular Malays, speak different languages and are animists or Christians. The Chinese belong to various clans and speak different dialects. Traditionally they are Buddhists, but many have now embraced Christianity or are non-believers. The Indians belong to different castes, and though most are Hindu many are Christian and Muslim.

The second significant development is an increase in social stratification with the formation of new and diverse classes. For a long time the various ethnic groups were identified with different geographical locations and economic activities. Rural Malays were mainly engaged in traditional rice cultivation and worked in rubber or palm-oil smallholdings, while a large number of Chinese worked in tin mines or engaged in petty trading in the rural areas and other business enterprises in the towns. The Indians have always generally been associated with work on the rubber estates.

Industrial, commercial, educational, administrative, political and other developments have induced people to enter new occupations and raise their socio-economic status. Many Malays have left their *kampung* (village) to become soldiers, industrial workers, clerks and teachers. Some have risen much higher as civil servants, politicians and corporate businessmen. Children of Chinese miners or small businessmen have become lawyers, engineers and doctors, or achieved success in the corporate world. Likewise, a large number of Indians have entered into the business and professional fields.

People can now be categorized into upper, middle and lower classes. However, the members of these social strata still do not have a strong *esprit de corps* among themselves. At present the pull towards ethnicity is much stronger than that towards class, even among workers (Hussein Ali 1984).

A large number of those in the lower stratum, especially peasants and estate and industrial workers, live in or near poverty. In 1990 about 17 per cent of the population had incomes below the poverty line. In rural areas the percentage was 22 and in urban areas, eight. The incidence of poverty is higher amongst Malays than Chinese and is highest among rubber smallholders and rice farmers. The states of Kelantan and Sabah record the highest incidence (over 30 per cent). The persistence of poverty implies socio-economic inequity, which often results in unequal access to social facilities.[1]

Economic

Under British rule, Malaya may be said to have become a dual economy. In the subsistence sector rice growing and rubber tapping dominated, while in the capitalist sector, rubber plantations, tin mines and commerce, largely owned by British capital, were the major economic activities.

After *Merdeka* a diversification policy was adopted and oil palm and cocoa were introduced at the smallholding and estate levels. A rural development plan was launched in 1959, focusing on drainage and irrigation, rubber replanting and resettlement schemes. An import-substitution policy initiated by the British continued after *Merdeka*. Factories were established to process natural resources and manufacture import substitutes locally.

In the wake of the May 13 Incident, the New Economic Policy (NEP) encouraged a combination of export promotion and import substitution. Foreign investment was attracted by the introduction of tax-free incentives under pioneer status for industries. A number of Free Trade Zones (FTZs) were opened. The manufacture of electronics, textiles, garments and footwear products was stepped up. The production and export of natural products, especially petroleum, palm oil, rubber and timber, were also promoted more actively.

The NEP was implemented under the Second Malaysia Plan (1971–5). Its main target was to achieve national unity through a two-pronged economic strategy: eradication of poverty irrespective of race; and restructuring of society to allow for greater *Bumiputera* participation in industry and commerce. The NEP succeeded to a large extent in reducing poverty and increasing Malay ownership of share capital.

Nevertheless, a large group of rural hard-core poor still remains, intra-ethnic socio-economic gaps, especially among Malays, have grown, and the share equity for Malays is monopolized by a privileged few. In its implementation the NEP has tended to emphasize bridging of the inter-ethnic gap in industry and commerce, and has neglected the growing intra-ethnic socio-economic inequity.

The imprint of the present prime minister, Mahathir Mohamad, on the Fifth Malaysia Plan (1986–90) is very marked. The plan emphasizes the role of the private sector in development, increased privatization of government-owned enterprises, adoption of Japanese work ethics through the Look East Policy, and acceleration of the industrialization process. In 1991 the Second Outline Perspective Plan was announced, delineating development until the year 2000, followed by the publication of the Sixth Malaysia Plan (1991–95). These two documents embody the vision of the Prime Minister, which aims at making Malaysia fully industrialized by the year 2020.

Undoubtedly, Malaysia is in transition from a primarily agricultural to a relatively industrial economy. This may be observed from the employment pattern. In 1970 49.1 per cent of employment was in agriculture, but this fell to 30.2 per cent in 1990. Even though employment in agriculture expanded by 210,000 between 1986–90, its growth rate (2.3 per cent) has lagged behind that of manufacturing (6.2 per cent). This transformation has taken place within the framework of a free-market system, encouraging foreign investment and stressing deregulation.

The labour situation

History

Political and economic changes have influenced the situation of labour and the labour movement in Malaysia. Before the Second World War, small and scattered trade unions already existed in some parts of the country. After the war, the General Labour Union (GLU) was formed, which incorporated existing unions and established new ones. The GLU's powerful bases were in the rubber estates and tin mines.

The British regarded its leaders with suspicion as militants using the labour movement for a wider anti-colonial struggle.

In an attempt to reduce the influence of the GLU, the British brought in trade union advisors from Britain to help organize moderate unions and leadership and counter the allegedly pro-communist ones (Awberry and Dalley 1948; Dass 1991; Gamba 1962). They were quite successful in this strategy among Indian workers. Malay workers had never been responsive to the GLU as its leadership was dominated by Indians and Chinese. Ethnic differences and conflicts were used by the colonial power to divide and weaken the labour movement, especially the GLU.

Following the proclamation of the emergency on 18 June 1948, some leaders were detained or executed, while others fled to the jungles or were forced underground. The emergency affected the economy adversely. With trade unions weakened, employers were able to retrench workers and reduce wages. The elimination of militant trade union leaders and organizations opened the way for further promotion of moderate leaders and unions such as the National Union of Plantation Workers (NUPW), the Malayan Trade Union Council (MTUC) and later the Congress of Unions of Employees in the Public and Civil Services (CUEPACS).

The Korean War in the early 1950s induced a rubber boom and the unions succeeded in negotiating higher wages. This led to an expansion of union membership. Political and economic uncertainty just before and after *Merdeka,* however, had a negative effect on the workers' movement. In 1960 the whole country was proclaimed 'white' (free of communist military threat), the trade union movement was allowed more space and membership began to increase. Simultaneously, the number of industrial workers grew, due to the government's industrialization policy.

Union activity intensified in the early 1960s when a number of Nanyang University graduates and cadres of the SF organized Chinese workers in the industrial and commercial sectors. They were more willing to confront employers and the government in order to advance the interests of workers. During the Indonesian Confrontation and following the declaration of the second emergency, many union activists were also roped in under the ISA and several of their unions were deregistered. Some managed to survive, but after the third emergency, declared after the May 13 Incident, they were virtually wiped out.

With the formation of the broad-based NF under his leadership, Prime Minister Tun Razak introduced a tripartite approach in labour relations. This approach fizzled out, however, towards the end of the 1970s, especially after the government detained 22 leaders of the Malaysian Airlines Employees Union (MAEU) under the ISA, banned their union and replaced it with an in-house one, as a consequence of a lockout staged by the MAEU to demand higher wages and better working conditions.

The idea of in-house unions was further promoted by the present prime minister under his Look East Policy. However, his attempt to emulate the so-called Japanese industrial relations model stressed almost exclusively the need for hard work to increase productivity (Jomo 1989). Labour was hit hard during the recession and fiscal crisis that occurred in the mid-1980s. Many workers in estates, mines and factories were laid off. The public-sector workers had to face pay or allowance cuts while new rules were introduced to tighten control over unions.

Several trends can be discerned in the labour situation:

- by 1985 about 66 per cent of the labour force was in agriculture and industry, and the remainder in the public sector;
- while employment generally increased, the rate of increase was fastest in the industrial sector;
- more Malays have entered the industrial labour market where they now constitute about half of the labour force;
- the number of women in the industrial sector has also increased, particularly in textile and electronics manufacture in FTZs;
- the level of unionization in the total labour force is low, around 10 per cent, but even lower among women;
- more in-house unions have been formed, but the majority of them are in the public sector and statutory bodies;
- there has also been a tremendous increase in immigrant labour, mainly from Bangladesh, Indonesia, the Philippines and Thailand.

Two conferences were held by unions and the MTUC in the 1970s to discuss the participation of unions in politics. They rejected direct union participation but allowed union leaders to be involved in political parties and to stand as candidates in general elections. Unions could endorse candidates from different parties considered to be pro-labour. However, current legislation forbids unions from forming links with political parties and the latter are not allowed to form unions identified with or affiliated to them (Dass 1991).

Therefore, no union is currently linked directly with any political party. A small number of union leaders and activists have remained involved in politics, however, in both government and opposition parties. It is interesting to note that the Council of the MTUC comprises more members affiliated to the government than to opposition parties, though some top leaders have been actively involved with opposition parties. For instance, the previous secretary-general was in the leadership of the Democratic Action Party, while its present president was a prominent member of the Semangat 46.

Political parties are involved in various activities among workers and unions but they have little impact on the labour movement. It is the government which continues to have a big say. The government has adopted two main strategies to weaken the labour movement. One is to encourage and later recognize more pro-government leaders and unions. The other is to launch sustained attacks on leaders and unions that are considered uncooperative with the government. The MTUC has often been accused of being disloyal for allegedly conniving with foreign labour organizations to discredit the country.

In the past, under the ISA, many trade union leaders were detained without trial. While the ISA hangs like a sword of Damocles over the heads of union and other activists, a number of other laws and regulations also directly govern and regulate the unions. The Employment Ordinance of 1955 governs industrial relations and stipulates certain rights relating to working conditions, compensations and various types of leave. Ironically, it does not protect workers from unfair dismissal. In fact, workers can be dismissed without notice for 'misconduct'.

The Trade Union Ordinance of 1959 regulates various aspects of unions. It gives wide powers to the Registrar of Societies, including that of deregistering unions. It also prohibits the use of union funds for political purposes. Finally, the Industrial Relations Act of 1967 regulates strict procedures for strike action and incorporates elements of compulsory arbitration. It prohibits union officials from holding key positions in political parties and designates many services in the private and public sectors as 'essential', thus limiting the power of unions representing workers in these services to take industrial action. An illegal strike is punishable by imprisonment under this Act. Over the years, these laws have undergone several amendments, which in many cases have made them far worse and even more oppressive.

Formal organization

Malaysia's total labour force now exceeds seven million, only a small proportion of which is organized through the more than 300 unions in the public and private sectors. Since Independence union membership has ranged between 8.5 and 13.7 per cent. It was highest during 1975–77, reaching over 13 per cent, but since then membership has been declining slowly. Current estimates indicate a union membership of about 10 per cent.

Union membership

The unions are organized in different ways. They may be based at the work place, some being in-house unions. A factory or department may have more than one union, representing workers of different skill levels or pay. A sector or trade may also have separate unions based on differences in ethnicity.

The proportion of Malays in union membership has increased rapidly and now exceeds 50 per cent. Chinese membership fell after the banning of many left-wing unions and the detention of their leaders. It has dropped steadily to about 15 per cent of the total membership. As for Indians, their share has decreased to around 22 per cent.

Two factors have contributed to the Malay increase. First, following the NEP Malays were encouraged to enter industry; the Malay working-class component grew and to some extent influenced union membership. Second, Malays form the majority of the labour force in the public sector and this sector's level of organization is much higher than that of the private sector.

Women's participation

For all years and all sectors the participation of women in the labour force has remained below that of men. However, some interesting observations can be made. Between 1970 and 1990 there was a striking increase in female employment in the modern sector: from 28.1 to 46.4 per cent in manufacturing, and from 18.2 to 38.6 per cent in the wholesale and retail trades and hotels and restaurants. In contrast, female employment in the traditional agricultural sector has decreased, albeit quite slowly, from 38 to 34.4 per cent.

The women's unionization rate is between 5 and 10 per cent, lower than the overall 10 per cent. The membership share of women in unions has always been relatively low. It fell below 20 per cent between 1968 and 1974 but then rose to nearly 30 per cent in 1988, and is still increasing steadily.

Women do not play a significant role at the leadership level; they hold fewer than 10 per cent of the leading positions in unions.[2] A number of explanations have been suggested for this: that women do not have much time to be active in unions because of their duties at home. Sharing of housework by spouses is not very common; that these organizations have a higher number of male members and women can win elections only if they are considered to be outstanding; finally, that the leadership is male-dominated and most of the leaders seem to be ill-disposed to having women at the top levels.

The MTUC has a Women's Section which organizes activities for and about women, particularly as workers. The chairperson of this section, who is elected at a convention confined to women, becomes one of the MTUC's vice-presidents. Her election usually depends on the support given by the larger organizations and more powerful male leaders. In contrast, in the CUEPACS women have to stand against men in order to gain office. If they win, it is on their own strength and merit. They are consequently less beholden to male leaders.

Whereas the career paths of women leaders in the MTUC can be constrained if the male leaders do not favour them, at least in theory this is unlikely to happen in the CUEPACS, especially when they receive wide support. Nevertheless, even in the CUEPACS, no powerful woman leader has emerged so far.

Umbrella organizations

Some unions, like the electronics in-house unions, stand on their own. Others are affiliated to larger organizations. By law these are based on the same trade. They can be multi-ethnic or focus on particular ethnic groupings and/or on similar training levels or professional status. There are also much larger organizations which serve as umbrella organizations. The four most prominent ones are discussed below.

MTUC: The Malaysian Trade Union Congress was formed in 1951 as the Malayan Trade Union Council. It is neither a federation nor a union, but merely a centre to coordinate common policies for trade unions and to represent them in government bodies and international organizations or at international meetings (Bahari 1989). It has no power to organize any industrial action or to negotiate for any union at the bargaining table.

The MTUC claims a following of about 135 affiliates and over 300,000 members. From its very beginning it has steered clear of party politics but nevertheless tried to cooperate closely with the government, sitting on various boards and committees with government representatives though its views are seldom taken seriously. Consequently, the relationship between the MTUC and the government has become increasingly stormy.

The MTUC's initial membership included both private- and public-sector unions. However, as a result of amendments to various trade union laws introduced during the 1970s, public-sector unions were discouraged from affiliating with the MTUC. Subsequently, internal conflicts also led to the departure of many government unions. Although it still has some government unions as affiliates it is now regarded as a private-sector organization. Following the privatization of some state undertakings, like telecommunication and electricity, unions in these enterprises have joined the MTUC.

Organizationally, the MTUC is governed by a council consisting of representatives from member unions. The daily management of the MTUC is in the hands of an executive committee, whose most important members are the president, secretary-general and finance secretary. Usually the MTUC's leadership originates from the large unions. For some time the NUPW and Transport Workers' Union (TWU) played a major role, not only as brokers to determine leadership but also as a source of MTUC leaders. As for the trade union movement as a whole, the MTUC's leadership has been oligarchic, with only a small number of powerful leaders who remain in office for prolonged periods.

CUEPACS: The Congress of Unions of Employees in the Public and Civil Services was formed on 23 October 1957. Its predecessor was the Government Services Staff Council, which was set up as a society in 1948. The CUEPACS also serves as a workers' centre but, unlike the MTUC, it is a federation of unions that has been granted powers to function as a union. Since its formation, it has remained the largest of such federations, claiming to have about 90 affiliates with approximately 124,000 members.

The CUEPACS is a public-sector organization, open only to workers in higher grades. Since almost every work process in the public sector is determined by the government, one would expect the CUEPACS to play a marginal role only. However, in the 1970s the CUEPACS frequently took up cudgels with the government; for example, to secure equal pay for women, particularly nurses and teachers.

Generally, the CUEPACS is more conservative and closer to the government than the MTUC. It adheres strictly to the policy of separating unionism from politics, particularly opposition politics. But a few of its national leaders have been known to be active as UMNO members or members of its labour bureau. In the past, a number of strikes was undertaken by CUEPACS affiliates, like the postal, forestry and railway unions.

Following the railway strike, new rules were introduced to make it difficult for public-sector workers, particularly those in essential services, to go on strike. The Industrial Relations Act details the procedures required before a strike can be initiated. In the 1980s many public-sector unions withdrew from the MTUC. Some joined the CUEPACS while others, like the Amalgamated National Unions of Local Authority Employees, remained on their own.

The CUEPACS structure is quite similar to that of the MTUC. The governing council comprises representatives of affiliated organizations and daily management is looked after by an executive committee. As with the MTUC, the CUEPACS is also dominated by its larger affiliates, such as the National Union of the Teaching Profession (NUTP) and the Malaysian Technical Staff Union. Its leadership tends to be oligarchic, too.

MKTR: The National Council of Industrial and Low-Income Group of Workers (MKTR) is the smallest of the trade union centres. It was founded on 17 May 1956 as the Industrial and Manual Group Staff Council. The MKTR has 22 affiliated unions and about 45,000 members. The MKTR membership consists of the lowest or subordinate groups from the public sector, quasi-government and local authorities, but none from the private sector.

The MKTR does not qualify for membership of the CUEPACS, which is only for higher grades of workers. However, some of its affiliates, like the KSATRIA (a union catering for workers in the armed forces), can also join the CUEPACS. The MKTR joined with the National Union of Banking Employees (NUBE) to form the Malaysian Labour Organization (MLO).

MLO: The Malaysian Labour Organization is a recent creation, largely a result of misunderstanding and conflicts amongst a few union leaders in the MTUC. It was registered in August 1989. The MLO serves as an umbrella organization but, like the MTUC, it cannot function as a trade union.

The MLO's creation was initiated by the NUBE, a member of the MTUC until 1987, which still forms its backbone. It has been able to attract the MKTR into its fold. At present the MLO claims to have 30 affiliates and about 150,000 members. It seems to be even closer to the government than the CUEPACS and is very critical of the MTUC. Its national leadership is quite new, despite the prior prominence of its general secretary in union circles.

Informal organization

As noted, merely 10 per cent of the workforce is presently unionized. Various explanations have been suggested for this low level:

- that a large section of the labour force, consisting of immigrant workers, cannot be organized because the workers have entered the country illegally.
- that in many sectors no organization of workers has yet occurred; for example, in construction and among shop workers. As for electronics workers, they have been constantly obstructed from forming unions, especially when organized on a national basis.

- that there is a general apathy and/or low level of consciousness regarding the importance of unionization. Some workers consider their conditions already good, while others think that they need not become union members to improve their conditions since these are determined by the employers (especially the government). Moreover, they believe they will benefit anyhow from any improvements in wages and working conditions won by unions even if they are not members.
- that the general weakness of the unions and the perception of union leaders as insincere and self-serving have lessened confidence in their ability to truly and effectively represent workers' interests.
- that an atmosphere of indifference or even fear has developed among many workers as a result of the banning of unions and detention of their leaders in the past. At the very least there is the fear of the possibility, especially in government service, of being transferred to faraway places or denied promotion if one is too active.
- that ethnic differences have been used to weaken and split unions and to discourage workers from joining.

Undoubtedly, various combinations of these reasons at different times and places are relevant to individual workers.

Migrant labour
It is estimated that more than one million migrants are working in Malaysia, of whom about half are registered with the government. Most came in search of jobs while some claim to be refugees. Rampant exploitation and neglect of migrant workers, particularly the illegal ones, exist. In most sectors they receive only about two-thirds of the local wages. Their passports are often held by their employers to prevent them from leaving their work sites. Their living conditions, especially in less-accessible areas, are known to be appalling; no proper housing or sanitation is provided.

It is well-known that migrant labour can and has been used by employers in the agricultural and building sectors to weaken unions, depress wages and even displace local workers. The plantation, building and business sectors frequently employ contract workers who have no job security and are often at the mercy of their employers. Local contract workers find their position increasingly threatened by the influx of migrants, making any attempt at unionization even more difficult.

Electronics workers

The number of electronics workers has been increasing rapidly since the first semiconductor assembly plant was established in Malaysia in 1972.[3] By 1984 it was estimated that there were about 60,000 electronics workers, but 12,000 were retrenched as a result of a downturn in the economy. Soon afterwards the electronics industry expanded again, following the government industrialization policies. Currently it is estimated that there are more than 200,000 electronics workers in the country. The majority are women, who are preferred because they are believed to be more suitable for the job, more diligent and less susceptible to trade union activism.

Workers in the lower rungs of the electronics industry, where women constitute the majority, initially receive a basic monthly wage of 250 to 300 Malaysian dollars. They work in three shifts and many of them are able to earn twice or even three times as much by doing extra or overtime work. During recession in the industry many workers, especially the more senior and higher paid ones, have been retrenched only to be replaced by new workers earning less pay.

There have been attempts in the past to organize the workers. Though the MTUC has been making strong demands for the organization of a national union for electronics workers, it has not been as active in meeting and organizing these workers at their workplace. Following an intense campaign by the MTUC locally and the International Metalwork Federation internationally, the government announced in September 1988 that electronics workers could form only in-house unions. So far only six of these unions have been formed. Five of them, formed with assistance of the government, are affiliated to the MLO.

Organization of workers by NGOs

Several Malaysian NGOs are involved in community work as well as organization of unorganized workers at the grassroots level. They are active at the workplace, especially estates and factories, and in squatter areas where many workers are settled. However, due to shortage in human and financial resources, the activities of NGOs are often localized and limited in their range. One example of such an NGO is the Worker Organization (WO), which operates mainly among estate workers. One WO leader was also very active in the attempts to form the first electronics union (Grace 1990).

A number of NGOs are targeted at women, such as the Women Development Centre, Malaysian Women Organization (AWAM) and Friends of Women (Sahabat Wanita). They do not confine their activities to workers only, but also operate among women in the villages and squatter areas. They concentrate on educational activities to raise consciousness on women's issues and aspects of human rights. They have organized seminars on rape and violence against women and children, and have successfully campaigned for the promulgation of new laws to protect women. To a very limited extent they also try to organize women as workers. Usually these organizations carry out their activities on their own.

International contacts

Most trade union centres and some of their affiliates have been able to establish international links. The MTUC used to be the sole workers' representative to the ILO, but since 1980, at the government's insistence, it has agreed to share this on an alternate basis with the CUEPACS. However, this issue was disputed by the MTUC recently. The MTUC is affiliated with the International Confederation of Free Trade Unions (ICFTU). Some affiliates of the MTUC, like the Railway Workers' Union and the TWU, are also direct members of the International Transport Workers' Federation.

The CUEPACS is affiliated with the Public Services International. Some CUEPACS affiliates are also linked with other international organizations. For example, the NUTP is affiliated with the International Federation of Free Teachers' Unions and, thus indirectly, also with the ICFTU.

The MLO has not established any international links yet. The government has hinted recently that it may raise the MLO's status to one of the alternate workers' representatives to ILO meetings in the future. The MKTR, on the other hand, is directly linked to the Brotherhood of Asian Trade Unionists, which is the regional organization for the World Confederation of Labour.

Through these associations with international organizations, leaders of Malaysian trade unions are able to attend international meetings and be elected to serve on some international committees as well. This provides them with opportunities for wider interaction and association. However, foreign trips appear to be highly prized and are often monopolized by the top echelons and their associates, which has become a source of dissatisfaction. The government is also known to sponsor various other leaders for foreign trips, especially in an effort to co-opt or win over some of these leaders to its side.

A certain number of the international organizations also raise funds which from time to time have been channelled to local unions for specific projects such as organizing seminars, workshops, training courses and so forth for local union members and leaders or for maintaining workers' centres, hostels or educational institutes. NGOs also receive funding from various international sources to help them carry out their activities.

While political, economic and social factors have all influenced the growth of trade unions in Malaysia, political factors appear to be the most important. Through its actions and the various laws and regulations it has promulgated, the government seems to have succeeded in stifling the growth of a strong and healthy workers' movement in Malaysia. Here, as in most Southeast Asian countries, workers are perceived as a potential threat to national stability, which their government regards as of prime importance for achieving economic growth. The general opinion appears to be that not only workers' rights but even human rights can be sacrificed to ensure such economic success.

The Malaysian state undoubtedly is less favourably disposed to labour than to capital. Allowed only limited freedom, labour has been unable to fight effectively for the development of a strong workers' movement and, consequently, better wages and employment conditions. The state strongly links wage increases to productivity. Even when productivity has increased or been maintained at a high level, as on rubber plantations and in the electronics industries, wages and incomes remain low and sometimes even below the poverty line. The determination to maintain a docile trade union movement does not augur well for the workers' future.

The union leaders also have to shoulder part of the blame for the weakness of their movement. Union leadership tends to be oligarchic, controlling several unions simultaneously in an interlocking manner, and not fully committed to serving the interests of workers. These factors, together with the lack of workers' consciousness, have resulted in low overall unionization and even lower participation by women. For these reasons, unions have not fully benefited from the employment expansion in the wake of the industrialization process. Indeed, the struggle towards developing truly united, democratic, responsible and genuinely pro-worker trade unions remains a great challenge in Malaysia.

Notes

1. See Chee (1990) for a discussion of unequal access to health care.

2. Ariffin (1991) contains a fuller discussion of women's participation in unions.

3. Grace (1990) provides a discussion of the industry's development and attempts to form unions.

References

Abdullah, F.H. (1985) *Radical Malay Politics: Its Origin and Early Development*. Pelanduk Publications, Kuala Lumpur.

Ariffin, R. (1991) 'Women and Trade Unions in Peninsular Malaysia With Special Reference to MTUC and CUEPACS', Ph.D. Thesis. University of Malaya.

Awberry, S.S. and F.W. Dalley (1948) *Labour and Trade Union Organization in the Federation of Malaya and Singapore*. Government Press, Kuala Lumpur.

Bahari, A. (1989) 'Malaysian Trade Union Congress (MTUC) 1948–81', Ph.D. Thesis. University of Warwick, Warwick.

CARPA (1988) *Tangled Web – Dissent, Deterrence and the 27 October 1987 Crackdown in Malaysia*. Haymarket, Australia.

Chee, H.L. (1990) 'Health and Health Care Among the Poor: A Case Study of an Urban Squatter Settlement in Peninsular Malaysia', Ph.D. Thesis. University of Malaya.

Dass, A. (1991) *Not Beyond Repair – Reflections of a Malaysian Trade Unionist*. Asia Monitor Resource Centre, Hong Kong.

Gamba, C. (1962) *The Origins of Trade Unionism in Malaya*. Donald Moore Press, Singapore.

Grace, E. (1990) *Shortcircuiting Labour: Unionising Electronic Workers in Malaysia*. Insan, Kuala Lumpur.

Hussein Ali, S. (ed.) (1984) *Ethnicity, Class and Development – Malaysia*. Malaysian Social Social Association, Kuala Lumpur.

Jomo, K.S. (ed.) (1989) *Mahathir's Economic Policies*. Insan, Kuala Lumpur.

Stenson, M.R. (1970) *Industrial Conflict in Malaya: Prelude to the Communist Revolt of 1948*. Oxford University Press, Kuala Lumpur.

4. Relative Stagnation: Pakistan's Labour Movement

Charles Amjad-Ali

The state, the economy and labour markets

Political system and social developments

In 1947, after the end of British colonial rule, the sub-continent was partitioned into Pakistan and India with the former having two parts, the east and the west, separated by some 1,000 miles of Indian territory. The partition was implemented largely on the basis of religion, with Pakistan perceived as the fulfilment of the aspirations of the Muslims of India.

From its very inception the state had two major preoccupations. It was based on the assumption of a transcendent and homogenizing religious ideology and identity, which was an internal compulsion because of the multi-ethnic identity of the population. Second, it was inimical to class ideology, since the latter negated its religious identity, at a time when the working class was asserting its identity as well as its political and economic demands. Both ethnic and class identities had, therefore, to be suppressed. At the same time the country had to industrialize and grow economically. This required passive manpower and cheap labour. Beside the ideological suppression, a coercive suppression was built into the state system from its beginning.

The nexus of state power has always consisted of the militocracy, the bureaucracy, the feudal structure, industrialists and the *ulema* (religious leaders). It was and is fundamentally opposed to democracy and has therefore worked consciously against the democratic forces in Pakistan and those demanding the rights of the people. One of the most victimized groups in this context are the unions, because of their potential ability to challenge the power of these elites.

Ethnic and religious factors have always been crucial issues in the political and social life of Pakistan. Pakistan is overwhelmingly a Muslim country. Of the total population of 117,320,000,[1] Muslims comprise 96.67 per cent. Respective rates for Christian, Hindu and other religions are 1.56, 1.51 and 0.26 per cent (CRP 1984: 18). This has led not only to overlooking the concerns of non-Muslims, but also to intra-Muslim sectarian tensions. These tensions, deliberately exacerbated during the martial law period of General Zia-ul-Haq to diffuse and control possible opposition, are played out in the political and labour arenas as well and limit some of the organizational abilities of the workers.

Pakistan's ethnic divisions are reflected in its linguistic divisions. According to the 1981 census, Punjabi is the mother tongue of 48.2 per cent of households, Pushto is spoken by 13.1 per cent and Sindhi by 11.8 per cent. The respective figures for Saraiki, Urdu, Baluchi and other languages are 9.8, 7.6, 3.0 and 6.5 per cent (CRP 1984: 186). While Urdu ranks only fifth in terms of mother-tongues, it has a special status as *lingua franca*. English still operates as an official language in most public transactions.

Ethnic tensions have a genuine basis, in that certain nationalities in Pakistan have remained deprived. Their recent manifestation, however, which pits Urdu speakers against other linguistic groups, is the product of the political cynicism of General Zia. Ethnic tensions have had a particularly deleterious effect on the labour movement as they are concentrated in Karachi, the country's main industrial city. A number of unions have become ethnically oriented and function largely as extensions of ethnic political parties.

Economic developments

At Independence, West Pakistan was overwhelmingly agricultural, with very little in the way of major industries or infrastructure. Since then there has been commendable progress, at least in terms of macro-economic indicators. For example, in 1950–51 the sectoral shares of GDP of the agricultural, manufacturing and other (i.e. service) sectors were 65.3, 9.5 and 25.2 per cent respectively (Ahmed and Amjad 1984). In 1990–91 their respective shares had become 28.21, 28.37 and 43.41 per cent.[2]

In the 1950s, economic policy was based on a five-year plan system developed on the recommendation of Harvard University. Industries and infrastructure were built from scratch following the import-substituting industrialization (ISI) model. On the face of it, this policy developed an open economy, but the emerging power of the industrialists in social and political spheres was vigorously controlled.

General Ayub's martial law period (1958–69) was a time of rapid industrialization (the 'Decade of Development') and a shift to export-oriented growth. At the same time, agriculture was transformed by the introduction of high-yielding crop varieties, fertilizers and mechanization as part of the 'Green Revolution'. Both industry and agriculture became highly capital intensive. Industrial development was geographically concentrated in a few areas, Karachi and central Punjab (Lahore, Faisalabad, Gujranwala, etc.), while control over industry was concentrated in a few hands, the '22 families'.

The democratically elected government of Zulfiqar Ali Bhutto (1971–77) adopted a socialist economic approach. All major industries, banks and financial institutions were nationalized. While the policy was an attempt to break the control of the 22 industrial families, it resulted in state monopolies, bureaucratization, corruption and inefficiency.

The martial law period of General Zia (1977–88) was basically a continuation of existing patterns although there was a new emphasis on the development of consumer industries. Pakistan received massive aid from the US, mainly directed at the military. The result was a skewed national budget, with a bloated defence establishment receiving a major portion of the country's resources and a growing debt burden incurred from aid which had done little or nothing to improve the social or infrastructural situation of the country.

The economic policies of the most recent period (1988 to date) have been determined by the agendas of the World Bank and International Monetary Fund (IMF): liberalization, privatization, foreign investment and the removal of state subsidies. Changes in the political regime during this period have not affected this economic agenda, although its mode of implementation has varied under different administrations. The first Benazir Bhutto government (1988–90) was unable to implement policy in any sector because of the active opposition of the state structures. Nawaz Sharif's regime (1990–93) was marked by a high level of fiscal irresponsibility and corruption and the rapid privatization programme actually developed into the de-assetization of the state for the benefit of certain elite groups. The caretaker government of Moeen Qureshi (summer 1993) and the most recent Benazir Bhutto government (October 1993 to date) have shown greater fiscal restraint and there has been a serious attempt to mobilize resources and widen the tax base.

The liberalization policies should have some beneficial effects, including efficiency increases and a lessening of the stranglehold of the bureaucracy. However, this is not yet reflected in economic performance which, instead, is marked by a stagnation in industrial output and high inflation (currently about 14 per cent). This poor economic performance may be the result partly of the political instability and a culture of corruption. The prolonged history of martial law may be a direct cause, but there are also many structural problems which need to be addressed.

Labour-market developments

Some fundamental problems in the Pakistani economy and labour markets have persisted since Independence, others have become prominent in the course of the country's development. In the long term, these problems will have to be faced and dealt with.

The population growth rate remains high, although some improvement has occurred recently. The annual growth rate in 1991 was at least 3.1 per cent,[3] while the current (1993–94) rate is reliably estimated at 2.9 per cent. It would be unrealistic, however, to expect a continued dramatic reduction in the growth rate in the near future. One result of this high growth rate is an ever-increasing number of young people entering the labour market.

The labour force is primarily rural, at around 68 per cent, and around half the labour force is directly employed by agriculture.[4] There is a steady rural–urban migration, with the population of the rural areas declining by approximately 0.32 per cent annually. This is due to the agricultural sector's inability to absorb the rural labour surplus, a problem which began with the Green Revolution, and the attractions of modernization which was perceived as a primarily urban phenomenon. Rural–urban migration increases the number of people looking for work in the industrial sector in addition to overburdening the fragile infrastructure of the large urban areas. It is, however, not increasing as rapidly as might be expected due to the urbanization of rural areas. This process is a result of improved infrastructure and communications networks, and is located largely in central Punjab. This, however, exacerbates already existing regional inequalities. It is also almost completely a product of informal-sector development.

These factors have led to a serious un- and underemployment problem. Government statistics for 1991–92 show an unemployment rate of 3.14 per cent and a labour-force participation rate of 28.83 per cent.[5] In addition, over 10.32 per cent of the population are estimated to belong to the category of disguised unemployed, that is persons who worked less than 35 hours during the reference week. If all disguised unemployed persons are included, the unemployment rate jumps to at least 13.45 per cent.

The government is the largest employer of non-agricultural labour due to the nationalization of major industries and the service and education sectors. State employment is highly prized as it provides security of tenure and social-welfare benefits not available elsewhere. It is also one of the most common forms of political patronage. As a consequence, the public sector is highly overstaffed, but the current privatization policy as well as the need to contain government expenditure make it unlikely that the public sector can generate further employment. Development in the formal industrial sector has been and continues to be capital intensive and remains unable to absorb the urban workforce.

Overseas labour migration has provided an outlet for excess labour, although it has been decreasing steadily in the last decade due to economic changes in the Gulf. This trend was amplified by the Gulf crisis. While overseas labour migration has begun to pick up again recently, and some new markets have opened up in East Asia, it is unlikely that it will be as significant as in the past.

This circumstance has further encouraged the growth of the informal sector. Accurate data on this are almost impossible to obtain, and the estimates that exist tend to be unsystematic and concerned only with specific areas. In the 1970s it was estimated that over 70 per cent of Pakistan's labour force worked in the informal sector. Since then there has been a large increase in the use of contract labour, even by large industries, and so the informal sector has grown even further.

Present problems

The informal economy presents perhaps the biggest challenge to sustainable development. On the one hand, it is a vibrant sector of the economy, labour-intensive and responsive to new needs and opportunities. On the other hand, it is largely undocumented, which distorts both official statistics and existing analyses of the economy's performance.[6] More importantly, it escapes the government's taxation and regulation network. Labour in the informal sector is not governed by the various labour laws or regulations on working conditions. This means that workers have no paid holidays, no job security, no medical cover, no pension or provident fund, no limit on the hours worked and no overtime pay.

Another vital issue is the gross neglect and denial of women's role and contribution to the economy. Official figures give incredibly low female labour-force participation rates: 3.2 per cent according to the 1981 census or 12 per cent according to the Labour Force Survey of 1987–88. A World Bank report suggests that 42 per cent of the economically active persons in agricultural households are women, working primarily as unpaid family labourers (World Bank 1989: 65).[7] Based on the under-reporting in the rural sector, the same report suggests that a similar level of under-reporting in the urban sector may be estimated. Thus, the full-time equivalent labour-force participation rate of women would be around 25 per cent, of whom around 80 per cent are employed in the informal sector.

The failure of the educational system is also a problem. The official literacy rate is 34 per cent, the functional literacy rate probably much lower. This implies that the vast majority of the workforce is illiterate. While primary education has languished, there has simultaneously been a rapid expansion of higher education. This has led to serious distortions in the labour market. There is a premium on skilled artisans and those with technical qualifications, many of whom migrated to the Gulf areas, but both the totally uneducated and the comparatively highly educated often find it either impossible or unrewarding to get employment.

Currently, about 55 per cent of all manufacturing employment is located in Karachi and central Punjab (Bengali 1991: 1). This regional concentration of both formal- and informal-sector industrial development also creates problems and growing tensions between areas and between ethnic groups which have to migrate to urban areas, particularly Karachi, to find work.

The labour situation

The legal environment

With a rapidly expanding population and a high under- and unemployment rate, labour finds itself in a buyers' market with all the power on the side of the employers. Furthermore, at the level of the local bureaucracy and law-enforcement apparatus, the state routinely supports employers against workers.

According to the Constitution, labour is a 'concurrent subject', which means that it is the responsibility both of the federal and provincial governments. Labour legislation is usually enacted at the federal level, but the responsibility for enforcing this legislation belongs to the provinces. By law, trade unions are organized on a plant or establishment basis and industry-wide organization is forbidden.

Pakistan's labour legislation is based on an elaborate institutional framework inherited from the British. This recognized workers' rights to form trade unions and to strike in restricted circumstances, set up compulsory conciliation and arbitration procedures and laid down standards for working conditions in the workplace.

The first significant piece of labour legislation passed by the Pakistani government was the Pakistan Essential Services (Maintenance) Act (ESA) of 1952. The Act deprives workers of the right to organize and the right to bargain collectively. Initially the Act was applied to all central government employees and a large number of workers in industries declared to be 'public utility services'. This was a crushing blow to the labour movement as most of the pre-Independence unionization had developed in the service and state sectors.

Later legislation extended the list of public utility services to cover all major categories of industry and denied the right of association to employees of security services, managerial and administrative personnel, and non-industrial government servants including employees of prisons and hospitals. The ESA has plagued the labour movement to date. The most recent example is the Finance Act of 1992, which exempts industries exporting over 20 per cent of their production from labour laws.

The most important piece of labour legislation which still regulates labour relations is the Industrial Relations Ordinance (IRO) of 1969. Under the IRO workers seeking to form a union must apply to the Registrar of Trade Unions for registration. The IRO allows the formation of more than one union in a single establishment. Registered trade unions may seek the status of 'certified bargaining agent' (CBA), which is the only body within an establishment empowered to conduct negotiations with management, sign a labour contract, collect union dues through check-off, and be represented on the various worker–management committees. If there is more than one union in a workplace, the CBA must be selected every two years through secret ballot. The result is a strong tendency towards factionalism in the unions. It becomes very difficult for workers to collectively press for their needs beyond a more than strictly local basis.

The IRO sets up a mandatory conciliation process. Only if this process fails can the CBA call a strike or take the matter to the Labour Court for adjudication. Even then, a mandatory waiting period is required before a strike can be initiated. However, under the IRO the government can ban a strike even before it commences if it is likely to cause 'serious hardship to the community'. This whole process makes legal strikes virtually impossible even in the small number of industries where unionization is allowed. Illegal strikes are dangerous, leaving the workers vulnerable to police harassment.

The labour laws contain a complex array of welfare provisions, including maximum working hours, paid annual holidays, rest periods, social-security system, an old-age benefit fund, cost-of-living increments and transportation allowances. The 1973 Constitution also bans all forced labour and child labour. The problem is that only a small minority of Pakistan's workforce is covered by most of these welfare provisions. Small establishments (employing fewer than ten or in certain cases 50 workers) are exempt, and many benefits are only payable to workers earning less than 1,500 rupees per month. Employers evade the welfare, health and safety provisions either by employing contract labour or by under-reporting the size of their workforce. Even where workers are covered, the provincial welfare departments are either unwilling or unable to enforce protective laws or health and safety standards. Forced labour on the basis of debts, particularly in the agricultural, carpet-weaving and brick kiln sectors, is rampant.

Subsequent governments have repeatedly been criticized by the ILO and others for failing to abide by the ILO Conventions they have ratified: Conventions 87 and 98 on the rights of association and collective bargaining, and Conventions 29 and 105 on forced labour. The system of industrial relations is

> devised basically to fulfil the needs of rapid industrialization with phenomenal profits for local as well as foreign capital. While ensuring their secure and unhindered operation, this system is geared towards securing permanent subordination of the workers on the one hand and the removal of conflicts from the work place, besides preventing such conflicts from developing into class conflicts on the other. To this end, the system seeks to turn the unions, whenever and wherever they are allowed, into instruments for disciplining the workers. (IFBWW *et al.* 1991: 141)

Trade union analysis

Prior to Independence there were two major trade union federations in India, the All India Trade Union Congress which was dominated by the Communist Party and the India Federation of Labour which was reformist with socialist leanings. These became, respectively, the Pakistan Trade Union Federation (PTUF), with 38 affiliated unions, and the Pakistan Labour Federation, with 49 affiliated unions.

During the 1950s, in the context of the Cold War, the state attempted to control the trade union movement through patronage, particularly the formation of the All Pakistan Confederation of Labour (APCOL) in 1950, and through harassment and suppression of non-conforming organizations. Nonetheless, prior to the imposition of martial law in 1958 there was an unprecedented level of workers' militancy protesting the continuous decline in wages and blatant anti-union attitude of employers. This upsurge was led by the shopfloor leaders, and APCOL was increasingly marginalized. With the martial law of 1958, existing rights of collective bargaining, strikes, freedom of speech, etc. were all annulled.

The rapid industrialization during General Ayub's Decade of Development led to union growth and the emergence of many new federations. However, workers and unions were controlled by an alliance of government, industrialists and bureaucracy.

In 1968, workers joined again in the mass movement against Ayub's regime and were the backbone of the Pakistan People's Party (PPP) street power. This led to a substantial growth in union activity. At the same time, workers, by taking direct action such as work stoppages, were rejecting the legal channels of conflict resolution. Leadership passed from the professional trade union leaders to the shopfloor level and the official trade union federation leadership became isolated.

The PPP government of Z.A. Bhutto (1971–77) was, at least in its rhetoric, pro-labour. It liberalized the regulations for the registration of unions, which led to the proliferation of small unions. The number of registered unions rose from 1,997 in 1971 to 8,332 in 1977. Union membership grew at an annual rate of approximately three per cent to reach a peak of just over one million in 1977. However, the growth in the number of unions did not necessarily add to their strength. When martial law came in 1977, the trade union movement was divided and weak, unable to face a hostile regime which was openly anti-labour.

The rights of workers were fiercely and viciously suppressed during the martial law period of General Zia. Labour strikes and protest demonstrations were forbidden, strikers were arrested, imprisoned without trial or tried by special military courts, tortured, flogged, shot and killed. Trade union activities were banned. The martial law regime also encouraged sectarian and ethnic groups to make inroads into working-class politics to break the hold of the PPP on this segment of society. Organizations like the Jamaat-i-Islami (JI) and later the Mohajir Qaumi Movement (MQM) received full state patronage to strengthen their involvement in union activities.

Some of the pressure on unions eased following the return to civilian rule in 1985 and the democratic elections of 1988. In 1990 there were 7,080 registered trade unions with 952,488 members. Of these unions, 1,957 were registered CBAs with a membership of 419,801 (PLG 1991: 133–4). Union membership, however, still comprises only approximately six per cent of the non-agricultural labour force. Unions are concentrated in Karachi and Lahore and in just a few industries. Expansion into other areas is restricted either because of the application of the ESA or the increasing use by employers of contract labour.

The nature and character of the unions
The history of organized labour in Pakistan has left trade unionism weak and divided. The movement is without political influence and subjected to severe official restrictions and controls. Unions have real influence only in a few large public-sector industries and in a small number of larger private-sector and multinational companies, again concentrated mainly in the service enterprises.

Unions are also polarized along the same ethnic and religious sectarian lines as the rest of society, and disadvantaged by the fact that the workforce is largely uneducated. One means of dealing with the latter problem is by appointing outsiders, people not employed by the plant concerned, as trade union executives. Under the law, up to 25 per cent of an executive body can be composed of outsiders. Such people are often ex-employees who have been dismissed due to their union activities, or educated individuals who sympathize with the unions's cause. The position of outsider can, however, also be used by bureaucrats, employers and political or sectarian groups to control a union.

Trade unions have been unable to address the wider political or human rights issues, or overarching economic issues such as unemployment. Due to legal structures and restrictions, they are bound to be concerned with local issues such as wages, working conditions and job security.

The complex arbitration and conciliation processes mandated by law mean that much of the energy and scarce resources of trade unions are expended on legal matters. The whole structure discourages the use of strikes. In 1988, for example, there were only 18 major strikes involving 8,231 workers. Since, ultimately, a worker's only weapon is the withdrawal of labour, unions have little power in negotiations.

Excessive state intervention, restrictive legislation, the lack of a democratic environment and an extremely fragmented social situation have all contributed to the present condition of the union movement, and they have also had an impact upon the organizational forms, leadership and politics of trade unions and federations. It is important to gain an understanding of these impacts on existing organizations as they, in turn, will decisively influence the future course of development of the union movement.

Since no comprehensive study of plant- or enterprise-level unions has been conducted so far, no information is available about even the most important of them. However, a limited assessment can be made by a study of some of the more important and larger federations.

There are around 100 or more federations, of which only 10 to 15 are considered important in terms of their share in total membership and influence on politics, the relative permanence of their structures over time (at least three decades) and their linkages with the international trade union movement.

These federations can be divided as follows:

- *those claiming to be free and independent.* These include all three affiliates to the International Confederation of Free Trade Unions (ICFTU),[8] namely the All Pakistan Federation of Trade Unions (APFTU), the Pakistan National Federation of Trade Unions (PNFTU) and the All Pakistan Federation of Labour (APFOL). These three are splinter groups from the APCOL, reconstituted in their present form after the APCOL's demise in 1962. Another federation in this category is the All Pakistan Trade Union Conference (APTUC), formed in 1974 and affiliated to the World Confederation of Labour (WCL).

- *party-affiliated political federations*. These include the JI-sponsored National Labour Front (NLF), created in 1969; the labour wing of the Pakistan People's Party, the People's Labour Bureau; the labour wing of the Pakistan Muslim League; and the recently formed Pakhtun Labour Front of the Awami National Party.
- *non-party political federations,* such as the Muttahida Labour Federation, the All Pakistan Trade Union Organization (APTUO), the PTUF, and the Lahore-based All Pakistan Trade Union Federation (APTUF) fall in the third category. All of them profess some variant of Left or social-democratic politics.
- *ethnicity-based federations, or labour-wings of ethnic political groups* are a more recent phenomenon and confined to the provinces of Sindh and Baluchistan. They include organizations in Sindh such as the Labour Division of the MQM; the Sindhi Porhiat Sangat, labour wing of the Jiay Sindh Movement; and the Sindhi Mazdoor Tehrik, labour wing of the Sindhi Awami Tehrik; and the Baluchistan Labour Federation in Baluchistan.
- *industry-wise federations,* such as the All Pakistan Newspaper Employees' Confederation and the All Pakistan Bank Employees' Federation.

The federations listed above collectively can claim to represent a clear majority of the registered and affiliated trade unions in the country. Therefore, they can be considered representative of the broad trends within the movement. For practical purposes, the ethnicity-based organizations are left aside. They do not deal as much with the broader trade union issues as with the specific political interests of their respective parent organizations, and confine themselves to workers belonging to a particular ethnic group.

Hierarchic and non-participatory structures

Although the federations listed in the first three categories differ markedly in their origins and claim widely different political orientations, there is a striking similarity in the way they were created and conduct their day-to-day affairs. For instance, all of them are top-down organizations. In most cases they were created by individuals who got themselves appointed to the leadership positions and continue to hold them even after two or three decades. These organizations are known for their complete lack of democratic and participatory norms. There is hardly any process by which leaders can be held accountable to the rank and file, be it in policy matters or financial affairs.

The result is that not a single organization has been able to develop a second generation of leaders, and most of them, with the exception of the part-affiliated federations, may be unable to survive beyond the lifetime of their founder leaders. This situation is the exact opposite of the one prevailing in plant-level unions where regular elections, often through the ballot, and continual change in leadership have gradually become the norm.

Union rivalry and exclusive concentration on permanent workers
These federations concentrate exclusively on the permanent workers in the large-scale industrial and services sectors, and even then only on the less than five per cent who are already unionized. Within this limited sphere, they are locked in severe rivalries and confrontations. This explains to a large extent the widespread proliferation of unions: on average there are now three to four unions at every unionized plant/enterprise. Surprisingly, the rivalries become more fierce when the unions involved belong to federations that are affiliated with the same international confederation. In this process, the basic principles of unity and solidarity are completely ignored. Moreover, they prefer to turn a blind eye to the non-permanent workers and those employed in the small-scale urban sectors, as well as to the rural workers.

Federation leaders' politics and workers' interests
Leaders of the mainstream federations have, with rare exceptions, always been found on the wrong side of the fence whenever an uprising of the workers has occurred. This was the case during the great movements of 1962, 1968–69 and 1972–73. While the workers, led by shopfloor leaders, struggled heroically and made tremendous sacrifices, the federation-level leaders were at best able to play the role of middlemen between workers and the state. Such influence on these leaders by the state or particular governments has blocked the development of a genuine trade union movement in Pakistan.

Under the last military dictatorship of General Zia, the trade unions suffered not only under the repressive regulations and policies, but also because of the extraordinary behaviour of some of the important trade union leaders. At least four major federations – the PNFTU, APFTU, APFOL (all ICFTU affiliates) and the JI-sponsored NLF – deemed it fit to cooperate with the dictator when, in 1981, he set up a phoney, nominated parliament (the *Majlis-e-Shoora*) in total violation of all democratic norms. The top leaders of these federations personally joined this mockery of democracy, both at the federal and provincial levels, in a context where fundamental trade union rights remained completely suppressed under various martial law regulations.

Even in an earlier period, after the imposition of martial law on 5 July 1977, various federations united in the form of the Pakistan Labour Alliance, to participate in the movement against the civilian government of Z.A. Bhutto, and made an open appeal to the armed forces to take over. More recently, when the elected government of Benazir Bhutto was dismissed by the president, the PNFTU congratulated him publicly and urged him to impose the Shariah law through an ordinance.

While such undemocratic behaviour is understandable in the case of the JI federation, the NLF, it is surprising that the trade union leaders professing to be committed to the cause of free and independent trade unionism see no contradiction in their actions.

The leaders of the other party-affiliated and 'independent political' federations are hardly much better. Their allegiance to or deference towards particular parties or governments has always taken priority over the workers' interests.

Inflated membership
Another common, and totally inexplicable, feature in all federations is that they always provide highly inflated membership figures. For example, according to the *Pakistan Labour Gazette*, by 1990 there were 6,897 registered unions with 927,351 members (PLG 1991). However, the three ICFTU affiliates alone provided the following account of their membership to the South Asian Regional Trade Union Congress, published in its 1989 report:

PNFTU	150,000
APFOL	265,000
APFTU	520,529
Total	935,529

A study conducted for the ILO in 1991 was provided with the following incredible figures by the 11 major federations: number of affiliated unions – 1,292 total membership – 2,052,007. These numbers make a correct assessment of the state of the Pakistani trade union movement impossible.

International affiliations
Eight federations have affiliations with international confederations. The APFTU, PNFTU and APFOL with the ICFTU, the APTUC with the WCL, and the PTUF, APTUF, APTUO and APFOL (Durrani Group) with the WFTU. Some are also affiliated with various International Trade Secretariats (ITSs). This has not, however, led to

any awareness about the international trade union movement among their rank and file members. In most cases the contacts are restricted to a handful of federation-level leaders. None of the federations has produced any information material on the respective confederations or the ITSs in local languages.

Current issues

In the light of the foregoing analysis, it is clear that a number of important issues confront the trade union movement. Foremost among these is the structure of economic activity in the country. The fact that the informal sector extends well beyond family businesses to include major segments of the industrial sector clearly affects the structure of the formal sector. There is a trend among employers to redirect as much work as possible to sub-contractors and daily wage earners. This both limits the application of existing legal welfare provisions and makes it difficult to register unions, as non-permanent workers can simply be disowned by the employer.

This leads to a dichotomy in the labour force. Within the existing formal sector, unions have a certain degree of collective bargaining power and have been able to protect the wages and conditions of workers. Permanent workers also have a large degree of job security. Many traditional labour problems abound outside the formal sector. The use of child labour is common, working conditions are virtually non-regulated and terms of employment are oppressive. Formal-sector and particularly government employment comes to be regarded almost as a sinecure and the efforts of unions are largely limited to trying to contain the shrinkage of the traditionally unionized areas. Union activity on the whole is remote from the realities facing the overwhelming majority of the labour force. If unions are to serve their purpose of defending the interests of the working class as a whole, they need to find ways of addressing the needs of workers in the informal sector.

The trade union movement also needs to look at the role and position of women in the labour process. The unions must take the lead in ensuring that the full contribution of women to the country's economy is recognized, that women workers, who are particularly vulnerable to management pressures, are properly organized and that women are granted equal status within the unions and federations themselves.

The trade union movement needs to develop a democratic and progressive culture within its membership and leadership. This will involve worker education on workers' rights, human rights and participatory structures. In particular, it will involve action to deal with ethnic and sectarian divisions within the movement.

Serious reflection on the situation of workers and development of the trade union movement to truly benefit workers will also depend upon a serious and thorough analysis of the trade union movement. Unless a proper quantitative and qualitative picture of the labour movement is developed, effective strategies cannot be devised. This task should, therefore, be assigned top priority. The experience of many countries has shown that the labour movement in the Third World cannot be built or sustained without strong and independent education and research input and back-up systems.

The need for international cooperation is obvious. However, international assistance can only be successful if the recipient labour movement itself has the commitment and the capability to utilize effectively such assistance and achieve the desired objectives. Given the extremely limited outreach of the Pakistani union movement, it will be necessary to interact with and support organizations whose work falls in line with the general objectives of trade unionism. These include relevant NGOs, women's groups, human rights groups and similar institutions. Moreover, it may also be asked whether, after the end of the Cold War, it remains necessary to continue to work through the present affiliates only. The time may be appropriate, especially with the demise of the WFTU, to initiate a process of bringing together all the genuine trade unions to develop a truly free and democratic union movement.

The current circumstances of IMF-determined privatization, foreign investment and the development of Free Trade Zones unrestrained by such things as labour laws do not add up to a conducive environment for labour in Pakistan. By and large this is true for the whole of the sub-continent. Moreover, the trade union movement in Pakistan remains extremely weak, hopelessly divided and fragmented. Its greatest misfortune, however, lies in the fact that it is controlled by a totally undemocratic, myopic and self-seeking leadership.

Despite the utter bleakness of the present scene, one can discern a silver lining in the emergence, even if in small numbers, of an enthusiastic, energetic and eager-to-learn layer of shopfloor-level unionists in the past few years. There have been many occasions when such unionists, belonging to different federations, have been brought together in joint education courses or seminars organized by some ITSs or independent educational institutions. During these interactions, they have demonstrated an unambiguous commitment to developing a genuinely free, unified, democratic and informed trade union movement. They reject the existing sectarian and divisive tendencies and are conscious of the special problems faced by their women colleagues and by the workers in the informal sector. They are also aware of the need to understand the broader socio-political and economic issues, and of the need for an independent intervention by the labour movement.

Some of the plant-level unions have exhibited a much broader horizon by making serious efforts to develop South Asian trade union networks. For instance, there is growing cooperation among workers of the various multinationals that operate in different countries in the region. A committee is already active in the region, attempting to develop this cooperation further. Similar trends can be observed among the various women's organizations in the region, especially those aimed at women workers. Nobody can predict the outcomes of these regional initiatives, but such efforts should be considered a positive development and may also lead to more cooperation within trade unions and federations inside Pakistan itself.

These particular developments are still at an embryonic stage and will need a lot of nurturing before they can lead to major changes in the structure and perspective of the trade unions. The potential for such a change, nonetheless, definitely exists.

Notes

1. *Economic Survey 1991–1992* (ES) (1992: 13). A careful analysis of these and most other statistics used in the text can be found in Amjad-Ali (1993). As noted there, the most recent census was carried out in 1981. All later statistics are ultimately extrapolated from this basis. It should also be mentioned that the accuracy of statistics from both government and private sectors cannot be relied on.

2. Statistical Appendix (ES 1992: 45).

3. Ibid: 13.

4. Ibid: 29.

5. Ibid: 19.

6. An exception is the study by Kemal and Mehmood (1993), a most-needed and solid report of a nation-wide survey of 1,500 small firms.

7. Similar figures are quoted in a more recent study conducted by Shirkatgah for UNICEF. The report is still not available publicly, but has been quoted widely in the press; see, e.g., Omar (1992).

8. The reformist/Western confederation which separated from the World Federation of Trade Unions (WFTU) during the Cold War.

References

Ahmed, Viquar and Rashid Amjad (1984) *The Management of Pakistan's Economy, 1947-82.* Oxford University Press, Karachi.

Amjad-Ali, Ch. (1993) 'Country Study: Pakistan' in H. Thomas *The Netherlands Trade Union Co-Financing Programme 1985–1989: An Evaluation. Asia.* Institute of Social Studies Advisory Service, The Hague.

Bengali, K. (1991) *Why Unemployment?* Pakistan Publishing House, Karachi.

CRP (1984) *1981 Census Report of Pakistan.* Government of Pakistan, Islamabad.

ES (1992) *Economic Survey 1991–1992.* Government of Pakistan, Islamabad.

IFBWW-ITGLWF-TWARO-IUF (1991) *Rights of Workers in South Asia.* Friedrich-Ebert Foundation, New Delhi.

Kemal, A.R. and Z. Mehmood (1993) *Labour Absorption in the Informal Sector and Economic Growth in Pakistan.* Friedrich Ebert Stiftung, Islamabad.

Omar, K. (1992) 'Women's Economic Contribution Grossly Underplayed', *The News,* 24 September.

PLG (1991) *Pakistan Labour Gazette. A Journal of Labour Affairs* (July 1990 – June 1991). Government of Pakistan, Islamabad.

World Bank (1989) *Women in Pakistan. An Economic and Social Strategy.* World Bank, Washington DC.

Part Two: Latin America

5. The Very Long March of History

Kees Koonings
Dirk Kruijt
Frits Wils

Labour's role[1] within the process of economic development and socio-political change in Latin America has acquired increasing significance since the early twentieth century.[2] This has gone hand in hand with the growth of the Latin American economies, first in response to a rising demand for primary exports and later as the result of rapid urbanization and inward-oriented strategies of industrialization. The first categories of labour to gain a voice were those employed in the large-scale export and transportation sectors during the first decades of this century.

Since the 1930s, urban labour, increasingly industrial, has been among the social sectors that sought active participation in the political process of many Latin American countries. The formation of syndicates and trade unions became an important part of the social incorporation and politicization of the Latin American working class. Between the 1930s and 1960s, organized labour in many countries was able to join, or in some cases be drawn into, populist alliances together with anti-oligarchic politicians, industrialists, civil servants and the military.

From the 1960s onwards, economic and political changes have affected the position of wage labourers and their organizations. The diversification and modernization of manufacturing industry in a number of countries provoked an increasing differentiation of the industrial labour force. At the same time, the rise to power of authoritarian regimes in important countries like Argentina, Brazil, Chile and Uruguay led to the political exclusion of organized labour. To a certain extent this contributed to the erosion of real wage levels for significant segments of labour in these countries. Finally, the capacity of formal urban labour markets to absorb labour stagnated relative to the expansion of the urban population, leading to an increase in social inequality, poverty and un- and underemployment.

Since the late 1970s the Latin American economies have faced a broader crisis which further complicated the situation of the working class in many countries of the region. In fact, from the early 1980s up to the present, profound socio-economic and political changes have affected labour, labour relations and trade unionism in Latin America. These developments are:

- The breakdown of the conventional model of closed, inward-oriented development in Latin America, based on import-substituting industrialization (ISI), and its replacement by structural adjustment, liberalization and a more open integration into the global economic order.
- The end of corporatist and populist socio-political models and concomitant forms of relations between labour organizations and the state, as a result of the retreat of authoritarianism and the transition to and consolidation of democracy.
- The process of informalization of livelihood strategies and social organizations in general, increasing the importance of the informal sector, informal labour processes and relations.

In various ways these current trends affect the nature and functioning of formal labour markets, the role of trade unions and the relations between organized labour and the state. To a certain extent this constitutes a clear break with the historic patterns of development and labour issues in the region that have predominated from the 1920s until the early 1980s.

This chapter aims to discuss these recent developments against the backdrop of the historic evolution of the economy, industry, labour, trade unions and the state in Latin America.[3] It discusses, first, the main features of the Latin American model of development, mainly industrialization and its consequences for the labour market prior to the 1980s. Second, the history of trade unionism in the region is traced and the development of state–trade union relations discussed. The next three sections deal, respectively, with the post-1980 consequences of economic liberalization, democratic consolidation and informalization for labour, labour markets and labour organizations.

The Latin American development model and labour, 1900–80

Following the seminal analysis of Cardoso and Faletto (1979), the general literature usually characterizes the Latin American model of development up till the early 1980s as one of ISI combined with primary exports. With some qualifications, this model can be applied to the larger countries of the region and divided into a number of phases. The result has been, to a certain extent, a regionally consistent pattern of production, labour absorption, income distribution and rural–urban relations.[4]

The expansion of world trade prompted by European and North American industrialization after 1850 led to the early incorporation of the Latin American economies into the global economic system. This expansion provoked a rapidly increasing demand for a number of primary export commodities from Latin America. Export sectors in Argentina (meat and wheat), Brazil (coffee), Chile (nitrate and copper), Colombia (coffee and gold), Mexico (metals and oil), Peru (guano), Uruguay (meat and wool) and Venezuela (oil) expanded vigorously between the 1870s and 1930. The effects of this on overall socio-economic change were tremendous: export growth brought in large quantities of investment and income as a result of which production and demand increased; infrastructure was expanded to meet the requirements of export activities; and large-scale mines and plantations were established mainly by foreign investors, while the first manufacturing firms were established by domestic agricultural or commercial entrepreneurs in the wake of the export boom (Cerutti and Vellinga 1989).

These processes contributed to the first wave of urbanization in the region. Wage labour made its appearance as a large-scale phenomenon in mining, plantation agriculture, railways, ports, and also in light industries such as food processing and textiles. Massive immigration from Europe and Asia contributed to the formation of a (mostly urban) wage labour force in countries such as Mexico, Peru, Chile, and above all Argentina and Brazil. The penetration of mercantile and capitalist relations into the countryside led to the advance of part-time wage labour among the peasantry, especially around large mines and plantations.

The second phase of the Latin American development pattern can be placed roughly between the crisis of the 1930s and the early 1950s. During these two decades, Latin America had to come to terms with the breakdown of the primary export boom of the pre-1930 era. At first by default, and from the late 1930s onwards by design, domestic manufacturing emerged as the new leading economic sector in the major Latin American countries. Many of the industrial firms that were able to expand during the 1930s had been founded in the previous decades of export wealth. Their growth was stimulated by the impossibility of maintaining previous import levels.

However, governments soon discovered the strategic importance of industrialization as a new strategy for national development. In one country after another, the late 1930s and the 1940s witnessed the onset of deliberate state intervention to complement the expansion of existing domestic industries. The latter were predominantly owned by domestic entrepreneurs and mostly covered branches of traditional mass consumer goods such as foodstuffs, beverages, cigarettes, textiles, footwear, clothing, furniture, soap and simple metalworking. However, the production of modern consumer goods expanded from the 1930s onwards (Weaver 1980: 125). Governments started to build up basic industries such as steel production, oil refining and electricity. This phase of easy import substitution received an additional boost immediately after the end of the Second World War due to the accumulation of foreign exchange during the conflict.

During these decades the urban working class, especially formal industrial wage labour, expanded. The domestic industries were mainly labour intensive and most labour in the industrial plants was low-skilled. The employment of women and children was commonplace. However, a gradual process of differentiation within the urban–industrial labour force set in as the size and the level of capitalization of the largest firms increased (Weaver 1980: 138–9). Workers in the larger factories tended to be more skilled and better paid than their colleagues in small- and medium-sized establishments.

From the 1950s onwards, the industrialization model of the major Latin American countries went through important structural changes. Economic historians speak of the transition from the easy to the advanced or dynamic phase of import substitution. In countries such as Brazil, Mexico, Argentina, Chile, Colombia, Peru and Venezuela this new phase was above all marked by a rapid increase in foreign direct investment in manufacturing. Transnational firms entered new industrial branches that were intensive in their use of capital and technology. They mainly catered to the fast-growing urban middle-class market for consumer durables such as cars, household appliances, radios and television sets. Foreign investors also entered or revitalized existing markets such as food processing, beverages, tobacco processing, pharmaceuticals and chemicals.

These developments were complemented by an often spectacular expansion of direct state involvement in industrial and related activities. Large public companies were established for steel production, oil refining, chemical production, electricity, transportation, mining and development banking. As a result, the establishment size and concentration ratios in the modern dynamic industries increased. Typically, the largest industrial groups evolved into tripartite ventures including transnational firms, state capital and privately-owned domestic firms.[5]

Consequently, the composition of the industrial sector in the major Latin American countries changed. The new dynamic sectors controlled by foreign or tripartite firms increased their share of total manufacturing output. Employment in these activities expanded, but not at the same pace as invested capital or manufacturing output. This reflected the increasing productivity of labour in the modern large-scale establishments as compared with small- and medium-sized workshops and plants. Still, total industrial employment in Latin America continued to expand rapidly throughout the 1950s, 1960s and 1970s.

In fact, the structure of the labour market underwent important modifications. Labour became increasingly urban, not only in manufacturing but also in the public sector and services. Informal urban labour proved to be a structural element of the urban economies (see pp. 116–120). Also in the countryside, wage labour became increasingly significant as large-scale commercial agriculture expanded in countries such as Argentina, Brazil, Colombia and Mexico. Brazil and Mexico, the two major countries that advanced most along the road of import substitution, recorded particularly impressive rates of growth of industrial output and employment. Argentina, a leading industrial country in Latin America during the first half of this century, lost ground from the 1950s onwards as the country entered a prolonged period of relative industrial stagnation (Infante and Klein 1991; Weaver 1980: 126 and 145).

Though the ISI model constituted the basis for impressive economic growth in a number of countries, especially between 1950 and 1975, it also incorporated a set of fundamental economic and socio-political difficulties. As far as industrialization performance was concerned, the emphasis on large-scale manufacturing for the domestic market did not eliminate the bottleneck of insufficient foreign exchange being generated by the export sector. Import needs shifted, however, from finished goods to more crucial intermediary goods, machinery, technology and energy. While dynamic industrialization advanced, the export sectors, however, retained their traditional characteristics in terms of composition, productivity and value-added. Furthermore, the policies of most Latin American countries discriminated against exports and agriculture in favour of industrial investment and urban income.

The continued dependence on increasingly strategic imports, unmatched by an expansion of exports, in combination with a rapid increase of direct state involvement in economic activities contributed to chronic trade imbalances and budget deficits, inducing permanent inflation (Furtado 1970). Furthermore, protective barriers led to an often inefficient and oligopolistic industrial structure. The prevailing patterns of manufacturing were aimed at a relatively reduced market consisting of elite and middle-class consumers. Combined with the limited labour-absorptive capacity of the dynamic industries, this pattern accentuated the tendency of social dualization and often extremely unequal income distribution. The often stagnant agricultural sector further aggravated these problems through an inadequate food supply to the urban sector, insufficient primary exports and persistent rural poverty. Rural poverty as well as the labour-saving effects of agricultural modernization, when it did occur, fed the increasing stream of rural–urban migrants and thus the informal labour market.

The economic and social drawbacks of the Latin American model of development came to light especially after the mid-1970s when both its internal and external macro-economic conditions took a turn for the worse and its adverse social consequences became manifest. After 1973 most Latin American countries took recourse to external lending to adjust their balance-of-payments and investment problems. Notably, countries like Brazil and Mexico hoped to weather the recession in this manner. Brazil even initiated an ambitious third phase of import substitution by promoting basic and heavy industry, domestic capital-goods production, high-tech manufacturing and non-traditional primary and manufacturing exports. As is well known, these and similar strategies employed by Latin American countries ran into decisive trouble after 1982 with the onset of the debt crisis. This crisis heralded the end of 50 years of inward-oriented development, calling for major reorientation of economic and social strategies in the region.

During these post-war decades of urban–industrial development a notable segmentation of the labour markets in the Latin American economies came to light. The sectoral distribution of the labour force underwent important transformations between 1950 and 1980. In 1980, only 32 per cent of the labour force was employed in agriculture as against 55 per cent in 1950. An enormous shift had taken place away from agriculture to industry (26 per cent) and services (42 per cent). The level of urbanization rose rapidly for most Latin American countries: the share of the urban population in Latin America as a whole increased from 48 per cent in 1960 to 62 in 1980 (Gilbert and Gugler 1983: 7). A second, relatively less-pronounced but nonetheless significant trend concerned occupational mobility towards higher-earning jobs in the private sector or the rapidly expanding public sector. By 1980 some 20 per cent of formal urban employment consisted of public-sector jobs (Infante and Klein 1991). Third, in spite of a decline in relative underemployment (from 46 to 40 per cent between 1950 and 1980), the absolute number of underemployed rose from 27 to 49 million people during the same period.

Finally, a pronounced segmentation into dual markets had become a persistent feature of both urban and rural labour markets. Despite the high mobility rates – from rural to urban and from low-wage to high-wage occupations – the inequalities in the overall structure of labour remuneration were not reduced. Furthermore, within the traditional peasant sector and the urban informal sector additional differentiation in remuneration was linked to occupational segmentation and increasing social stratification. In effect, workers in the large-scale private and public industries and associated public services consolidated as a relatively privileged minority within the working class (Weaver 1980: 158; Wynia 1990: 61). They earned better wages, acquired skills, had access to company – and public – welfare schemes, and were incorporated into influential trade unions. By and large, the material position of this segment of the labour force developed more favourably compared with workers in traditional, unskilled, small- and medium-sized manufacturing, the informal sector and agriculture (Touraine 1989: 72–3).

This segmentation of the labour market was also reflected in Latin American social structures. A number of authors (for example, Portes 1985; Touraine 1989) have pointed at the structural duality of Latin American societies.[6] Until the late 1970s economic growth did lead to increases in the absolute level of employment and in the total number of people living above specified poverty lines. A growing number of people, however, were forced to rely upon informal activities within the urban economies, and small-scale informal activities generally remained a large component of the urban–industrial sector. At the same time, the related phenomenon of urban poverty did not diminish very much prior to 1980, while increasing in absolute as well as relative terms after 1980 (Altimir 1981; Feres and León 1990). The implications of the post-1980 developments with regard to the economy, labour market and poverty are discussed below (pp. 108–112 and 116–120).

Trade unions and socio-political relations, 1900–80

The expansion of capitalist relations of production in primary exports and light manufacturing, increasing urbanization, and immigration of mainly European workers laid the foundations for the rise of workers' organizations and trade unions from the late-nineteenth century. Ideologies on workers' strategies were diffused from Europe through immigrants, pamphlets and other means. During the first two decades of the twentieth century, anarcho-syndicalist rather than social-democratic orientations dominated the nascent labour movement. After 1917 communism became influential among Latin American syndicates. Labour unions and federations were set up to unite these localized organizations of workers. Their actions varied according to country, period and sector, but usually entailed combinations of direct demands and more general manifestations of dissatisfaction with the social conditions of the workers. The strike was the most commonly used instrument to support demands against employers and the government.

Prior to 1930, some advances were made across the continent on wage levels, working hours, trade union rights and social welfare for urban wage labour. Especially in the countries where trade unions were most effectively organized, namely Argentina, Chile and Uruguay, headway was made in the adoption of progressive labour legislation and social-welfare policies by responsive governments: Battle in Uruguay, Yrigoyen in Argentina, and Alessandri in Chile. Rather more frequently, however, trade union activities were met by repressive legislation or state and employers' violence (Berquist 1986; Spalding 1977).

After 1930 the issue of labour's political incorporation decisively entered the considerations of contending political groups in the principal countries of the region. The social changes provoked by decades of economic growth started to erode the consensus underpinning the rule of the oligarchic elites linked to the export sector. The new contenders for political power included the military, modernizing political elites, urban entrepreneurs, the urban middle class and organized labour. A new configuration of power arose in a number of countries based on coalitions of these segments organized by populist politicians or regimes. Whether through elections (Argentina, Chile, Colombia, Uruguay), prolonged revolution (Mexico) or intra-elite rebellion (Brazil) populist regimes came to power. They adopted industrialization, popular mobilization and modest social reform as their main objectives.

The role of trade unions was modified in this new situation. Instead of standing in opposition against employers and the state, the labour movement became tied to what Touraine (1989) calls the national-popular state.[7] By and large, the role of trade unions shifted from direct revindication of workers' interests to being the vehicles for political action by organized labour in the populist alliances. In most cases increasing political participation reduced trade union autonomy. Co-optation, regulation or outright organization by the state affected the actions of trade unions. Notoriously, the state took control of organized labour through restrictive legislation, financial control and direct co-optation or control of union leadership. In exchange, the interests of labour were recognized as politically legitimate and given a place in the corporatist articulation of sectoral social interests. Furthermore the state ensured the protection of labour through legislation and the extension of social benefits, often making use of the institutions of trade unions themselves to distribute these.

This incorporation of organized labour in national–popular regimes assumed its most typical forms in Argentina (under Peronism or *justicialismo*), Brazil (under Vargas-inspired *trabalhismo*) and Mexico (under the post-revolutionary order organized by the Institutional

Revolutionary Party – PRI). The insertion of labour into the national–popular state also occurred under varying political conditions at different moments in time in other countries: liberal democracy (Chile, Uruguay and Venezuela), oligarchic democracy (Colombia) or different types of revolutionary or post-revolutionary regimes (Bolivia, Guatemala, Nicaragua).

The 1960s witnessed the onset of sudden and violent ruptures from this model in some of the principal Latin American countries. The military takeover in Brazil in 1964 inaugurated an era of institutionalized authoritarianism in Latin America. The rise of 'bureaucratic-authoritarian' regimes (O'Donnell 1973; Collier 1979) had profound effects on the socio-political role of organized labour. It meant the breakdown of the compromise state and national–populist alliances. Organized labour became suddenly marginalized politically in Brazil (1964), Argentina (1966 and 1976), Chile (1973), Uruguay (1973) and a number of other countries. The new dictatorships moved from the prior incorporation of popular sectors to their exclusion from power and policy making.

The underlying rationale of these regimes is often presented in terms of the increasing incompatibility of reconciling economic restructuring with popular socio-economic demands (O'Donnell 1973), but the political and ideological dimensions of the 'new authoritarianism' were at least as important.[8] At any rate, the reorientation of development policies conflicted with the material and political interests of organized labour. On the politico-ideological level the new authoritarian regimes represented an elite and middle-class response to real or perceived threats to the existing social and political order. Organized labour became part of the 'internal enemy' (Alves 1985; Perelli 1990). Military institutions took the lead in Brazil, the Southern Cone, Bolivia, Central America, and – more covertly – Colombia. Trade unions and workers' parties were prohibited or strictly controlled. Peru and Ecuador provided deviant examples of reformist militarism (Kruijt 1991), but although these regimes declared themselves in favour of mass popular participation, they did not resolve the problem of labour's incorporation as successfully as did the Mexican PRI.

According to some analysts (for example, Portes 1985: 31–3) the advent of the new dictatorships, in combination with the changing patterns of social relations in the urban domain in Latin America (see pp. 101–105) led to a shift in popular collective action from the classical capital–labour opposition towards a new type of confrontation between the authoritarian state and the 'new social movements'. While it cannot be denied that trade unions were seriously affected by the actions of the authoritarian regimes (and also by the not-so-openly authoritarian states as in the case of Colombia), this formulation overemphasizes the earlier significance of the classical Western European and North American model of organized-labour strategies in Latin America.

Already under populism, the state had become the principal interlocutor of organized labour. It is true that with the restriction of trade unionism under authoritarianism, the growing number of urban workers, including both formal and informal workers, was forced to develop alternative channels for organization and interest representation. Simultaneously, urban workers, together with other segments of the urban poor, confronted increasingly difficult conditions to gain their livelihood. To a certain extent their common condition as impoverished urban residents, sharing the same neighbourhoods, housing conditions and lack of access to basic public services, replaced the workfloor as the main focus of collective action. Nevertheless, trade unions made efforts to escape from the authoritarian deadlock.

The Brazilian case of 'new syndicalism' is the most noteworthy. From the late 1970s, vigorous new trade unions succeeded in sidestepping the tightly controlled trade union system set up under Getúlio Vargas and preserved by the military. Metal workers in the São Paulo agglomeration defied labour laws and national security legislation in order to demand wage increases from the large industrial firms in the area. Labour demands gradually evolved into open criticism of the trade union system and of authoritarian politics (Munck 1981). Not only did this massive movement lead to the foundation of the Partido dos Trabalhadores and the political ascendancy of Luis Inácio Lula da Silva, but the movement also developed close links to the new urban movements and to massive popular mobilization in favour of democracy and social reform (Alves 1985; Kowarick 1985). In Brazil as well as in other countries, trade unions played an active part in the retreat or collapse of authoritarianism and the transition to democracy in the 1980s (see pp. 112–116).

Economic liberalization, labour and trade unions

When Mexico announced its inability to continue its debt servicing in 1982, Latin America's debt problem was transformed into a major debt crisis. It triggered three years of profound and widespread economic crisis, followed by almost a decade of efforts by Latin American governments to counter the crisis through structural adjustment measures. In terms of macro-economic performance, structural adjustment [9] has produced widely diverging outcomes, but in terms of social consequences the outcomes have been more uniformly negative (Ghai and Hewitt 1990). It has become manifest that the short- and medium-term costs of crisis and adjustment have been borne by the poorer, less privileged and less organized groups in Latin American societies.

In general terms, the debt crisis meant severe balance of payment problems, which, in turn, led to a decreasing capacity to import, invest and maintain public spending. The overall consequences included economic recession, rising interest rates, declining welfare spending, increasing unemployment and growing poverty. This situation has driven governments across the region to adopt measures to restore the balance of payments, restrict government expenditure, counter inflation, restore economic growth through liberalization and attend to various often conflictive distributive demands. To complicate matters further, many countries faced the need to consolidate democratic political systems (Frieden 1989). These imperatives often proved to be economically and politically irreconcilable.

Here the discussion will be limited to the effects on labour and trade unions. Labour and its organizations are confronted with four consequences of the economic crisis and adjustment: a decline in the level of real wages, rising open unemployment, a liberalization and flexibilization of the economy, especially manufacturing, and socio-economic government policies that are unfavourable to workers or the poor in general. Each aspect will be discussed in turn.

Since the onset of the crisis, real wages have shown a declining trend. The decline was most severe in Mexico and Peru; only Brazil registered a positive trend in real wage levels, largely due to the price freeze of the Cruzado plan in 1986 (Roxborough 1989: 91–2). This decline was induced by the sharp economic downturn which forced firms to control labour costs. In many cases trade unions found it difficult to protect wage levels through collective bargaining or militant action. As a rule, well-organized workers in advanced industries, strategic sectors and public enterprises were more successful than workers in traditional low-pay, low-skill activities. Citing Tokman, Ghai and Hewitt (1990: 23) indicate an average decline in manufacturing wages of 8.4 per cent between 1980 and 1985, while the decline in income of minimum-wage earners, construction workers and informal-sector workers was significantly (up to three times) higher. In addition, high levels of inflation particularly affected the purchasing power of wage earners since they depended on periodic wage and price-level adjustments, often government regulated. Such adjustments were mostly too little and too late.

Rising open unemployment appeared as a relatively new phenomenon in the wake of the crisis. Both private firms and public agencies were forced to resort to massive lay-offs, either to realize payroll reductions because of competitive pressure or because of structural adjustment-induced downsizing. As is shown by Roxborough (1989: 92), the levels of open unemployment for Latin America as a whole rose from 6.3 per cent of the labour force in 1980 to 10.2 per cent in 1987 (see also Portes 1989). In the 1980s the loss of formal jobs was not as easily made up by the expansion of informal-sector activities as it had been previously. Increasing open unemployment not only contributed to the downward pressure upon wage levels but also hampered the trade unions' capacity to bargain for better wages and other benefits. The willingness of Latin American workers to engage in direct labour conflicts declined as the threat of job losses became more imminent. Increasingly also, governments revoked protective legislation that traditionally had secured job stability for important categories of industrial- and public-sector employees. By and large, trade unions in countries such as Argentina, Brazil, Chile, Mexico and Venezuela have been unable to counter these changing patterns within the labour market.

The need to defend the direct material interests of workers under these conditions has been a novel theme for Latin American trade unions as they were used to operating in a more political way to secure workers' benefits through state policies (Touraine 1989: 278–80). While trade unions have succeeded in gaining a larger measure of autonomy since the early 1980s in the countries where they had been particularly involved in corporatist arrangements (Roxborough 1989: 91–2), this, at the same time, meant the vanishing of the state's traditional willingness to respond favourably to organized labour's demands. By and large, trade unions have experienced a reduction in their capacity to circumvent labour-market pressures on wage levels and hiring through the collective bargaining process.

While the short-term effects of crisis and adjustment for labour are evidenced by wage declines and rising unemployment, a longer-term implication concerns the reformulation of development strategies and the re-insertion of the Latin American economies into the world economy. Most Latin American countries have adhered to the tenets of opening up their economies to international trade and investment. Therefore production must achieve international levels of competitiveness. Some countries, notably Chile, Mexico and Argentina, have had considerable success in recent years in reviving economic growth under conditions of economic liberalization. In fact, during the past few years economic growth has returned and analysts have become somewhat more optimistic about future developments (CEPAL 1991; IDB 1992). In addition to the expansion of exports and a recent boom of stock markets, the capital balance has shown timid positive figures.

For industry to recover, however, more is needed than the mere implementation of orthodox policy prescriptions under structural adjustment packages. Comparisons with the successful East Asian NICs show that technological development and the formation of human capital are essential preconditions for sustained industrial development which depends crucially on maximizing competitive, as against comparative, advantages within the global economic system (Gereffi and Wyman 1990). Latin American governments will have to pursue more autonomous policies in this field instead of yielding to the short-term interests of traditional economic groups such as large agricultural exporters, monopolistic industrialists, bankers or managers of public companies.

The implications for labour of such new directions are far-reaching. The macro-economic justification for relatively high wage levels under an ISI strategy is replaced by wage restraints as an element within the effort to enhance international competitiveness. Both the restructuring of economic sectors and the need to increase technological and skill levels call for the participation of labour in these changes, rather than its forced compliance. Sub-contracting and flexible management practices will have a profound impact on labour and its organizations. Many governments have abolished job security. The flexibilization of the labour force and sub-contracting have become legal and increasingly used methods to minimize costs and avoid the implications of stable employment contracts. As a result, large groups of workers and salaried employees have lost their job security and have been dismissed. Some of those who lose their jobs are rehired through sub-contracting or temporary employment, while many others have been forced to secure an income in the informal sector.

Trade unions will have to respond to these changing circumstances. Increasingly, unions in manufacturing industry and advanced service sectors are abandoning their traditional opposition to management strategies and technological modernization. This implies a reconceptualization of 'the enterprise', its vital interests, the combined responsibilities of management and labour, and the benefits of upgrading labour in terms of human resource approaches. Intra-enterprise and intra-sectoral problems and strategies become a focus of concern for trade unions.

During the past decade labour militancy has been directed increasingly against the overall socio-economic situation through the proliferation of political strikes. Greater autonomy and capacity to organize on the (con)federational level has pitched the trade unions against the general economic and social policies adopted by governments as part of structural adjustment programmes. The typical aspects attacked by (con)federations and their political allies were the orthodox adjustment policy in itself (since it foretold recession and hence loss of income and jobs), as well as specific elements such as the curtailment of welfare spending and subsidies by the state (since it diminished access to social services such as health care, education, housing, cheap basic foodstuffs and transportation), public-sector lay-offs, and even privatization schemes of public companies (since it threatened wages and jobs in these companies as well as other public-sector privileges and trade union influence).

As living standards dropped, especially for the urban poor, and general poverty levels increased, socio-political militancy sponsored by trade unions together with other popular, grassroots organizations often prevailed over more narrowly focused actions in defence of wages and jobs. This trend marks the difficult reorientation of the political position of organized labour in the complex environment of adjustment imperatives combined with the task of consolidating new and old democracies in the region.

Democratic consolidation and state–labour relations

Organized labour was a major actor in the recent processes of transition to democracy in a number of former dictatorships in Latin America. Exclusion and repression by the military regimes may have led to a temporary de-activation of trade unions, but these regimes never succeeded in totally eradicating the capacity of the unions to act. In countries such as Argentina, Brazil and Uruguay, organized labour resumed its militancy in the late 1970s. The unions moved from purely defensive actions to a more political stance, criticizing the dictatorships and demanding a return to democracy. In these three countries, organized labour was one of the galvanizing forces behind mass popular protests that contributed in important ways to the end of authoritarianism. But also in other cases (Bolivia, Ecuador, El Salvador, Honduras, Peru) organized labour participated in various ways in the popular campaigns and socio-political alliances that marked efforts at transition or democratic consolidation during the late 1970s and 1980s. Even in a semi-authoritarian situation such as the Mexican one, some sectors within the trade unions, but outside the government-backed Central de Trabajadores Mexicanos (CTM), tried to distance themselves from the PRI-dominated system.

The wider literature on democratic transitions and consolidation concurs on the following combinations of social forces and political mechanisms that made the demise of authoritarianism possible.[10] Within the regime itself, and especially within the military, the notion of giving authoritarianism a more legitimate appearance (in the form of a liberalized *dictablanda*) had to prevail against the view of hardliners within the regime.[11] Such a liberal persuasion within the regime might have been derived from existing doctrines about the political role of the military, as in Brazil, or an increasing awareness that closed authoritarianism was insufficient to guarantee the continuation of the regime (Argentina, Chile, Uruguay). This position was strengthened when the economic situation became more complicated, the intensity of social demands increased and groups formerly supporting authoritarianism, such as the elites and the middle classes, came out in favour of democracy.[12]

But such changes within the regime and its political constituency were in itself insufficient. Equally crucial were the reactivation of civil society, mass popular protests rejecting authoritarianism and calling for a return to democracy, and the construction of a viable political alternative capable of governing under democratic rules and, eventually, imposed upon or acceptable to the wielders of dictatorial power. In this scheme, organized labour re-appeared as an important actor pressing for the full return to democratic government.

Organized labour played this part in several ways. To start with, labour militancy served, often in combination with other forms of popular and grassroots mobilization, to explore and extend the limits of popular protest to express dissatisfaction with specific conditions existing under the authoritarian situation: low wage levels, adverse living conditions and the lack of civil rights, such as the right to organize or the right to go on strike. As such, labour militancy contributed to the resurrection of civil society and politicization of the public. Labour militancy also played an important role in organizing pressure upon the political actors in favour of a transition agenda and a political pact. In addition, organized labour contributed to the establishment of a credible political alternative by supporting or participating in opposition parties that could rely on widespread popular support. Especially in Argentina, Brazil and Uruguay, labour militancy accelerated the transition process by exerting pressure on the regime and the political opposition.

The role of trade unions in the re-democratization of Latin America inaugurated what appears to be a new period of state–trade union relationships. Not only have the repressive and exclusionary authoritarian regimes retreated or collapsed; a return to pre-authoritarian populism, and state paternalism towards the labour movement, also seems ill-favoured in the present political conjuncture. The participation of trade unions in the overthrow of the dictatorships has re-legitimized their role in society. At the same time, the new conceptualization of democracy in the region, whether in liberal or social democratic terms, means a greater scope for autonomy of the trade unions. This also means that adherence to democratic rules and principles has become an important obligation for current labour organizations in Latin America. Trade unions will have to take into account the effects upon governability of their socio-political attitudes and strategies.

This raises new dilemmas for organized labour. A clear example of this is the position taken by trade unions in post-transition environments in Argentina and Brazil. In both countries the civilian opposition that took over from the military in December 1983 and March 1985, respectively, had to deal with the problem of re-politicized and militant organized labour. The immediate task of both the Alfonsín and Sarney governments was to address the economic crisis, while at the same time democratic institutions had to be consolidated, or rebuilt, and the military kept at bay. Both governments tried to establish social pacts with business and labour in order to reach a consensus on economic and social policy. The intention was to forestall protest actions by trade unions which could jeopardize economic policy and the institutional consolidation of democracy. Both Alfonsín and Sarney met with little success: social pacts failed since the trade unions did not feel they obtained significant benefits in exchange for adherence.

In both countries, the trade unions felt that economic recovery and social redistribution could not be postponed indefinitely just to complete the uncertain political agenda of democratic consolidation. Furthermore, in both countries important sections of organized labour were aligned with the political opposition (the Peronist Partido Justicialismo in Argentina and the leftist Partido dos Trabalhadores in Brazil). Alfonsín and Sarney were thus confronted with continuous protest by trade unions as well as with open or covert moves of the military against their administrations.[13]

The overall balance of economic and political liberalization in Latin America is a complex one for the trade unions. Weakened by a long period of harassment and repression by authoritarian regimes and still affected by the consequences of structural adjustment and recession, the labour movement is now engaged in an effort to rebuild and reconsolidate itself. Aggression against union leaders is gradually diminishing. Yet in countries like Colombia where terrorism and drug-related violence are rampant, unions continue to suffer from persecution and physical attacks. Here, as in Central American countries such as Guatemala and El Salvador, violence and aggression against organized labour still persist although their incidence has declined somewhat. Still, new labour organizations and a new generation of labour leaders all over Latin America are confronted by a series of challenges related to economic restructuring and political democracy.

First, unions in many countries tend to engage more autonomously in collective bargaining at the enterprise or branch level with less interference from governments. The old style of bargaining under the threat of violence, a strategy oriented more towards government than to employers in order to obtain general or branch-level guidelines for wages and other conditions, is now being replaced by direct negotiation with employers. In the process, unions are becoming more professionalized.

This tendency is combined with efforts to increase the institutional and organizational autonomy of trade unions. The earlier domination and interference by populist, corporatist or authoritarian governments has diminished. With regard to the relationship between unions and political parties, the situation is more complicated. In the case of the *Peronista* labour movement in Argentina, for instance, a distancing between organized labour and the Peronist fraction in power around President Menem can be observed, although Argentinean unions are divided over this issue. In Brazil, Lula, former president of the metalworkers' union of São Bernardo (greater São Paulo) and presidential candidate in the 1990 and 1994 elections, was one of the founders of the Partido dos Trabalhadores (PT). Up till now close links exist between this party and the Central Unica dos Trabalhadores (CUT). The PT and CUT argue that workers' objectives cannot be reached at the level of trade union activities only. In Mexico, Costa Rica and Venezuela, unions remain very much related to, and dependent upon, political parties within the system. In Chile, trade unions try to preserve a pluralistic and independent position in the face of a political landscape that has been reconquered by the traditional political parties (Epstein 1989).

In this new environment of trade union autonomy, governments often seek social pacts or tripartite agreements to stabilize the economy and to control inflation. As we have seen, labour, as in the case of Argentina and Brazil, has remained sceptical. Only in Chile was a social pact established, but in very special circumstances: the economy was booming and the democratic government was able and willing to mount a major attack on unemployment and poverty. Moreover, the presence of Pinochet and the military loomed over the process. In Argentina and Brazil, no convincing effort has been made by governments to address the social issues that affect workers' livelihoods.

Still, it is important to note that part of the Latin American labour movement is not satisfied by bread and butter unionism. Quite consciously it attempts to transcend mere *revindicación* and become *propositivo*, that is, offering constructive proposals for a range of problems facing the economy and society in general. This new kind of political unionism propels organized labour into a broader role, discarding a mere defensive posture in favour of promoting alternative policies in fields such as energy, the environment, industrialization and social welfare. Trade unions may become increasingly aware that important opportunities exist to assume a broader role in civil society as part of the social consensus that is necessary to support development and democracy.

One of the most formidable problems that has to be addressed in this context is that of widespread poverty and ongoing informalization within Latin American economies and societies. Currently, it is not repressive state action but unemployment, poverty and informal livelihood strategies that are undermining the capacity of trade unions to mobilize and represent the Latin American workers in defence of their interests. If not taken into account, these issues may not only erode the capacity for representation and action of the conventional labour organizations themselves, but also pose a major threat to the long-term prospects of development and democracy in the region. Therefore, the problems of poverty and informalization and their consequences for labour are the subject of the next section.

Informalization, labour and new labour organizations[14]

A structural phenomenon affecting Latin America's economy and society in general, and labour and labour relations in particular, is the problem of poverty and informalization (see Table 5.1).

Table 5.1 Incidence of poverty, mid-1980s (%)

Country	Poverty	Extreme poverty	% of
Argentina	9	3	urban
Colombia	35	14	urban
Guatemala	68	43	total
Mexico	42	17	total
Panama	36	16	total
Peru	53	30	total
Uruguay	15	3	urban
Venezuela	31	11	total

Source: PREALC (1989).

In terms of income distribution, the richest five per cent of the population of the region increased or maintained their income, while the lowest 75 per cent experienced a significant reduction in theirs, making the contrast between wealth and poverty more acute. At the beginning of the 1990s, the percentage of Latin American households with income levels below the average varied from 68 per cent in the urban areas of Costa Rica to 78 per cent in the metropolitan areas of Brazil. The comparative patterns of income distribution among the countries in the region remained stable during the 1980s, with Argentina, Costa Rica, Uruguay and Venezuela having a significantly more egalitarian national distribution than Colombia and Brazil. In the latter countries, the households in the lowest quintile share just between four and six per cent of total income, compared to a range of eight to eleven per cent in the former.

Nowadays, poverty is particularly concentrated in the urban areas of Latin America. The urban poor represented between 55 and 60 per cent of the total poor in 1990, a significantly higher figure compared with 46 per cent in 1980 and 37 per cent in 1970.[15] There is a strong coincidence between poverty and informality. According to official estimates in the 1990s, 35 per cent of the Mexican population is considered to be informal; in Central America this percentage lies between 30 and 60 (Costa Rica and Guatemala, respectively); and 65 per cent of the population of Lima Metropolitana (Peru) is defined as informal. By 1980, between 75 and 80 per cent of those employed in the informal sector received an income below recognized national minimum standards. Similarly, in Lima, 62 per cent of those earning an income below the minimum were employed in the informal sector. For those with extremely low incomes the proportion was even higher, reaching 75 per cent. In Costa Rica and Venezuela, 71 and 79 per cent, respectively, of those working in the informal sector were members of poor households in 1982 (Tokman 1990).

The Latin American poor, like those of other continents, have displayed an infinite range of alternative strategies by means of which they manage to engage in economic production, survive and reproduce themselves. From the beginning of the 1970s the International Labour Organization popularized the new name by which these alternatives are known collectively: the 'informal sector', in contrast to a 'formal sector'. This model has been criticized not so much for being dualistic or imprecise as for the difficulty of distinguishing which units belong to one or the other sector. In effect, to distinguish between formal and informal, one has to use various criteria simultaneously: social, economic and legal. Nevertheless, the term has gained acceptance throughout the world and attempts have been made to apply it to diverse realities, not only in the underdeveloped countries but also in advanced societies. This has made the term somewhat obscure, imprecise, or at least polysemic as an analytical category. Still, empirical studies in

Mexico, Central America and Peru indicate some remarkably common tendencies.[16] Basically, one should note the stigmatization of the informal sector as the 'sector of poverty': it is marked by the over-representation of vulnerable social categories such as women, younger people, children, the aged, indigenous peoples, refugees and, in general, the victims of the Central American and Andean civil wars.

Be that as it may, the phenomenon considered in this chapter under the various terms 'informal sector', 'unstructured sector', 'subterranean economy', 'self-employment economy' or 'petty commodity production' applies to the world of the poor and their strategies for survival.[17] These terms comprise a multitude of forms of production, organization and consumption in which possibly the only common factor is their heterogeneity. Basically, however, we can distinguish two broad categories: small-scale enterprises that obey a logic of mere subsistence (which accounts for the immense majority) and those that combine simple reproduction with a modest capacity for accumulation (which is characteristic for the elite amongst the micro-entrepreneurs).

In the first group of enterprises, the purpose of the production process is not the maximization of utilities, as is the case in an adult capitalist enterprise, but equilibrium, subsistence. The second group, although starting at the same economic level as those of subsistence, consists of businesses generally owned by males, oriented according to other kinds of objectives. They tend to assume greater risks and may manage to overcome the restrictions imposed by their scant capital and difficult working conditions. Thanks to certain factors, among which may be highlighted the social and political relations of the small entrepreneurs but more especially their training, experience and organization, these sometimes achieve social and economic mobility, thus becoming examples of the capacity of the informal sector to jump, that is, to make the transition towards modern and formal activities.

Informality impedes the setting up of links between management and labour strictly in terms of wages or salaries, and it promotes a horizontal perception of labour relations within the establishment, relations which to a large extent originate in the familial characteristics of the small business. The absence of wage relations implies a kind of labour flexibility very different from that of enterprises ruled by the logic of accumulation and efficiency. The forms of remuneration adopted in the family business do not obey the mercantile rationale as much as the needs of each member of the family and the group as a whole. Mercantile relations yield to nexuses of a more affective type where solidarity and mutual support predominate. This does not deny the existence of a high level of self-exploitation within the informal sector. The fact that family members do not receive the market rates for their work in order to reduce costs and ensure the firm's survival in some cases means that the family micro-enterprise is unable to retain its members for very long. In other cases, family self-exploitation is seen as a payment deferred to the future, since the business will pass on to the proprietor's family (Cortés and Rubalcava 1990).

It is only by recourse to euphemism that the self-employed in the informal sector can be considered entrepreneurs. One of them demonstrates clearly in his own words how he perceives the situation:

> People like us, who have small businesses, to my mind we're workers. We're no different from people who work for a boss. We don't work the way a boss does, but more like an employee. We're our own employees. (Goldenberg and Acuña 1994: 51).

In informal economic activities, management–labour relations are other than in the formal economy and the differences between employer and employee in the informal economy are vague.

The emergence of Latin American informality is accompanied by the reduction, maybe partial disintegration, of the institutional pillars of formal society. In most Andean countries and in Central America, the Chambers of Industry and Commerce and the all-mighty labour confederations began to decline considerably in the 1980s in terms of membership as well in terms of political presence.

The informalization of society means in practice an alteration of the structure of class organization and representation. All over Latin America new associations or federations of micro-entrepreneurs and petty traders are coming into existence. One should remember that these informal businessmen form a relative elite; the informal employees have not made a comparable advance in terms of organizing themselves. It is worth noting, however, that the small-scale businessmen are often at the same time full-time workers in their own businesses. What is still more significant in the Andean countries and in the Central American capitals is a relative reduction in trade union activity in the formal sector, together with increasing organization on the part of the proprietors in the informal sector. In this process, curiously, the existing relations of direct dependency within the informal establishments – of workers upon owners – is being reproduced on a broader scale. Similar patterns of clientèlism and dependence are visible when organizations of small businessmen are fostered and guided by outside patrons: private and non-governmental development organizations (NGOs), churches and at times the financial institutions that offer credit to small-scale enterprises. The organizations of small-scale proprietors are at most semi-autonomous.

Maybe the most interesting manifestation of Latin America's informality is the emergence of these new social actors on the national scene: micro-entrepreneurs presenting themselves as organized poor, being more alike with their workers (mostly family members and relatives) than representatives of the formal economy. There is at least a similarity between the informal organizations of all kinds and tendencies and the formal organizations of the labour movement. Both are defensive organizations aimed at the improvement of economic and labour conditions of their members. But the labour movement is the formal representative of the legally protected national labour force organized in unions, federations and confederations. Its members are the *obreros* and *empleados* of the medium-sized enterprises and the big companies in the private and public sectors. They negotiate by means of collective bargaining, executed by highly-trained professional staff members who receive good salaries based upon the contributions of the affiliated members.

The *sindicatos* or *camaras* of the 'informals' such as the micro-entrepreneurs, the artisans and the self-employed are at best incipient organizations with a precarious institutionality, generally created to fulfil pragmatic and short-term objectives: a market place, a credit line, spontaneous publicity or the solution of a very specific problem with the local authorities. The same remarks apply to the variety of non-economic organizations: the *clubs de madres*, the *vaso de leche* committees, the popular–kitchen movements. Their *raison d'être* has been mostly an *ad hoc*, although essential necessity: food, safety, housing, health or an immediate source of income. In most cases, their creation was induced externally, by a private development organization, a church committee, a local financial agent, an entrepreneurial politician and sometimes by an international donor representative. In this sense, we may speak of the 'NGO-ization' of the formerly autonomous informal labour movement: the spontaneous affiliation of poor people becomes by necessity dependent upon the charity and support of others. The organizations of the informals and the poor have to look beyond the existing institutions of the formal national economy and society for stability.

Conclusions

In the course of the twentieth century, wage labour has risen as an important factor and actor in Latin American development and social change. The expansion of the primary export economies from the late nineteenth century onwards has placed the working class on the Latin American social and political stage. With the expansion of ISI throughout the region, especially after 1930, wage labour and its organization became fully integrated into social life and political strategies. In the early decades of this process, large-scale wage labour was limited to the big mining operations, plantation agriculture, public utilities and transportation. The rise of light industries and concomitant urbanization brought about the expansion of the industrial class. Initially this class was composed predominantly of former artisans and non-skilled workers, very often women.

Industrialization and urbanization in the major Latin American countries accelerated after the Second World War. The industrial sector was transformed as the principal Latin American economies entered into the dynamic phase of import substitution. This involved upgrading the branch structure of manufacturing industry towards more capital-intensive and technologically more advanced production of consumer durables, intermediary goods and some capital goods. In the course of this process, firm size and production scale in the leading industries grew. These industries absorbed increasing numbers of skilled and semi-skilled workers. Nevertheless, economic growth and investment tended to outpace the creation of urban–industrial jobs. Demographic growth and rural–urban migration started to have a permanent impact on urban job markets leading to the consolidation of informal activities and jobs as an important aspect of the Latin American economies.

The post-war industrialization pattern contributed to a marked dualization, or maybe even a 'triplification' of labour in Latin America: skilled, relatively better-paid, organized and protected labour in the large industries and the public sector; low- or unskilled, low-paid and unprotected labour in the traditional activities of often small and medium-sized firms; and finally informal labour, generally unproductive and unrewarding, for the persons who had or sought no access to formal jobs and who lived as a rule on or below established levels of poverty. The more adverse the conditions for jobs seemed to be, the greater the likelihood of finding vulnerable categories to occupy them, for example, women, children, recent migrants and ethnic groups.

In particular, female labour in labour-intensive, low-skill and low-wage industries has been important throughout the history of Latin American industrialization: initially in textiles and clothing, and food processing, later also in printing, pharmaceuticals and electronic parts and components. Low wages for women workers have always been based on the premise of the complementary role of women's income, a premise firmly entrenched in Latin American patterns of gender relations. In the informal sector, but to a certain extent also in the formal sector, female labour is very often the main source of household income.

Latin American trade unionism has risen with the expansion of wage labour. Often radical and fragmented prior to the 1930s, workers' organizations became united, institutionalized, and socially and politically incorporated. The 1930–80 period may be divided in two great cycles (albeit at the risk of oversimplifying): the populist-corporatist situation, in which organized labour was incorporated into often nationalist and developmentalist socio-political alliances; and the authoritarian–repressive situation, in which organized labour was mostly excluded from the political process. In both cases, however, the relationship between trade unions and the state in Latin America became a close one. Up till the early 1980s Latin American trade unions were not independent from the state. Their organizations and strategies were very often not the autonomous expression of workers' interests and demands but rather modelled on institutional, political and ideological control by the state.

Since 1980, three major trends have been affecting the position of wage labour and trade unions in Latin America: liberalization, democratization and informalization (related, respectively, to the market, the state and poverty). Their consequences will be summed up by raising a number of questions that are only beginning to be answered.

Liberalization has led to a shift from the protection of the vested interest of labour (or at least that of its elite segments) to a more open and dynamic confrontation of labour with market forces and employers' strategies. This means that, while firms are increasingly paying attention to productivity and performance, workers and their organizations are confronted with both the imperative of the upgrading of work and the threat of redundancy and unemployment. This may well prove to be a difficult challenge. Latin American trade unions are only now beginning to build up experience in constructive collective bargaining. Ideologically they are instinctively inclined to dismiss neo-liberal propositions. Still, some signs suggest that trade unions are turning towards the strategy of protecting workers' interests by supporting the companies in which they work.

An important and as yet uncertain complicating factor is the process of regional economic integration. Both NAFTA (North American Free Trade Association) and Mercosur, when fully evolved, will have a major impact on the labour markets in their member countries. It seems likely that trade unions, given the relative immobility of labour compared with capital, will be slow in their response to the economic and institutional changes brought about by market integration.

The consolidation of democracy, often achieved with the active participation of trade unionists, went hand in hand with the delinking of organized labour from the state. While trade unions in general welcome their increased autonomy, they also face new problems. Will greater autonomy also mean a depoliticization of organized labour? Can and should more independent trade unionism support democratic regimes despite the possibility that the latter's policies might be unfavourable to workers' interests? Organized labour is looking for a new role within civil society. Whether or not institutionalized social relations in Latin America develop towards a convergence with either the liberal labour–capital model of the United States, or the tripartite welfare-state labour–capital–government model of Western Europe, remains to be seen.

Informalization and endemic poverty pose a major threat to the capacity of trade unions to organize and defend the working population. The informal sector, as a realm of the poor, is expanding. Within it the harsh insecurity of the impersonal market is partly replaced by the security of primordial social relations within the labour process. The flip side of this security is low rates of remuneration, adverse working conditions and high levels of self-exploitation. Formal trade unions find it difficult to address and represent the informal workers. The trend since the 1970s of the new social movements to fill the gap in mobilizing the poor is in many cases being continued by the rise of new organizations of the informals.

However, this process is shot through with ambiguities. How can the interests of the heterogeneous category of informal producers and workers be defined? Should owners of small-scale enterprises unite with their workers, or should the latter try to set up their own organizations? Could these organizations be linked to the formal trade union system, or would this weaken or marginalize the position of the informal proletariat? How should the issue of donor-dependency and tutelage of the organizations of informals be addressed? Can these organizations develop into firm pillars of civil society, or is it more likely that they will support conservative neo-populist leaders and regimes? The last dilemma touches upon the tricky relationship between poverty and the threat of social disintegration on the one hand, and democracy and social consensus on the other. These dilemmas mark the crossroads Latin American countries seem to be facing towards the end of the twentieth century.

Notes

1. This chapter refers mainly to urban labour, i.e. formal blue-collar wage labour in industry, construction or (public) services, as well as workers and self-employed in the informal sector. This does not suggest that rural labour is

less important. Labour forms in the agricultural sector have evolved from traditional nineteenth-century forms (for example, slavery, debt peonage, sharecropping, tenant farming) towards the increasing significance of wage labour in the plantation sector, commercial agriculture and agro-industry.

2. Since the 1960s, labour and labour organizations have received increasing scholarly attention. Opinions on the importance of labour in Latin American social change differ. Touraine (1989: 72) states that the Latin American labour movement only played a secondary role, while Berquist (1986: 1) refers to the 'decisive role' played by organized labour in the region. This debate will not be addressed here. Only a few studies analyse the labour issue on a continental scale (for example, Alexander 1966; Berquist 1986; Epstein 1989; Katzman and Reyna 1979; Spalding 1977). A number of monographs analyse the role of labour and trade unions in different sectors in specific countries (for example, Humphrey (1982) on Brazil; Kruijt and Vellinga (1983) and Payne (1985) on Peru; Pécaut (1973) and Urrutia (1969) on Colombia; and Vellinga (1979) on Mexico).

3. For reasons of space and expertise, the Caribbean region will not be considered. While there are some basic similarities between the Dominican Republic and other Latin, especially Central, American countries, the often small independent or quasi-independent countries of the non-Spanish Caribbean demonstrate different socio-economic and political patterns from those in continental Latin America. The economic and political trajectories of both Cuba and Puerto Rico are too singular to allow for their inclusion in this general survey.

4. See, for example, Furtado (1970) for an early structuralist treatment of Latin American economic development, and Weaver (1980) for a detailed analysis of industrial development in the region. Touraine (1989) and Wynia (1990) provide useful general overviews. Harris (1986) and Gereffi and Wyman (1990) offer comparisons between Latin America and East Asia.

5. Evans (1979) has analysed this tripartite pattern in the case of Brazil. He generalizes the pattern to all cases of 'dependent development' to show that dependence on foreign capital and technology in manufacturing does not necessarily entail industrial stagnation or the subordination of domestic agents (such as the state or the domestic bourgeoisie).

6. However, Portes rejects the conventional notion of 'dualism' derived from modernization thinking: 'The multiple relations between the informal proletariat and capitalist production and circulation suggest that the common description of Latin American economies as "dual" is inappropriate. These economies can be better described as unified systems in which the modern capitalist sector articulates with and relies on the continuing existence of backward modes of production and the associated labor supplies' (1985: 16).

7. See, for example, Conniff (1982), Di Tella (1972), Dix (1985), Laclau (1977) and Weffort (1980) for various ways in which the phenomenon of Latin American populism has been analysed. As rightly observed by Touraine (1989: 161 and *passim*), a major characteristic of Latin American populism has been the use of mass popular support and mobilization by a state that sets out to organize and control limited economic and social reforms.

8. See, for example, the contributions to the debate on bureaucratic-authoritarianism contained in Cammack and O'Brien (1985) and Collier (1979). Recent interpretations of militarism can be found in Goodman *et*

al. (1990) and Rouquié (1989). Koonings (1991) provides an overview of the literature on modern militarism.

9. Structural adjustment itself has assumed a wide variety of forms, from liberalist orthodoxy to structuralist heterodoxy. Frequent policy shifts are characteristic of many countries between 1982 and the present. The record of successes and failures in macro-economic terms has recently compelled most countries to adopt more conventional orthodox adjustment and stabilization policies. The latest to do this has been Brazil, which in July 1994 adopted a new currency pegged to the dollar as part of a liberal adjustment scheme designed by the former Minister of Finance, Fernando Henrique Cardoso. See, for example, Ruccio (1991) for a conceptual discussion of orthodoxy versus heterodoxy. Stallings and Kaufman (1989) provide a collection of general analyses and country cases on the macro-economic, social and political dynamics of the debt crisis.

10. For a widely cited analytical approach, see the three volumes edited by O'Donnell, Schmitter and Whitehead (1986a/b/c). Important contributions to the debate and valuable case studies appeared in Baloyra (1987), Diamond, Linz and Lipset (1989) and Lopez and Stohl (1987). Calderón and Dos Santos (1988) include essays on less-often discussed smaller countries. A useful summary is provided by Munck (1989).

11. See Goodman *et al.* (1990) and Kruijt and Torres-Rivas (1991) for discussions on the politicization of the military and the importance of civil–military relations.

12. See Higley and Gunther (1992) for a framework and case studies on the role of elites in democratic transition and consolidation. The thrust of their argument is that political consensus among elites is crucial for the consolidation of democracy after the breakdown of authoritarian regimes.

13. In Argentina, military dissatisfaction was largely a matter of violent political protests by young insurgent officers. In Brazil, the military ministers, the combined chiefs-of-staff and the Serviço Nacional de Informações inherited from the military regime made labour unrest one of their prime objects of attention.

14. Many of the ideas presented here are analysed more explicitly in Alba Vega and Kruijt (1994).

15. See Alba Vega and Kruijt (1994: 1–6), Feres and León (1990), Menjívar Larín and Trejos (1992) and Stallings and Kaufman (1992: 55).

16. For Mexico, see Arias (1985), Escobar (1987), Gabayet (1987), Gabayet *et al.* (1988), and Gonzáles de la Rocha (1986). For Central America, see Menjívar Larín and Pérez Saínz (1990, 1993). For Peru, see Toledo and Chaubert (1991).

17. See, for example, Lubell (1991), Middleton (1989) and Tokman (1992) for conceptualizations.

References

Alba Vega, C. and D. Kruijt (1994) *The Convenience of the Minuscule. Informality and Micro-Enterprise in Latin America*. THELA Publishers, Amsterdam.

Alexander, R.J. (1966) *Organized Labor In Latin America*. Free Press, New York.

Altimir, O. (1981) 'Poverty in Latin America', *CEPAL Review* Vol.13: 65–91.

Alves, M.H.M. (1985) *Estado e Oposição no Brasil, 1964–1984*. Vozes, Petrópolis.

Arias, P. (ed.) (1985) *Guadalajara. La gran ciudad de la pequeña industria*. El Colegio de Michoacan, Zamora.

Baloyra, E.A. (ed.) (1987) *Comparing New Democracies. Transitions and Consolidation in Mediterranean Europe and the Southern Cone*. Westview, Boulder.

Berquist, Ch. (1986) *Labor in Latin America. Comparative Essays on Chile, Argentina, Venezuela, and Colombia*. Stanford University Press, Stanford.

Calderón, F. and M. Dos Santos (eds) (1988) *Hacia un Nuevo Orden Estatal en América Latina? Democratización/Modernización y Actores Socio-Políticos*. CLACSO, Buenos Aires.

Cammack, P. and Ph. O'Brien (eds) (1985) *Generals in Retreat. The Crisis of Military Rule in Latin America*. Manchester University Press, Manchester.

Cardoso, F.H. and E. Faletto (1979) *Dependency and Development in Latin America*. University of California Press, Berkeley.

CEPAL (1991) 'Balance preliminar de la economia de América Latina y el Caribe 1991', *Notas sobre el Desarrollo de la Economia* No. 519/20. CEPAL, Santiago.

Cerutti, M. and M. Vellinga (eds) (1989) *Burguesías e Industria en América Latina y Europe Meridional*. Alianza, Madrid.

Collier, D. (ed.) (1979) *The New Authoritarianism in Latin America*. Princeton University Press, Princeton.

Conniff, M. (1982) *Latin American Populism in Comparative Perspective*. University of New Mexico Press, Albuquerque.

Cortés, F. and R.M. Rubalcava (1990) *Autoexplotación forzada y equidad por empobrecimiento* (Jornadas 120). El Colegio de Mexico, Mexico.

Di Tella, T. (1972) 'Populism and Reform in Latin America', in C. Veliz (ed.) *Obstacles to Change in Latin America*, pp. 47–74. Oxford University Press, London.

Diamond, L., J.J. Linz and S.M. Lipset (eds) (1989) *Democracy in Developing Countries. Vol. 4: Latin America*. Lynne Riener and Adamantine Press, Boulder and London.

Dix, R. (1985) 'Populism: Authoritarian and Democratic', *Latin American Research Review* Vol. 20, No. 2: 29–52.

Epstein, E.C. (ed.) (1989) *Labor Autonomy and the State in Latin America*. Unwin Hyman, Boston.

Escobar, A. (1987) *Con el sudor de tu frente. Mercado de trabajo y clase obrera en Guadalajara*. El Colegio de Jalisco, Guadalajara.

Evans, P. (1979) *Dependent Development. The Alliance of Multinational, State, and Local Capital in Brazil.* Princeton University Press, Princeton.

Feres, J.C. and A. León (1990) 'The Magnitude of Poverty in Latin America', *CEPAL Review* Vol. 41: 133–51.

Frieden, J. (1989) 'Winners and Losers in the Latin American Debt Crisis: The Political Implications', in B. Stallings and R. Kaufman (eds) *Debt and Democracy in Latin America*, pp. 23–37. Westview, Boulder.

Furtado, C. (1970) *Economic Development of Latin America.* Cambridge University Press, Cambridge.

Gabayet, L. (1987) *Obreros somos. Diferenciación social y formación de la clase obrera en Guadalajara.* El Colegio de Jalisco, Guadalajara.

Gabayet, L. *et al.* (1988) *Mujeres y sociedad. Salario, hogar y acción social en el occidente de México.* El Colegio de Jalisco, Guadalajara.

Gereffi, G. and D.L. Wyman (eds) (1990) *Manufacturing Miracles. Paths of Industrialization in Latin America and East Asia.* Princeton University Press, Princeton.

Ghai, Dh. and C. Hewitt de Alcántara (1990) 'The Crisis of the 1980s in Africa, Latin America and the Caribbean: An Overview', in Dh. Ghai (ed.) *The IMF and the South. The Social Impact of Crisis and Adjustment*, pp. 13–42. Zed, London.

Gilbert, A. and J. Gugler (1983) *Cities, Poverty and Development. Urbanization in the Third World.* Oxford University Press, Oxford.

Goldenberg, O. and V.H. Acuña (1994) *Género en la informalidad. Historias laborales centroamericanas.* FLACSO, San José.

Gonzáles de la Rocha, M. (1986) *Los recursos de la pobreza. Familias de bajos ingresos de Guadalajara.* El Colegio de Jalisco, Guadalajara.

Goodman, L.W., J.S.R. Mendelson and J. Rial (eds) (1990) *The Military and Democracy. The Future of Civil–Military Relations in Latin America.* Lexington Books, Lexington.

Harris, N. (1986) *The End of the Third World. Newly Industrializing Countries and the Decline of an Ideology.* Penguin, Harmondsworth.

Higley, J. and R. Gunther (eds) (1992) *Elites and Democratic Consolidation in Latin America and Southern Europe.* Cambridge University Press, Cambridge.

Humphrey, J. (1982) *Capitalist Control and Workers' Struggle in the Brazilian Auto Industry.* Princeton University Press, Princeton.

IDB (1992) *Economic and Social Progress in Latin America 1992 Report* (Special Section: Latin America's exports of manufactured goods). Inter-American Development Bank, Washington DC.

Infante, R. and E. Klein (1991) 'The Latin American Labour Market, 1950–1990', *CEPAL Review* Vol. 45: 121–35.

Katzman, R. and J.L. Reyna (eds) (1979) *Fuerza de Trabajo y Movimientos Laborales en América Latina.* El Colégio de Mexico, Mexico.

Koonings, K. (1991) 'La sociología de la intervención militar en la política Latinoamericana', in D. Kruijt and E. Torres–Rivas (eds) *América Latina: Militares y Sociedad* Vol. 1, pp. 19–61. FLACSO, San José.

Kowarick, L. (1985) 'The Pathways to Encounter: Reflections on the Social Struggle in São Paulo', in D. Slater (ed.) *New Social Movements and the State in Latin America.* CEDLA, Amsterdam.

Kruijt, D. and E. Torres-Rivas (eds) (1991) *América Latina: Militares y Sociedad* (2 vols). FLACSO, San José.

Kruijt, D. and M. Vellinga (1983) *Estado, Clase Obrera y Empresa Transnacional. El Caso de la Minería Peruana, 1900–1980*. Siglo XXI, Mexico.

Laclau, E. (1977) *Politics and Ideology in Marxist Theory*. New Left Books, London.

Lopez, G.A. and M. Stohl (eds) (1987) *Liberalization and Redemocratization in Latin America*. Greenwood Press, New York.

Lubell, H. (1991) *The Informal Sector in the 1980s and 1990s*. OECD Development Centre, Paris.

Menjívar Larín, R. and J.P. Pérez Saínz (eds) (1990) *Informalidad urbana en Centroamérica. Evidencias e Interrogantes*. FLACSO, San José.

―――― (eds) (1993) *Ni héroes ni villanas. Género e informalidad urbana en Centroamérica*. FLACSO, San José.

Menjívar Larín, R. and J.D. Trejos (1992) *La pobreza en América Central*. FLACSO, San José.

Middleton, A. (1989) 'The Changing Structure of Petty Production in Ecuador', *World Development* Vol. 17, No. 1: 139–55.

Munck, R. (1981) 'The Labor Movement and the Crisis of the Dictatorship in Brazil', in T.C. Bruneau and Ph. Faucher (eds) *Authoritarian Capitalism. Brazil's Contemporary Economic and Political Development*, pp. 219-38. Westview, Boulder.

―――― (1989) *Latin America: The Transition to Democracy*. Zed, London.

O'Donnell, G. (1973) *Modernization and Bureaucratic Authoritarianism: Studies in South American Politics*. Institute of International Studies, University of California, Berkeley.

O'Donnell, G., Ph.C. Schmitter and L. Whitehead (eds) (1986a) *Transitions from Authoritarian Rule: Latin America*. Johns Hopkins University Press, Baltimore.

―――― (1986b) *Transitions from Authoritarian Rule: Comparative Perspectives*. Johns Hopkins University Press, Baltimore.

―――― (1986c) *Transitions from Authoritarian Rule: Tentative Conclusions about Uncertain Democracies*. Johns Hopkins University Press, Baltimore.

Payne, J. (1985) *Labor and Politics in Peru. The System of Political Bargaining*. Yale University Press, New Haven.

Pécaut, D. (1973) *Política y Sindicalismo en Colombia*. La Carreta, Bogotá.

Perelli, C. (1990) 'The Military's Perception of Threat in the Southern Cone of South America', in L.W. Goodman, J.S.R. Mendelson and J. Rial (eds) *The Military and Democracy. The Future of Civil–Military Relations in Latin America*, pp. 93–105. Lexington Books, Lexington.

Portes, A. (1985) 'Latin American Class Structures: Their Composition and Change during the Last Decades', *Latin American Research Review* Vol. 20, No. 3: 7–39.

―――― (1989) 'Latin American Urbanization in the Years of the Crisis', *Latin American Research Review* Vol. 24, No. 3: 7–44.

PREALC (1989) *Magnitud de la pobreza en ocho países de América Latina en 1986*. PREALC, Santiago de Chile.

Rouquié, A. (1989) *The Military and the State in Latin America*. University of California Press, Berkeley.

Roxborough, I. (1989) 'Organized Labor: A Major Victim of the Debt Crisis', in B. Stallings and R. Kaufman (eds) *Debt and Democracy in Latin America*, pp. 91–108. Westview, Boulder.

Ruccio, D. (1991) 'When Failure Becomes Success: Class and the Debate over Stabilization and Adjustment', *World Development* Vol. 19, No. 10: 1315–34.

Spalding, H. (1977) *Organized Labor in Latin America. Historical Case Studies of Urban Workers in Dependent Societies*. Harper & Row, New York.

Stallings, B. and R. Kaufman (eds) (1989) *Debt and Democracy in Latin America*. Westview, Boulder.

———— (eds) (1992) *The Informal Sector in Mexico*. Secretaría del Trabajo y Previsión Social and US Department of Labor, Mexico and Washington DC.

Tokman, V. (1990) 'The Informal Sector in Latin America: Fifteen Years Later', in D. Turnham, B. Salome and A. Schwartz (eds) *The Informal Sector Revisited*. OECD Development Centre, Paris.

———— (ed.) (1992) *Beyond Regulation. The Informal Economy in Latin America*. Lynne Riener, Boulder.

Toledo, A. and A. Chaubert (eds) (1991) *Las otras caras de la sociedad informal. Una visión multidisciplinaria*. ESAN/IDE, Lima.

Touraine, A. (1989) *América Latina: Política y Sociedad*. Espasa Calpe, Madrid.

Urrutia, M. (1969) *The Development of the Colombian Labor Movement*. Yale University Press, New Haven.

Vellinga, M. (1979) *Economic Development and the Dynamics of Class. Industrialization, Power and Control in Monterrey, Mexico*. Van Gorcum, Assen.

Weaver, F.S. (1980) *Class, State and Industrial Structure. The Historical Process of South American Industrial Growth*. Greenwood Press, London.

Weffort, F. (1980) *O Populismo na Política Brasileira*. Paz e Terra, Rio de Janeiro.

———— (1992) *Cuál democrácia?* FLACSO, San José.

Wynia, G. (1990) *The Politics of Latin American Development*. Cambridge University Press, Cambridge.

6. Free Market Economics and Belated Democratization: The Case of Chile

Patricio Frías
Jaime Ruiz-Tagle

The political system

After Chile's Independence from Spain in 1818, the political system developed through various changes from oligarchy to presidential democracy. From 1891 to 1925 the country was governed by a parliamentary system based on powerful political parties. In 1925, a new constitution built around a presidential system was adopted, which remained in force until the military coup of 1973. The stability of Chile's political system, rare in Latin America, was an important source of prestige for the country.

Until the 1973 coup the Chilean armed forces were recognized as highly professional and respectful of the constitution. Since the turn of the century, they had accepted co-existence with Marxist political parties (especially communist and socialist) which had gained great popularity and influence.

A number of factors have contributed to the emergence of a difficult political climate in recent decades. The national electorate was almost equally divided between the parties of the right, centre and left for a long period preceding the coup. This political fragmentation made it difficult to address the nation's main problems and fostered instability. The lack of synchronization between presidential and parliamentary elections compounded the problem and made it difficult for presidents to obtain a solid parliamentary majority.

The reinstatement of a limited democratic system in 1990 saw the re-emergence of the political divisions that had existed prior to 1973. However, some differences can be discerned, the most important of which were the strength of the Christian Democratic Party at the centre of the political spectrum, the division of the right into two equally prominent parties and the deterioration of the political influence of the Communist Party on the left. Also, the new willingness to collaborate, unknown two decades previously, has eased the task of governing the country.

The common political front formed by the opposition parties won a decisive victory in the 1989 elections. It elected the new president of the republic and secured a majority in the House of Representatives. However, the provision of designated (non-elected) senators, inserted in the constitution by the previous political regime, blocked the attainment of a similar majority in the Senate. This made it difficult to pass new legislation, especially when aimed at labour-system reforms. Not surprisingly, the government has proposed a constitutional reform to eliminate the system of designated senators to the National Congress.

The ruling coalition has generally been sympathetic to the demands and interests of trade unions. However, three factors have limited its capacity to respond to their demands: the special status of designated senators created by the military prevented the achievement of a senate majority; the necessities of the macro-economic management of an open economy induced pressures on wages; and the adherence to the political imperative to allocate sufficient resources to poverty alleviation. Since the coalition again prevailed during the 1993 parliamentary and presidential elections, further reforms favourable to the trade unions can be expected.

The Ministry for Social Security and Labour is the most important ministry for trade unions. Through its Labour Directorate it is responsible for the control and enforcement of labour laws and standards. The current ministry has encouraged several forms of dialogue and social harmonization and prepared legislation to improve labour relations. Furthermore it has initiated an important programme to train young people for work.

To a lesser extent, the ministries of finance and economics are also important to trade unions. The importance of the former resides in its power to determine the guidelines for minimum wage, pension and family allowance adjustments. In a nutshell, it determines the level of subsidies that benefit the majority of the population.

Since the restoration of democracy, trade union leaders have had easy and frequent access to the various ministries and public agencies, although many feel that their points of view have not been sufficiently incorporated into public policy. Most executive trade union leaders are also members of political parties and have easy contact with members of parliament, especially those of their own party. Thus, it can be argued that the trade union movement, though relatively independent, is suitably integrated into the national political system.

Social development

Chile is a socially well-integrated nation in comparison with many other Latin American countries. *Mestizos* comprise 75 per cent of the population, 20 per cent are white and five per cent indigenous. Other, culturally isolated ethnic minorities account for an even smaller proportion of the population.

Risking an oversimplification, it can be said that ethnic problems carry relatively little weight in urban trade union activities. Within the rural environment some existing ethnic problems overlap with the difficult conditions in which poor peasants live and work. This is particularly the case in the Ninth Region where sizeable groups of Auracan Indians still maintain part of their identity.

Chile has a Catholic tradition, though Church and government have been separated since 1925. The legitimacy of this tradition has been reaffirmed by the Catholic Church's defence of human rights during the Pinochet dictatorship. The Church, therefore, strongly continues to influence public opinion. Church institutions dealing with social issues, such as the Workers' Vicarage, have been remarkably pluralistic, accepting diverse ideological streams, including Marxist.

Living standards are still highly inequitable. Social differences between classes remain large and averages often obscure the real depth of problems relating to poverty or social marginalization. Despite the progress achieved during the past few years it is estimated that 33 per cent of the population, approximately four million people, live below the poverty line. Life expectancy is high (71.9 years in 1992), but much lower among the poor. The official illiteracy rate is low at 6.6 per cent, but functional illiteracy and the low quality of education remain widespread among the disadvantaged groups. Moreover, income distribution is highly uneven, in fact more so than at the end of the 1960s. According to data from the Ministry of Planning, the poorest 20 per cent of the population received only 4.5 per cent of the national income in 1992, whereas the richest quintile received 55.4 per cent.

Trade unions currently face the difficult problem of defining their position on the distribution of power and income in the country. To become significant social actors nationwide, they need to support the demands of the poor. They also need to support the large segment of their members who have relatively high incomes, such as workers in the copper industry, banking and the telephone service. To date, the labour movement, particularly its national leadership, has legitimized its position by defending the interests of the least-favoured groups. In the annual negotiations with government and the business community the unions have argued for increases in minimum wages, family allowances and the lowest pensions.

The new generation of trade union leaders are relatively highly educated. Most have completed at least secondary school. Older generations have developed a broad informal culture of participating in national and international seminars, the number of which multiplied during the Pinochet dictatorship. Exile also facilitated access to knowledge about trade unions and social realities abroad. This strengthened the confidence of these leaders in their dealings with the government, business community and public opinion. However, it should be mentioned that the knowledge acquired by executive leaders has been insufficiently transmitted to grassroots leaders. Indeed, many newly-elected leaders require substantial training in trade union operations.

Economic development

By the middle of the nineteenth century, the Chilean economy gained momentum as the mining sector developed and became a source of accumulation and wealth. These resources enabled the state to develop major public works such as the railroad system and to increase education and health services which fostered the development of a middle class.

In the 1930s, the previous outward-oriented economic model was replaced by a domestic-oriented approach. The new strategy aimed to accelerate import-substituting industrialization (ISI) by introducing measures to protect national industries and according a fundamental role to the state in the creation of new enterprises (Pinto 1959 and 1964).

Within this new orientation, the National Development Corporation (CORFO) was established in 1939. This institution created a variety of large public enterprises in key sectors of the economy, amongst them the National Petroleum Company, Pacific Steel Company, National Electricity Company and the National Sugar Industry. Their creation had an important impact on the labour movement as less confrontational unions evolved within them. These unions were linked to the middle class and, consequently, more concerned with improving labour relations than with radical political change.

In 1964 the Christian Democratic president Eduardo Frei launched the 'revolution with liberty'. Though primarily a response to the pressures exerted by the Cuban revolution and the Alliance for Progress, it initiated a series of transformations in the economic system.

During Frei's government an agrarian reform was implemented, the copper industry was partly nationalized, economic modernization was promoted and popular participation encouraged.

The Socialist government of Salvador Allende (1970–73) decided to deepen these structural changes. His government extended Frei's agrarian reform and nationalized the entire copper industry and large industrial and banking monopolies. It also strengthened trade unions and other social organizations (Ruiz-Tagle 1973).

The coup of 1973 interrupted this process of social and economic change. In 1975 a 'shock policy' was implemented as a response to existing economic imbalances which were exacerbated by the first oil crisis. This policy had serious consequences for workers since their employment and wage situation deteriorated considerably. Simultaneously, the agrarian reform was reversed and previously nationalized enterprises were reprivatized.

After six years of economic growth Chile was affected by the debt crisis (1982–83) even more seriously than were other Latin American countries. Employment and salary levels deteriorated even further and external debt and debt servicing grew considerably. The trade unions, which at the time were in the midst of a process of reorganization, were deeply affected by this new crisis.

A structural adjustment policy was adopted in response to the situation. Successive devaluations were carried out to restrict imports and stimulate exports. Both large cuts in fiscal expenditure and the privatization of enterprises were used to balance public finances, and salary reductions were imposed to lower domestic demand. The economy eventually regained its positive growth rate. Between 1986 and 1989 the Chilean economy experienced large increases in exports, rapid economic growth, a reduction of external debt and a growth in investment (Ruiz-Tagle 1991).

Immediately after its inauguration (March 1990), the new democratic regime had to intervene with another small adjustment to avoid the economy's overheating. Unlike the dictatorship, it could not resort to lay-offs or salary reductions to achieve this. Nevertheless, the new approach was effective and the economy recuperated to an annual rate of growth of over six per cent. This growth rate was achieved while reducing inflation and external debt, and increasing employment, salaries and social expenditure.

The desired diversification of exports has so far remained limited. Copper and other minerals together with marine products, fruits, wine and forestry products continue to make up the bulk of exports. Manufactures still represent only 17 per cent of total exports. Due to this stagnating development, some analysts predict that the period of easy export growth is nearing its end and that a technological jump is required to launch a new export phase.

The informal sector remains important and sizeable despite the economy's recent strong growth performance. This reality and the current low levels of formal unemployment have convinced the economic authorities of the country of the necessity of increased efforts to improve the quality of employment in terms of stability, access to social security, and health and working conditions.

While trade union leaders do not dispute the success of the macro-economic policy and the social progress achieved in recent years, they frequently express dissatisfaction with the current situation. They favour a more interventionist government policy to speed up social progress, and though they agree that Chile should increase its participation in world markets, they tend to reject the excessive reliance on market mechanisms in the allocation of resources. Trade union leaders continue to support the democratic process and limit their criticism in order to maintain the current political stability. At the same time, however, they reject the excessive neo-liberal influence visible in the economic policies currently pursued (Frías 1992).

Trade union growth and membership

Before 1973

The military dictatorship was preceded by long periods of democratic rule during which close ties between political parties and unions developed. The primary reason for the development of such ties was the party system's crucial role in the introduction of new legislation favourable to workers through parliamentary initiatives. In this way unions became progressively more subordinated to political parties, and this subordination, which was already evident during the 1953–73 period and reached its peak during the Allende years, considerably weakened the autonomy of the labour movement.[1]

The Pinochet years

After the coup the relationship between trade unions and political parties became more functional. The need for both parties and unions to adopt defensive strategies played a significant role in shaping this new relationship. Political repression, as well as the enhanced public role of trade unions and the development of the union leadership, was conducive to the evolution of a more autonomous position for the trade union movement. However, the tendency towards close political involvement still prevails.

Trade union rights and activities were severely repressed during the early years of the Pinochet regime. Official figures, though, still show a slight increase in their membership between 1973–77.[2] The 1979 Labour Plan redefined traditional unions (manufacturing, professional and agrarian) and replaced them with four types of unions: company, inter-company, independent and transitory.[3] Of these, only company unions could engage in collective bargaining. Existing unions and other organizations had to adjust their by-laws to comply with the new regulations and obtain legal recognition.

The procedures to collect information and prepare official statistics were simultaneously changed to eliminate inactive unions, those in recess and those whose registration had been cancelled. These legal and statistical changes make it difficult to trace the impact of the economic policies and repression on the evolution in membership and number of unions across the entire period.[4]

In response, the trade union movement went through a process of organizational restructuring and initiated a process of social mobilization. From 1983 onwards, these activities resulted in an increase in the number of unions and their membership; and a reinforcement of their intermediate levels (federations and confederations). While the labour force grew at an annual rate of 5.8 per cent during the 1983–88 period, the respective rates for growth in the number of unions and membership were 7.9 and 6.8 per cent.

The trade union movement during the transition to democracy

The creation of the Unitarian Central Workers Union (CUT) in August 1988 was a new step in the process of consolidating the labour movement. Overall trade union membership continued to display strong, sustained growth, and by 1993 close to 700,000 workers were affiliated. This figure represents an increase of 53.4 per cent over the number of workers registered in 1988. During 1990 and 1991 growth of 19.5 and 15.5 per cent was realized. Once this re-activation period was over, membership growth dropped to only 3.2 per cent in 1992, and actually decreased by 5.5 per cent in 1993.

The growth in membership was primarily achieved in the new democratic environment after March 1990, which permitted the organization of the first national congress of the CUT in October 1991. This congress had a positive impact on the process of regrouping workers. The level of representation achieved by the CUT during this congress, later to be confirmed by its constituent bases, can be seen in Table 6.1.

Table 6.1 National organizations affiliated to the CUT

Organizations	Foundation August 1988	October 1991 Congress	April 1994 Congress
Fed. and Confed	72	78	45
Associations	3	3	2
National Unions	3	7	5
Unions	20	–	–
Profess. Associations	1	1	1
Total	99	89	53
Membership	307,016	522,848	423,748

Source: Programa de Economia del Trabajo (PET), based on CUT data.

The most recent figures available indicate a sizeable fall in the CUT's membership in 1994. This decline appears to outstrip the drop in the total figure of registered members (see Table 6.2 totals) indicating an erosion of the CUT's very strong position.

In 1993 a total of 11,389 trade unions were registered with 684,361 members, 13.7 per cent of the total labour force of 4,985,700. Their distribution by type of union is presented in Table 6.2.

Table 6.2 Number and membership of unions by type, 1993

Type of union	No.	No. of members	Average membership per union
Company	7,408	460,219	62
Inter-company	861	75,436	88
Independent	2,762	115,295	42
Transitory	358	33,411	93
Total (1993)	11,389	684,361	60
Total (1991)	9,858	701,355	71

Source: Labour Directorate 1994.

Most company unions have the power to bargain collectively. However, it should be noted that 34.6 per cent of all union organizations still could not engage in collective bargaining in 1993. Since the latest labour reforms, non-company unions that were not allowed to negotiate during the military regime can do so with the consent of the owners.

Eighty-six per cent of union leaders are male and they hold the majority of executive positions in the trade unions. The low representation of women in leadership positions contrasts with their large overall presence in the unions, and leaves ample room to expand their participation beyond the traditional secretarial role (16.8 per cent). Precise gender data on trade union membership are not readily available, though women have a significant presence in sectors such as textiles, food, agro-industry, financial services, health, teaching and public administration.

The average number of 60 workers per union is relatively low compared with similar organizations in industrialized countries. Average numbers are larger in mining (130), construction (112), electricity, water and gas (145), and financial establishments (102). The average union size in the latter two branches is now larger than in manufacturing (56), which was traditionally a stronghold of the labour movement. This underscores the increasing importance of the service industry for the trade union movement.

A comparison of the sectoral distribution of union membership with the sectoral distribution of the labour force reveals that considerable scope for trade union expansion still exists in most sectors. In 1993 only 13.7 per cent of the labour force was unionized. Only in mining, energy and transportation have unions achieved a degree of representation that exceeds 50 per cent of these sectors' workforce. The low score of the service sector (7.2 per cent) stands out particularly.

Table 6.3 Trade union membership by economic activity

	1971 %	1991 %
Agriculture	31.5	10.1
Mining	9.1	9.2
Manufacturing	29.8	25.5
Utilities	2.1	2.4
Construction	4.1	7.2
Services	23.2	45.0
Other	0.03	0.4
Total	100.0	100.0

Source: adapted from Table 8 (Ruiz-Tagle and Frías 1993).

However, a longitudinal comparison of the sectoral division of union membership (Table 6.3) reveals the deep transformations that have already occurred. By 1991 the service sector (commerce, finance, transportation, personal and other services) had become the largest sector. This changed structure points to a new challenge: how to incorporate the interests of the service sector in the trade union movement.

Collective bargaining

At the enterprise level, collective bargaining can be carried out not only by trade unions but also by groups of workers organized on an *ad hoc* basis (bargaining groups). Negotiations can result in either collective contracts, settled strictly according to legal procedures and including the right to strike, or conventions with employers on a more voluntary basis. Trade unions have been more successful as compared with bargaining groups in negotiating for the more secure collective contracts.

The official collective bargaining process has been considerably strengthened under the democratic government. There has been a substantial increase in the number of collective agreements as well as in the number of workers involved. From 1989 to 1993, the number of collective agreements grew by 9.2 per cent. The number of workers covered by collective agreements increased by 24 per cent in 1991 and 12.8 per cent in 1993. Thus 255,337 workers were covered in 1993 as compared with 128,513 in 1988. Furthermore, wage adjustments have become progressively closer to 100 per cent of the consumer price index since 1989.

Conflict levels have been notably low. During 1991, less than 10 per cent of all collective negotiations resulted in strikes. However, the intensity of strikes has been rising since 1989 due to the more democratic conditions that prevail. It is still much lower, though, than the intensity observed in previous democratic periods. For instance, between 1966 and 1970 the average number of days lost through strikes was 2,330,000 per year whereas in 1991 this was only 720,517. In 1992 and 1993 the losses were 344,708 and 311,979 days respectively. Considering that the total number of workers today is 1.7 times greater than during the previous period this difference becomes even more significant.

Labour reforms

Since 1990 a number of reforms have been presented to the National Congress and subsequently incorporated into the new Labour Code published in January 1994.

Law No. 19.010 of December 1990 established the principle that all lay-offs must be justified on factual grounds. This eliminated the 'termination of contract' under which an employee could be dismissed summarily by an employer provided s/he was given compensation. While the law still recognizes the need of employers to adjust or reorganize their labour force as a valid cause for dismissal, a formula for the required level of compensation in such cases is now included in the law. Workers can also challenge their dismissal before the Labour Tribunal (Rojas 1991). These new norms make dismissals more difficult or expensive, but do not strengthen the stability of employment in any real sense.

Law No. 19.040 of February 1991 recognized the right to form central trade unions; established new and less demanding regulations to create them; and generally increased their freedom. This law not only authorizes the affiliation of private-sector trade unions, but also allows the affiliation of organizations such as those of public-sector workers and professional associations (of, for example, teachers and secretaries) and organizations from the passive sector (pensioners). The legal recognition of central trade unions entitles their leadership to some exemptions, grants and free time for union activities. Legal recognition has also opened up a wider range of funding options.

Law No. 19.079 of August 1991 concerns trade union organization. It strengthens trade unions, federations and confederations, broadening their objectives and allowing a wider range of financial possibilities. This law includes a number of other measures, such as lowering the quotas required to form trade unions; the widening of possibilities to form trade unions for casual workers; increased time allotment for union activities; and more exemptions for their leadership. It also expands the range of issues that can be included in collective bargaining and allows for negotiations above the enterprise level. Law No. 19.079 also restricts the right of employers to hire substitutes during strikes or to reach agreements with individual workers during negotiations. In addition, it sanctions indefinite strike periods.

Law No. 19.214 of April 1993 concerns the creation of a fund for trade union education and training. This fund provides trade unions with resources to develop such activities during a four-year period.

Law No. 2.950 of September 1993 contains a number of amendments to the Labour Code relating to individual labour relations. It includes improvements in some labour rights such as legal formalities for the settlement and modification of the individual labour contract, working day, bonuses, minimum income, holidays and protection of seasonal workers. It also includes reforms of Labour Tribunal procedures to expedite judicial proceedings.

Another initiative still under discussion concerns the organization of public-sector workers. To date these are not allowed to form trade unions and must resort to civil procedures to form private legal entities operating as public employee associations without union objectives.

Current labour issues

While the institutional strength and stability of trade unions have increased since the inauguration of the Aylwin government in March 1990, a number of crucial issues remain for the coming years.

Forging new relationships and institutional consolidation

The relationship between the trade unions and the government has been consolidated within the new democratic framework and a new type of relationship has emerged with the entrepreneurs. These new arrangements have enabled a series of achievements that have resulted in new benefits to trade union members.

The General Agreement of April 1990 is a good example of such new developments. This agreement established the main guidelines for regulating the relations between capital and labour. It included norms to determine minimum salaries and wage adjustments, establish procedures to resolve conflicts and specified labour reforms that will be implemented in the near future. The agreement has been renegotiated annually with employers since 1990. In 1993, for instance, it was agreed that minimum wages should follow expected changes in inflation and productivity.

In the same vein, major agreements on salary adjustment have been reached by workers' organizations in the public sector representing tax officers, health workers, and teachers, all affiliated to the CUT, among others. These, too, have been renewed annually in the past years.

The labour movement has also benefited from a series of agreements with various ministries, universities, local governments, associations of entrepreneurs, and other similar groups. These agreements deal with a broad range of issues, such as housing, education, health and recreation. Of special relevance has been the training programme for young people aimed at enrolling 100,000 young persons in four years. By September 1993, it had enrolled more than 70,000, surpassing by far any previous programmes.

The trade union movement has gradually accepted the requirements of an open and competitive economy and is relinquishing its ideological over-commitment of the past. Moreover, new issues have become important to trade union activists. These include health conditions, industrial sanitation, technological challenges, the quality of life and preservation of the environment.

The trade union movement is still in the midst of a process of institutional consolidation. Formation and training have received considerable attention with the creation of labour schools in the CUT as well as in several other confederations. The regional structure of the trade union movement has also been reinforced with the creation of local and regional organizations. These latter are progressively assuming a more prominent role in the promotion of regional development.

The creation of tripartite commissions (government, entrepreneurs and the CUT) has formed part of the consolidation process. These commissions discuss a number of issues such as employment, training and retraining of workers, the application of norms and controls, health and work, and unemployment insurance. Bipartite commissions (government and the CUT) addressing labour problems in the public and coal sectors and specific issues concerning women and work also play a role in the consolidation process.

In 1993 relations cooled considerably between the government and labour. As recently as July 1994, a major protest rally was organized by the CUT in support of its demands for labour reforms and more control over the employers, among other issues. The rally provided the impetus for a new accord between government authorities and workers, containing a commitment towards joint work and dialogue, as well as the decision to emphasize and favour mutual consultation and tripartite arrangements for the resolution of conflicts.

Development cooperation

Development cooperation grew enormously in the 1970–1980s, especially in support of the people's resistance against the military regime. A new trend is discernible following the installation of the democratic government. Bilateral cooperation (government to government) has increased while the North–South cooperation between non-governmental organizations (NGOs) has decreased. This trend occurred despite the explicit efforts of the new government, frequently reiterated in public by the Minister of Planning and Cooperation, to facilitate multilateral cooperation.

A variety of organizations has supported trade unions in the past. Organizations from outside the labour movement (of secular or religious origin) channelled private and government resources in support of the trade union movement and/or institutions that collaborated with them. Organizations linked to political parties in developed countries also supported trade union activities, but usually imposed more or less explicit political guidelines. Finally, organizations linked to international (central or sectoral) trade union federations made their cooperation contingent on the acceptance of ideological options and have mostly supported like-minded organizations.

Most organizations preferred to finance training for trade union activities. However, in some cases they also supported initiatives to strengthen the institutional development of the labour movement. For future cooperative efforts it is important to stress that the extraordinary growth of trade unions and their leadership demands a very substantial effort towards training them adequately. In this respect it should be remembered that Chilean law forbids businesses to use tax rebates to finance educational activities by the unions. This obviously restricts their possibilities of obtaining local resources.

Moreover, educational activities require specialized professional staff. This staff will need to engage in continued research on labour issues to avoid a curriculum and training that is outmoded or ill-informed and thus unconducive to efficient trade union development in a rapidly modernizing state. International cooperation will be indispensable to achieve these objectives but should not limit the autonomy of the Chilean labour movement. Although trade unions can learn much from international experiences, excessive dependence and ideological commitment must be avoided.

Finally, international cooperation should not restrict its support to research and training activities by professionals from the trade union movement only. The contributions of relatively autonomous intellectuals who are respected by business, government and the general public alike are fundamental to a true strengthening of the labour movement (Sepi 1992).

The urban informal sector
The informal sector has been difficult to define ever since the concept was formulated. Various indicators are in use to characterize the sector: a small number of workers per unit; high labour intensity coupled with modest capital outlays; predominantly unskilled labour;

low utilization of modern technology; unstable employment; low compliance with legal norms and regulations; low wages and poor working conditions (see, for example, PREALC 1990).

This inherent imprecision complicates the introduction of further distinctions such as sub-sectors. One part of the sector, the self-employed, does not compete with formal workers nor does it constitute a direct problem for trade unions. But another segment, made up of those aspiring to formal-sector employment, has a major impact on the labour market and affects the scope for trade union activism. Its existence limits the possibilities of industrial action since it represents an uncontrolled and competitive group which can influence wage levels and threatens job security. The co-existence of workers in formal shoe factories and garment industries next to many small workshops and/or self-employed workers engaged in similar work is one example of such a relationship (De Laire 1992).

Second, it is important to note that *within* the informal sector micro-enterprises and popular economic organizations form 'a popular economy'. This sub-sector is not well-structured but has sufficient institutional and organizational links to be considered an emerging social actor (Razetto 1991).

Notwithstanding such limitations, some inferences about labour in the informal sector can be made. In 1990, urban informal workers represented 19.7 per cent of total employment, a figure which excludes domestic service workers (5.3 per cent). A similar estimate for rural areas is more difficult to obtain since rural workers move much more frequently between formal jobs, informal jobs and unemployment.

The PET surveys in metropolitan Santiago indicate a slight decrease in informality during the last years, from 24.5 to 22 per cent (but from 6.2 to 6.9 for domestic services) in 1988–90. Though the Santiago figures are somewhat above the national average, other, national, surveys have confirmed this slow decline in labour-market informality.

In general, the trade union leadership has experienced difficulties in establishing relationships with popular leaders in the informal sector since the latter lack a clear, identifiable constituency. However, the trade union movement considers informal workers a part of the wider world of the poor. Moreover, although trade union members do not originate from the poorest strata in the country, Chilean trade unions have historically considered themselves defenders of the poor and there is little doubt that they will continue to do so in the future.

Conclusions

Despite the recent advances and achievements, the trade union movement resents the inadequacy of the labour reforms. It does not easily accept the idea that it needs to develop without the direct support of an interventionist state. Unions also resent the continuation of traditional authoritarian practices by employers. Furthermore they have not adjusted to the lack of resources and have been unable to close the gap between the leadership and the grassroots membership (see Frías 1992).

Such conditions carry a danger that a large part of the unions' innovative positions *vis-à-vis* business, modernization, the role of trade unions in development, etc., will remain limited to speeches or confined to a small section of the union leadership. Furthermore, greater creativity in the diversity and provision of services to members would be desirable. Much still needs to be done to address the needs of the workers and their families in the areas of education, health, recreation and housing.

The legalization of the CUT has led to a process of ratifying new membership. This affiliation process has gone hand in hand with the continuing challenge to move towards the financing of all CUT activities out of contributions by active members. The latter process is not without difficulties given the narrow range of services which the national and intermediate organizations can currently offer to their members. More importantly, the leadership of the CUT is divided into factions with confrontational and collaborative tendencies. This division may threaten the unity of the movement.

The labour movement faces the challenge of defining a new identity within the changed socio-economic and political framework. Although it has maintained its representativeness in general terms, it fails to reflect the recent transformations that have occurred in the productive structures. The heterogeneity of its constituent bases is not adequately reflected in its leadership. Many of the new labour force entrants, particularly women and unskilled young workers, are engaged in activities in which trade union organization is notably weak.

There is a recognition that political realities and positions have changed and that traditional forms of struggle and social mobilization appear to be no longer valid. Social change no longer concerns 'the problem of access to the State's control in order to drive the transformation of society' as it did in the past: 'The new conceptions of social change should emphasize the technological and productive transformation in the industrial restructuring and in a new culture of labour relations' (CUT 1991).

This new orientation goes in hand with a reappraisal of the firm, industrialization, and development processes and the character of the labour relations.[5] The trade union movement has supported the *social concord* within this new view of its role and contribution. This tacit understanding has facilitated the increase in firm productivity as well as the democratization of its functioning. It was within this perspective that the General Agreement of 1990 was formulated and implemented by employers and workers and renewed annually under the coalition government.

However, the efforts of the trade union movement towards defining new roles and identities have not been reciprocated, as was expected, by the government, parliament, entrepreneurs and political parties. Notwithstanding the significant progress achieved, the labour movement considers that levels of injustice and unbalanced distribution of wealth still remain that 'dramatically contradict the proclaimed modernization of the society' (CUT 1993). It strongly vindicates the state's role in the development process and maintains that the market is incapable of solving the problems of poverty and inequality while also criticizing the insufficiency of labour reforms.

In summary, the Chilean trade union movement is currently dedicated to: consolidating its existing strengths; enlarging its representativeness by incorporating new emerging groups; reinforcing the instruments for training of grassroots members as well as cadres; and achieving an independent financial status. To pursue these objectives the Chilean trade union movement tries to utilize fully all the support that the government and employers can provide.

The intermediate levels in the organization of the trade union movement (confederations, federations and provincial CUT) will play a substantial role in deepening the movement and disseminating its ideas to its membership. Increased professional advice and the active support of training and services will be required to accomplish these tasks.

Intermediate institutions, such as the federations and confederations, and grassroots unions have never before played such a key role. A modern economy demands professional unions with leadership that can understand fully the implications of their activities in terms of competition and productivity. To fulfil this role they must have full knowledge of their enterprises and industries and access to adequate training and advisory services. Furthermore, to guarantee independence from other social groups, unions must be financially independent and in a position fully to pay the cost of such services.

In this new context, the role of the CUT is different from the one it played previously when it sought to destabilize the system and re-establish democracy by revitalizing the political parties and mobilizing the various social groups. Its key role today is linked to grassroots activities that may assist in overcoming poverty.

Notes

1. See, for example, Almeyda (1989), Barrera (1988) and Noé (1986).

2. For analyses of trade union activities after 1973, see Campero and Valenzuela (1984), Frías (1985) and Ruiz-Tagle (1985).

3. Company unions are the real trade unions, while inter-enterprise unions assemble workers belonging to different enterprises. Independent unions consist of own-account workers (self-employed), while transitory organizations are made up of workers in temporary or sporadic jobs, such as construction workers and dockworkers.

4. See, for example, Frías (1985) on this aspect.

5. '...the scientific and technological revolution and its impact on new forms of production...questions the organizational structure of firms and challenges labour skills, the flexibility of the labour market and mechanisms of workers' participation in the process of production and technological management, and the form of economic incentives linked to productivity levels and the quality of production' (CUT 1991).

References

Almeyda, C. (1989) 'Interacción de lo Político y Sindical en Chile'. CES, Santiago.

Barrera, M. (1988) 'Consideraciones acerca de la Relación entre Política y el Movimiento Sindical. El Caso de Chile'. CES, Santiago.

Campero, G., and Valenzuela, A. (1984) 'El Movimiento Sindical en el Regimen Militar Chileno, 1973–1981'. ILET, Santiago.

CUT (1991) 'Plan de Trabaja de la CUT', in *Informativo CUT: Unidad y Trabajo* 17. CUT, Santiago.

―――― (1993) 'Propuesta de la CUT a los Candidatos Presidenciales', in *Informativo Unidad y Trabajo* 37. CUT, Santiago.

De Laire, F. (1992) 'Nuevas Formas de Organización del Proceso Productivo en la Industria del Calzado: El Caracter Escindente de la Modernización', in *Economía y Trabajo en Chile, 1991–1992, Informe Anual*. PET, Santiago.

Frías, P. (1985) 'Afiliación y Representatividad del Movimiento Sindical bajo el Regimen Militar: 1973–1984'. Documento CED, No. 83. Santiago.

―――― (1992) 'Desafíos de Renovación Sindical', in *Economía y Trabajo en Chile: 1991–1992. Informe Anual*. PET, Santiago.

Noé, M. (1986) 'La Acción Política del Sindicalismo'. Documento CIASI, Santiago.

Pinto, A. (1959) *Chile un Caso de Desarrollo Frustrado*. Ed. Universitaria, Santiago.

—————— (1964) *Chile: Una Economía Difícil*. Fondo de Cultura Económica, México.

PREALC (1990) 'Más allá de la Regulación. El Sector Informal en América Latina'. Programa Regional del Emplleo para América Latina y el Caribe, Santiago.

Razetto, L. (1991) 'Las Organizaciones Económicas Populares: Balance de 17 Años y Perspectivas', in *Economía y Trabajo en Chile: 1990–1991. Informe Anual*. PET, Santiago.

Rojas, I. (1991) 'Las Reformas Laborales', in *Economía y Trabajo en Chile: 1990–1991. Informe Anual*. PET, Santiago.

Ruiz-Tagle, J. (1973) 'Poder Político y Transición al Socialismo. Tres Años de la Unidad Popular'. ILDIS, Caracas.

—————— (1985) 'El Sindicalismo Chileno después del Plan Laboral'. PET, Santiago.

—————— (1991) 'Crisis de la Experiencia Neo-liberal en Chile. Cambios en las Relaciones Laborales y Respuesta Sindical: 1981–1988', in *Trabajo y Economía en el Retorno a la Democracia*. PET, Santiago.

Ruiz-Tagle, J. and P. Frías (1993) 'Country Study Chile', in H. Thomas *The Netherlands Trade Union Co-Financing Programme 1985–1989: An Evaluation. Latin America*. Institute of Social Studies Advisory Service, The Hague.

Sepi, M. (1992) 'El Sindicalismo y los Intelectuales', in *Sidicalismo y Democracia* (August). ISCOS-CISL-CLACSO, Santiago.

7. Decline of an Oil Economy: Venezuela and the Legacy of Incorporation

Domingo Mendez-Rivero

The Venezuelan economy has been heavily subsidized with oil revenues. Basic class compromise and a system in which both labour and capital have refrained from making any serious threats to each other has ensured the survival of democracy. Labour costs have been controlled and labour peace maintained through mechanisms which include specific agreements between labour and management, as well as state regulation of union formation and collective action, and partisan control over the labour movement (Davis and Coleman 1989).

Until the late 1970s this model made the Venezuelan case unique in the region. However, it proved to be no guarantee for protection of the various actors once the crisis of the 1980s seriously weakened the economic basis on which the agreements had been made. In the absence of economic expansion following the downturn in the oil market, insufficient resources were available to accommodate a rise in real wages as well as the capital formation required for growth. Consequently, the state began to experience serious difficulties in managing the collective bargaining process and extending benefits and privileges to labour.

Political and socio-economic development

State–societal relationships have passed through three stages in Venezuela. Until the 1920s the state played no major role in the process of national unification and was unable to develop its capacity to provide public services to the population. The situation changed when considerable revenues were generated by the oil industry, which gave the state the capacity effectively to become a national state. Furthermore, the oil revenues enabled the state to play the role of social provider and distribute oil-rents among the different socio-economic actors and interest groups. From the 1940s onwards, Venezuela became a positive-sum society and experienced a virtually total absence of social conflict.

The decline of oil revenues in the 1980s radically altered the situation and eliminated the state's capacity to manage social conflicts through the, more or less, fair distribution of the oil-rents. In this phase, new conflictive elements emerged in the interactions of the trade union movement and other socio-political actors as evidenced by two attempted military coups in 1992, followed by the president's dismissal by the Supreme Court and the Congress on charges of corruption in 1993.

The political system and the labour movement

There has always been a strong relationship between the labour movement and party politics in Venezuela. The birth of the political parties was simultaneous and related to the same socio-political events that prompted the creation of the modern trade union movement. In many cases, the founding fathers of political parties were trade union leaders and *vice versa*. Therefore, with few exceptions, trade union struggles have also been political struggles (Ellner 1987). This political involvement is one of the greatest challenges confronting the labour movement today.

The current relationships between the political system and the trade union movement have their origins in the early 1930s and developed in the context of the struggle to re-establish democracy and create modern political parties. This initial struggle for democracy was fought between the socio-political actors – commercial petty bourgeoisie, agro-export bourgeoisie, workers of the oil industry, educated elites – rather than in the sphere of political ideologies.

Struggle for democracy: 1920–58

Throughout the nineteenth century, politics was characterized by fragmentation and regionalization. The rise to power of General Juan Vicente Gómez in 1908 marked the beginning of the process that would lead to the consolidation of the national state. Several factors contributed to this development:

- in addition to the support received from multinational oil companies, General Gómez succeeded in creating a national army and defeating the regional chiefs;
- the exploitation of oil generated sufficient resources to develop a national infrastructural network independently of the resources of the regions and the agro-export bourgeoisie;
- and the population displayed a favourable attitude towards peace following more than a century of civil wars.

The first public expression of the struggle for democracy occurred in 1928. In February, university students belonging to the higher and middle classes transformed the election of the carnival queen into a protest movement and demanded the establishment of a representative democracy. The regime's reaction was extremely violent. Most participating students were sent to jail or exiled. The latter did not return until after the death of the dictator. This event is important in the political history of Venezuela since these students constituted the first urban-educated group of leaders and later became the backbone of the modern political parties.

Gómez' death in 1935 was the start of a period of strong political activity which focused on the democratization and modernization of Venezuelan society. Twenty-two years later this period ended with the overthrow of the last military dictatorship (Pérez Jiménez 1948–58) endured by the country.

The beginnings of the labour movement

Modern trade unionism first manifested itself in 1919 when the first-known collective contract was signed. Paradoxically, it was signed in the transport sector, between workers and management of the German railroad enterprise, a Krupp subsidiary, rather than the emerging oil industry. It included agreements on salary increases, a work-day of 8.5 hours, paid holidays and some forms of social security. The paradox can be explained by the Germans' relatively long-standing tradition of collective negotiation which contrasted with the practice of American oil companies.

The first important strike led by a modern trade union occurred in 1936 in the expanding oil industry. In 1925, oil revenue had already accounted for more than 50 per cent of total public-sector revenue, and by 1936 the industry had become the key economic sector and was operating at full capacity. The strike led to the founding of the Venezuelan Confederation of Workers (CVT), which became the present Workers' Confederation of Venezuela (CTV) in 1944. Both the strike and the CVT's founding owed much to the active support of political parties. The Communist Party (ORVE, the forerunner of the present Acción Democrática which has a social-democratic orientation) and the Venezuelan Federation of Students played important roles in this process.

The Great Social Pact: the consolidation of democracy and incorporation of organized labour

In 1958, after a long period of military dictatorship, the Venezuelan elites were committed to building a new state in which the occurrence of another coup would be unlikely. It necessitated the formation of a 'great coalition' to permit accommodation of the interests of the elite as well as create manoeuvring space for other social actors. The aim was to avoid polarization which could be a motive for either the left or right to impose a political solution by force (Davis and Coleman 1989).

Two accords played a fundamental role in creating the new political order: The Statement of Principles and the Minimum Programme of Government (1958); and the Pact of Punto Fijo, signed by the three major parties of the time,[1] in which they agreed to respect election results and contain conflict. These agreements also recognized the economic interests of all the major contenders for power. These included the domestic capitalists, who were guaranteed the right to pursue private capital accumulation, the large landowners and the multinational companies. Addressing the needs of the working classes, the Minimum Programme committed the state to the pursuit of full employment, the freedom to organize unions, a new labour code and widespread social legislation in health, education and social security. To finance this programme, the elites relied heavily on the achievement of economic expansion with low inflation and on the continuation of the oil bonanza.

The Great Social Pact determined the institutional structure of the labour market for a long time to come. This structure may be described as a pact between the unions (especially the CTV), the employers' organization (Federacion de Asociaciones y Camaras del Comercio y la Industria – FEDECAMARAS) and the state. The Ministry of Labour was the principal administrator of the pact. Once the favourable conditions started to deteriorate in the late 1970s, the first cracks in the system of control appeared and the breakdown of the Great Social Pact became unavoidable.

Socio-economic development

Economic development

An import-substituting industrialization (ISI) strategy was adopted in the 1940s to encourage faster industrialization. It was, however, only weakly related to endogenous forces or explicit political decisions. The decision owed much to the combined effects of a number of circumstances: the rising demand for (semi-)durable consumer goods, originating from the urbanized part of the population; the increased participation of the labour force in the expanding service sector; the increased purchasing power as a result of the redistribution of the oil-rent; and the high price of many imported goods, as a consequence of the Second World War, which increased the profitability of local production or assembly of such goods (Purroy 1982).

The trade union movement grew rapidly during the mid-1940s, from 113 in 1936 to 252 in 1945 and 1,104 in 1948 (Betancourt 1969). This momentum was related to the democratic experiment of 1945–48 and the stimulus provided to industrialization by the ISI strategy adopted after 1945.

The impact of ISI on the economic structure and employment was significant. Total manufacturing employment grew from 165,000 in 1950 to 655,000 in 1978, a shift of 10.8 to 16.8 per cent in its share of total employment during that period. Measured as the quotient between industrial and total Gross Domestic Product (GDP), the level of industrialization increased from 10 to 18 per cent during the 1950–80 period (Bitar and Troncoso 1983). The speed of this process, measured as the ratio between the rates of growth of industrial and total GDP, was more than 1:1 throughout the entire period. All indicators of investment and production growth in the industrial sector were above the GDP growth rate.

Although the share of manufacturing employment as a percentage of total employment increased constantly during the 1950–80 period, the growth of manufacturing was constrained by a shortage of skilled human resources. This negatively influenced the capacity to generate new projects and the absorption of savings in productive investments. Excluding the oil sector, manufacturing employment registered annual growth rates of 6.1 per cent for the 1950–78 period and of 8.7 per cent for 1971–8. These extremely high rates of growth were not accompanied by a commensurate upgrading of the skill levels of the labour force. This qualitative bottleneck became more apparent in the more expansive phase of manufacturing growth during 1974–77. This shortage of skills and qualifications, together with accelerating international technological progress and Venezuela's surplus of capital and foreign exchange, directed the industrialization process towards a more capital-intensive path (Bitar and Troncoso 1983).

Another important outcome of the ISI period is the high degree of concentration and monopolization of production that resulted. In 1977, large-scale industry accounted for only 7.2 per cent of the number of establishments and 74.2 and 57 per cent of the total value of production and employment respectively. For small-scale industries the respective percentages were 68.6, 8.3 and 20, the remainder being accounted for by medium-scale industries (OCEI 1977). The high degree of industrial concentration reflects the prevailing class alliances during the entire ISI period. Apart from a few brief interludes, an alliance between the state and the industrial bourgeoisie dominated the political scene. The trade union movement did not participate in any of the alliances.

Urban shift

The rapid urbanization after 1936 is a key explanatory factor for the socio-political role played by the trade union movement and its current structure. The expansion of the tertiary sector, the sector most characteristic of the urbanization process, is the most important process that needs to be emphasized in this context.

Between 1936 and 1988, the rural–urban distribution of the population changed drastically. The share of the rural population declined from 70 to 12 per cent. The growing demand for urban goods and services instigated by the oil bonanza played a major role, but the adoption of the ISI strategy accelerated the process considerably.

Rapid urbanization, combined with the state's self-proclaimed role of social provider, resulted in the early development of the tertiary sector as a major source of employment, especially in public services. This has had two major implications for the trade union movement: public-sector employees became the largest group of workers affiliated to the CTV and, until recently, constituted its major political base; and, due to the use of public employment as a mechanism of political patronage, an excessively large bureaucracy came into existence.

One of the biggest challenges currently confronting the trade union movement is its position on employment and social-income distribution problems. These are partially caused by the process of state- and public-sector restructuring initiated in 1989 because of shrinking per capita oil revenues. Between 1980 and 1988 revenues fell by more than two-thirds in a society that had become much more complex and socially demanding. With an estimated fiscal deficit of nine per cent of GDP by the end of 1994, the state has no option left but to reduce the size of the public sector. If successfully completed, this will further erode the trade unions' capacity to be a valid and legitimate actor in future social developments. The corruption within the CTV and its failure to accomplish egalitarian distribution of the hardships caused by the crisis will alienate an increasing number of workers from the organized labour movement and push them towards more radicalized, authoritarian and fascist, alternatives. An indication of such a development is the massive popular support still enjoyed by Colonel Hugo Chávez, the leader of the first 1992 coup attempt.[2]

Trade unions

There are currently four central unions with a national character. The CTV is the most important and represents more than 90 per cent of the unionized workers. Though all political parties are represented in the

CTV, the Acción Democrática (AD) is clearly the dominant force and elects more than 60 per cent of its executive committee representatives. The CTV also maintains the most important international contacts. It is affiliated with the Organizacion Regional Internacional del Trabajo (ORIT), and through it with the International Confederation of Free Trade Unions (ICFTU).

Which of the remaining organizations is second in importance is hard to determine. The Confederacion de Sindicates Autonomes (CODESA) which has Christian Democratic leanings has some political importance, while the Confederacion Unificada de Trabajadores de Venezuela (CUTV), linked to the Communist Party, is clearly the least significant. The fourth organization, the Confederacion General de Trabajadores (CGT), is a recent creation and not linked to any political party. The CGT is affiliated with the Latin-American Workers' Central (CLAT), and through it with the World Confederation of Labour (WCL).

The present labour situation is characterized by the breakdown of the institutional agreements that regulated capital–labour relations after 1958. Several factors have contributed to this collapse: the exhaustion of the ISI model, the implementation of structural adjustment and macro-economic stabilization policies, the informalization of the labour force, and the current political and institutional crisis in the country.

Political parties and trade unions
In addition to its close ties to political parties, the labour movement has also been highly dependent upon government paternalism. The federal government, for instance, grants handsome subsidies to the CTV and other confederations based on the periodic submission of a budget of anticipated expenses. In certain cases, it has also furnished labour organizations with headquarters, while various state governments provide supplementary financial aid to individual unions.

Not only does the CTV continue to be heavily subsidized by the government, enjoying the biggest subsidy among the labour confederations, it also has privileged access to the Ministry of Labour. This is another explanatory factor for the CTV's support of the status quo. The CTV has traditionally supported the economic programmes of AD governments and acted as a loyal opposition under COPEI governments, protesting against the economic policies through strikes and wage demands.

Under no circumstances, however, has the CTV posed a systematic threat to the democratic regime. Instead, the orientation of the dominant national labour confederation since 1959 has been predicated on a doctrine of class compromise and conciliation with active support of the democratic regime. (McCoy 1989)

An analysis of the relationship between the AD and its Buro Sindical, an internal trade union division, is illuminating in this respect. The distinction between the union and the political leadership is extremely tenuous within the party. In fact, the substantial role played by trade union leaders in the selection of party presidential candidates reveals their ability to act as political brokers (Ellner 1987). Until the 1980s, this blurring of trade union/political roles and responsibilities did not restrict the union's effectiveness in representing its constituency and achieving significant improvements in the standard of living for Venezuelan workers.

The state and benefits to organized labour
The 1958 Minimum Programme committed the state to looking after the interests of organized labour. Without doubt, the labour movement achieved some significant gains in the post-1958 era, especially through the reform of labour law, which is the primary vehicle for extending privileges and benefits.

Through the revision of labour law, the state secured profit-sharing plans, subsidized retirement plans, social security, paid vacations, the eight-hour work day, and health and safety regulations for labour. Collective bargaining was rarely highly conflictive. The primary concern during this period was to obtain improved wages and benefits for workers in a non-conflictive labour-relations environment in which wage demands did not pose any serious threat to capital accumulation.

The state guaranteed access to collective bargaining and introduced favourable wage policies that enabled the earnings of workers to keep pace with inflation until the late 1970s. In 1974, a national minimum-wage was decreed by President Carlos Andrés Pérez and the 1979 Law of General Salary and Wage Increases also included a minimum wage provision, doubling the 1974 level. By one measure, this legislation helped to reduce urban poverty 'in that the proportion of urban wage earners who earned less than the subsistence-level income fell from 32 per cent in 1979 to 13 per cent in 1980' (Cartaya 1989). This process of across-the-board wage increases ended in 1990 when the *Ley Caldera* was passed by the Congress, legalizing the decrees of previous governments.[3]

The crisis of the 1980s and the breakdown of the Great Social Pact
After 20 years of significant growth, the economy started to stagnate in 1979 and went into recession in 1980. Increased inflation from the late 1970s, the weakening of world oil prices after 1981 and the

emergence of a foreign-debt crisis led to significant declines in real wages.

Cumulative inflation reached 71 per cent between 1980 and 1984, indicating a loss in purchasing power of six per cent in real terms. Inflation has continued unabated since. In 1989 the inflation rate was an historic 81 per cent, while in the period 1990–92 inflation never dropped below 30 per cent. It stood at 46 per cent in 1993 and is expected to cross 60 per cent by the end of 1994. Workers in small-scale enterprises were especially hard hit, since 44 per cent of these workers receive the minimum wage or less. Oil revenues registered a decline of 20 per cent in 1982, followed by a further dramatic fall in oil prices in 1986, which forced the government to sign its first loan in a decade with the Inter-American Development Bank (IDB) to help finance an industrial credit plan for the private sector.

The government responded to the economic and debt crises by devaluing the national currency. The bolivar was devalued 237 per cent between 1983 and 1986 at the official rate, and nearly 500 per cent at the free-floating rate. Between 1988 and June 1994 the value of the bolivar fell by more that 400 per cent, partly due to inflation and, more recently, to capital flight induced by the political unrest since 1992. Capital flight was only halted in July 1994 when the government imposed a system of exchange controls. Both inflation and successive devaluations had a major impact on a country accustomed to consumerism and foreign travel for the medium and upper classes.

As the fourth-largest Latin American debtor with an external debt structured in such a way as to be most troublesome – a large portion was short term, maturing in 1983–4 – and with its economy in recession, Venezuela suddenly faced a dilemma common to other Latin American countries: how to meet its external financial obligations, reactivate the domestic economy and, simultaneously, sustain the well-being of its citizens.

Though statistics vary depending on their source, there is a general recognition of a sustained decline in real wages after 1979. After a sharp rise in 1977–8, real wages declined abruptly in 1979 as inflation shot up and collective bargaining failed to secure adequate compensation. Between 1981 and 1984, real wages in Venezuela registered a cumulative decline of almost 18 per cent compared to a Latin American average of 12.8 per cent (IDB 1987). The decline in real household income was more than 40 per cent between 1981 and 1989. For the poorest strata this decline was 54 per cent, against only 33 percent for the richest stratum, worsening an already inegalitarian income distribution (D'Elia and Cartaya 1991).

Unemployment levels were quite low during the oil boom, averaging 5.95 per cent between 1975 and 1978. However, with the stagnation and later decline of the non-oil economy, especially in the construction and service sectors, unemployment worsened, reaching a historic high of 14 per cent in 1984. Since then, it has never been less than 8 per cent and an official estimate indicates a level of 20 per cent for the end of 1994. According to some studies, Venezuela fell from having the third-lowest urban unemployment in 1978 to being seventh in a 13-country survey in 1983. Thus, within the regional perspective, Venezuelan workers became relatively worse off.

The economic crisis that started in 1979 particularly affected the CTV's capacity to sustain its members' income levels, and seriously weakened the CTV's bargaining power. For instance, while public employees still cannot stem the deterioration of their real incomes, financial and banking groups easily managed to obtain one billion bolivars to help solve the recent collapse of eleven Venezuelan banks.

Historically, the bargaining strength of the trade unions was concentrated in the politically most sensitive sectors such as the oil industry and the public sector. Even though the living standards of Venezuelan workers have deteriorated, the stability of relations between labour and capital has continued to increase in these highly-unionized sectors. As early as 1977, 89 per cent of the signed collective contracts had a proposed duration of over one year and almost 50 per cent a duration extending beyond two years. In 1958 scarcely 13.5 per cent of collective contracts had a duration of more than two years (Cordiplan 1986).

Venezuela has one of the highest unionization rates in Latin America: 25 to 30 per cent of the labour force. More than two-thirds of the workers, however, are not covered by collective contracts.

> Furthermore, the size of the enterprise determines to a great extent the coverage by collective contract. Nearly all workers in large enterprises (more than 100 workers) are helped by collective contracts, whereas only about 20 per cent in small enterprises, and practically none in micro-enterprises (one to five workers), are helped (Cartaya 1989).

As a result, the labour movement's activities have been paradoxical. The unions have been incapable of stopping the general decline in real wages while, simultaneously, they have been able to negotiate effectively for the strongly-unionized large-scale industries in key sub-sectors of the economy.

Organized labour took a cooperative stance and refrained from demanding a general wage increase to compensate for inflation during the first two to three years of economic austerity. The CTV was more concerned about jobs and employment than wages. This concern explains the political position taken by the CTV during the period 'when they openly supported the measures that will promote private sector investment and productivity, and thus prevent bankruptcies and further loss of jobs' (McCoy 1989).

However, the economy did not recover, and talks between the government, business and labour faltered. The close links of the labour movement with the democratic regime were under threat, with the state no longer able to finance the Great Social Pact. Despite its long-standing success, the state was unable to provide sufficient, and sustained, legitimization for austerity and adjustment measures. Resource scarcity generated precisely the type of conflicts that the Great Social Pact was designed to preclude.

Rising rank-and-file discontent with both the AD and COPEI policies created pressures on the union elites to reconsider union strategy. The CTV shifted from patient cooperation to union action. From 1985 onwards, strike activities and social disruption increased, together with the demands for across-the-board salary increments. However, the CTV lost control over the process. Enterprise or industry unions no longer hesitate to formulate demands and strike against private entrepreneurs and the state, with or without the CTV's permission. This recent development has created more pressure to exploit the fiscal crisis of the state and the already widespread political unrest.

Current labour issues
The demise of the Great Social Pact has left both the state and the trade union movement with a future series of conflicts which demand special attention.

The need for new structures
Radical changes in the way political parties and organized labour deal with each other in future are unavoidable. The previous structure and balance of power between trade unions, employers' organizations and political parties need to be replaced or adapted to the changed economic realities of structural adjustment and public-sector restructuring. This will force each party to reconsider and redefine its role and position.

New issues
Besides devising new structures to address traditional issues, it will also be necessary to formulate views and policies on new issues and problems that have surfaced or become more apparent. Wages, social benefits, retirement schemes and pensions for workers in the unionized sectors have traditionally been the main issues. However, the present era of structural adjustment, reorganization of the state and industrial restructuring has revealed major contradictions between the

characteristics of the traditional labour force and changing patterns of labour demand.

Issues such as the flexibilization of labour, the growing informal sector (see pp. 161–62) and the role and participation of women (both in the labour force and trade union movement) demand a response from trade unions. Both the state and labour movement will be pressed hard to evolve policies that allow for the political, economic and social participation of the emerging forces of unprotected labour and wider social movements. So far, the unions have generally taken a defensive attitude towards participants in the new social movements; for example informal workers, women and neighbourhood associations.

International cooperation
Both because of organized labour's intimate ties with political parties in the previous era and the booming economy, the international labour community's perceptions of Venezuela are as follows: high per capita incomes, the strong financial position of the CTV, a bad political climate and corruption in the trade unions. This has had a negative impact on the level, intensity and specific direction and forms of support given to the Venezuelan labour movement by international labour organizations.

The present conditions, which are particularly detrimental to the working class, call for an upgrading or development of international cooperative ties at the initiative of either Venezuelan or international labour organizations. In this respect the activities and orientation of the CLAT and CGT deserve particular mention.

Founded in 1954, CLAT has been based in Caracas since the early 1970s. CLAT's membership is made up of about 40 national organizations and 12 international trade federations, including organizations for pensioners and cooperatives. As early as 1961, efforts were undertaken to mobilize rural workers as well. In response to the new realities in the labour markets of the 1980s, such as informal-sector labour and highly marginalized workers, CLAT has developed a new comprehensive approach towards labour and work that addresses both the traditional trade union domain as well as the social area.

The CGT, founded in 1971, is affiliated with the CLAT and currently has 14 national federations, 16 regional federations and 5,048 trade unions affiliated with it. The affiliates include two social movements: the National Centre of Community and Pobladores (slum dwellers) Organizations, and the National Coordinator of Cooperatives. The following special commissions are included: the National Commission of Working Women, the National Commission of the Handicapped and the National Commission of Migrant Workers.

The organizational composition of the CGT reflects CLAT's ideological position on the consolidation of a broad-based social movement which represents the labour movement in general and not only organized workers. The CGT's major asset is its ability to present itself as an independent confederation which maintains its distance from the political system and so cannot be accused of the negative aspects that such dependence has previously engendered.

Informalization and the bargaining strength of trade unions

The informalization of the labour force, that is, the growth of the labour segment outside the institutional framework regulating labour relations, is a relatively recent phenomenon in Venezuela.[4] While the informal-sector debate started in most Latin American countries during the mid-1970s, the sector did not become an important issue in Venezuela until the mid-1980s due to its relatively small size until then.

In 1975, the percentage of informal workers in Venezuela was, on average, 10 points lower than in the rest of the region (19.6 vs 30 per cent).[5] The Venezuelan case is unique in the region in one more respect. Informality in Venezuela is not necessarily associated with increasing poverty, but rather with the structural changes experienced during the 1980s.[6]

The structural changes in the economy contributed to the following specific characteristics of the informal sector:

- Its expansion was rapid: in 1975 the sector accounted for only 19.6 per cent of employment, in 1988 this proportion had reached 39.6 per cent and in the second half of 1990 it was above 40 per cent.
- Micro-enterprises have constituted its fastest-growing segment, both in terms of employment and number of enterprises.
- The most dynamic segments within the sector's manufacturing activities are those engaged in the production of intermediate goods, that is, chemicals and construction. Traditional segments producing non-durable consumer goods such as shoes, garments and food are expanding more slowly.

In the course of the 15-year period during which informality developed, the level of formal education among workers in the informal sector has increased significantly. The percentage of individuals employed in the sector with higher education rose from one per cent in 1973 to seven per cent in 1988 while the incidence of illiteracy fell from 25 to less than six per cent, a percentage well below the national average in the same year. In recent years this trend of professionals and better-educated people being pushed into the sector has accelerated since open unemployment has increased, especially in the service sectors.

During the same period, the level of employment in the micro-enterprise sector has displayed three different behaviourial patterns *vis-à-vis* the economic cycle. Between 1975 and 1979 the micro-business sector showed an anti-cyclical trend. This corresponds with the predictions of the PREALC approach, the most popular theory in the region: a decreasing GDP is associated with increasing employment in the micro-enterprise sector.

Between 1980 and 1984, the behaviour was acyclical. No statistical relationship between employment in the sector and the level of economic activity was apparent. In spite of stagnant GDP, the sector experienced high growth. However, since 1984 the level of employment in the sector appears to correlate positively with the economic cycle and employment in the micro-enterprise sector is expanding at the same pace as in the rest of the economy (pro-cyclical).

Obviously, not all employment statistically classified as informal conforms to the characteristics usually attached to the sector. Similarly, not all informal employment corresponds with the features described above since survival strategies of the very poor are also known to generate informalization. There is strong evidence, however, to argue that a significant part of the sector has extensive links with what has been wrongly called the formal sector.

The growth of the informal sector has affected the position and role of trade unions. At the very least, the increased informalization of the labour force has weakened the negotiating position of the organized labour movement. The bargaining strength of formal workers has been squeezed between the emergence of a more flexible and largely unprotected labour market which introduced the trade-off between job security and the maintenance of previous wage levels and benefits.

Some inferences can be made on the basis of the evolution of average nominal salaries since their evolution is a function of the social forces that intervene in the labour contract. It appears that informalization has functioned as a vehicle to externalize part of the cost function of large enterprises and as a means of enforcing discipline and increasing managerial control over workers in large-scale enterprises. In almost all industries nominal earnings grew faster during the 1974–80 period than during the years 1981–88, the period in which the informal sector registered rapid growth. For instance, in chemicals, a key industry in Venezuela, nominal earnings increased at a rate of 30 per cent during the period 1974–80. From 1981–88 they increased only by 9.3 per cent while cumulative inflation was 165 per cent (Baptista 1991).

Update

On 4 February 1992, Venezuela experienced its first coup attempt in more than 30 years. Nine months later a second attempt also failed. Shortly afterwards, in May 1993, President Carlos Andrés Pérez was dismissed on charges of corruption. In the following December elections Rafael Caldera was elected president with less than 28 per cent of the votes.

Having won the elections on the basis of an anti-neoliberal platform, the new government was taken by surprise by the worst financial and banking crisis in Venezuelan history. It heralded not only a new phase in the economic crisis itself, but revealed that the political crisis had not passed. Given the worsening of the fiscal and political crises, the government has been forced to shift back and forth between a neoclassical stabilization programme and an interventionist one, including price and foreign exchange controls. By sending confusing messages to the political and economic actors, this has further deepened the political unrest.

By mid-1994, the political crisis had progressed to an atomization of the political arena. Economic and financial interest groups, political parties and trade unions alike were all unable to formulate or synthesize issues of common interest to the different social groupings and mobilize support for them. This has severely undermined Venezuela's democratic governability.

Thus, radical changes have been and are taking place in Venezuela following the breakdown of the Great Social Pact which contributed to the political inactivity of the trade union movement during the years of economic expansion and the oil boom and reduced labour's autonomy as a major power contender. Frequent allegations are made of trade union corruption, the qualitative deterioration of political leadership and about politics and politicians in general. The trade unions have been unable to fight successfully for redistributive policies, for a reorientation of the government's development strategy towards greater equity through social programmes to assist the rural and urban poor.

At the same time, these changes have opened the doors for the emergence of labour organizations and social movements that are politically independent and free from corruption. Though not yet constituting a majority, they are strongly committed to the challenges posed by the new economic and social conditions. Above all, it must be realized that the confrontation between neo-liberalism and state intervention is a misleading one. Trade unions should adopt pragmatic approaches to Venezuela's problems since the conditions that previously allowed the development of strong labour organizations with a potential for influence in all spheres no longer exist.

The Venezuelan labour movement will have to find answers to a long list of challenges confronting it, including:

- The needs and priorities of the ever-growing segment of informal sector workers.
- The uneven impact of adjustment processes on different segments of society, affecting mainly the vulnerable groups – the poor, the young, the aged and women.
- The conflictive and deteriorating conditions of migrant workers, especially those coming from Colombia, who are subjected to constant harassment and mobility restrictions by the authorities.
- The acute deterioration of real wage levels and per capita income.
- The increasing inequalities in income distribution, which in turn increase social unrest and threaten democracy.

The implementation of a new economic development model, and the current political and economic crises show that the subordination of the working classes to the political parties through social pacts is no longer a reliable mechanism. It seems that the current economic, political and social events are creating the basis and the environment for new developments in state–labour–management relations which will have impacts on labour-market structure. All this, clearly, will also demand a serious reappraisal by the international labour community of its attitude and present and future policies towards organized labour in Venezuela.

Notes

1. The Actión Democrática (AD), Comité de Organización Política Electoral Independiente (COPEI, the Christian Democrat Party) and Unión Republicana Democrática (URD, a centre–left oriented party).

2. As his public speeches demonstrate, his views on a solution to Venezuela's problems are based solely on mere nationalism and firing squads for politicians and entrepreneurs.

3. Named after Rafael Caldera, then a senator but now president.

4. Figures and arguments in this section are primarily based on Méndez Rivero (1991).

5. As measured by the PREALC (Programa Regional del Emplleo para América Latina y el Caribe) criteria: self-employment, domestic service and micro-enterprises.

6. From traditional theoretical perspectives on the informal sector and its role in development, especially the 'PREALC approach', this is a controversial statement. It is not implied that there is a positive relationship between informality

and better standards of living. See Cartaya (1989) for a discussion of the empirical basis for the Venezuelan case.

References

Baptista, A. (1991) *Bases quantitativas de la economia venezolano: 1830–1989*. Communicaciones Corporativas, Caracas.

Betancourt, R. (1969) *Venezuela politica y petrolo*. Editorial Senderos, Bogota.

Bitar, S. and E. Troncoso (1983) *El desafio industrial de Venezuela*. Editorial Pomaire, Buenos Aires.

Cartaya, V. (1989) *La Pobreza y la Economía Informal: Casualidad o causalidad?*, Mimeo. Simposio IESA, Caracas.

Cordiplan (1986) *Informe Social*, No.3. Cordiplan, Caracas.

D'Elia, Y. and V. Cartaya (1991) *Pebreza en Venezuela: Realidad y Political*. Cisor, Caracas.

Davis, Ch. and R. Coleman (1989) 'Political Control in a Semi-consociational Democracy: The Case of Venezuela', in E. Epstein (ed.) *Labour Autonomy and the State in Latin America*. Unwin Hyman, Boston.

Ellner, E. (1987) 'Venezuela', in C.M. Greenfield and S. Maram (eds) *Latin American Labour Organizations*. Greenwood Press, New York.

IDB (1987) *Social and Economic Progress in Latin America*. Inter-American Development Bank, Washington. DC.

McCoy, J.L. (1989) 'Labour and the State in a Party-mediated Democracy: Institutional Change in Venezuela', *Latin American Research Review* 24(2).

Méndez Rivero, D. (1991) 'Informalization of the Venezuelan Labor Force: Malfunctioning of Markets or Changes in the Labor–Capital Relationship? A Historical Inquiry for the Period 1975–1988', M.Phil. Thesis. Institute of Social Studies, The Hague.

OCEI (various years) *Encuesta industrial*. Oficina Central de Estadistica e Informatica, Caracas.

Purroy, M.I. (1982) *Estado e industrializacion en Venezuela*. Vadell Hermanos, Valencia.

Part Three: Africa

8. A Context of Sharp Economic Decline

Paschal Mihyo
Freek Schiphorst

This chapter aims to provide the wider framework within which labour relations operate in Africa. The analysis is limited to sub-Saharan Africa, a term commonly used to denote the 47 African countries south of the Sahara, excluding South Africa. First the chapter briefly addresses the problem of approaches to African studies before analysing political and economic developments. It concludes with a general survey of the labour-market situation, trade unions and unprotected labour.

Approaches to African studies

A variety of approaches has been adopted in African studies, which need examination before one can address the crisis in Africa. The first issue is whether the African state is on 'the decline' (Turner and Young 1985) or whether, in fact, the state has been gaining strength and becoming more capable of controlling the African population, thereby eliminating opposition. Related to this is the question of whether the African state is more appropriately characterized as a 'lame Leviathan' (Callagy 1987) or, in the same vein, as weak and suspended above society (Hyden 1983). The weakness of the African state is relative, depending on the aspect of it under consideration. The failure of the state to provide basic services or to develop clear policies for structural change may justify its characterization as weak or even 'soft' as has been done by authors such as Rothchild (1987). In terms of the way it has controlled political processes, however, incorporated all potential opposition groups, controlled the population through systems like the *kebele* system in Ethiopia, the ten-cell system in Tanzania, the committees for the defence of the revolution in Ghana or the dynamization groups in Mozambique, the state is neither a lame Leviathan nor suspended above society, nor is it 'omnipresent but impotent' as has been asserted by Chazan (Rothchild and Chazan

1988). In some cases it has been a killer state either through repression or neglect, and this is in no way a sign of weakness, decay, decline or omnipotence.

The second issue to be considered is whether the authoritarianism of the political parties which has led Africa to its present decline was endemic or acquired. Most existing studies that base themselves on decline and decay theories tend to project the authoritarian tendency of African states as an unfortunate trend into which regimes grew. The theory of the state in Africa as a patrimonial one characterized by growing corruption and personalization of authority, and the theories which look at the African state as a prebendal state (Jackson and Roseberg 1982) tend to confirm the notion of decay. However, they fail to investigate the possible authoritarian tendencies of African political parties prior to independence.

Such analysis could lead to a different assessment of the roots of authoritarianism. As early as 1963, Kilson (1963: 263) in a lonesome voice warned that the parties challenging colonial rule in Africa were organized on undemocratic lines, mobilized the people through threats and coercion, and had vindictive agendas for punishing their opponents once they came to power. The Kenya African National Union (KANU), the ruling party, emerged out of a tribal organization committed to the expulsion of all non-Kikuyus, black or white, from the Central Highlands. In Tanzania, the Tanganyika African National Union (TANU) warned its opponents that they would die in exile and would be denied water, jobs and clothing. The dominant parties in Ghana, Swaziland and Zambia had mobilization songs which conveyed similar threats.

In Ghana the persecution of the opposition commenced immediately after Kwame Nkrumah came to power in 1958 with 54 per cent of the vote. Within the first three years he passed censorship laws, and by October 1960 had detained 115 members of the opposition (the United Party). In Kenya, the opposition party, KADU (Kenya African Democratic Union), was offered an opportunity to join KANU in the interests of national unity. The current president, Daniel Arap Moi, was the leader of the KADU at the time. In 1986 he said the offer had been accepted because among other things 'Mzee Jomo Kenyatta was very insistent' (Moi 1986: 15). In Tanzania, the opposition was outlawed immediately after the first elections, which were won by an overwhelming majority by TANU. Thereafter, former opposition leaders were either given low-ranking administrative jobs in hardship areas, kept under surveillance or, when they challenged the system, detained or exiled (Mlimuka and Kabudi 1985). These are just a few examples which point to the endemic totalitarian nature of the parties that took over the colonial machinery in Africa, preserved it as it was and used it systematically to marginalize their people.

A third methodological issue is how economic and political trends in Africa should be categorized: on the basis of geographical divisions (East, West, Central and Southern Africa); or on their colonial background (for example, French, British, Belgian, Portuguese)? Or do economic and political trends in Africa defy such categorization? The second categorization may be the easiest to contest when one considers that Liberia and Ethiopia experienced only brief periods of colonial domination. In addition, post-independence patterns in the Côte d'Ivoire and Kenya have been similar although their colonial backgrounds differ. The colonial approach is also questionable on account of the fact that since 1960 most African countries have been exposed to the international environment. Their colonial past has had an important influence on the form, level and intensity of their exposure, but this has certainly not been the only, or in some cases decisive, factor.

On the other hand, a geographical division is also unconvincing as there are countries in East and West Africa that display economic and political commonalities without sharing borders or historical backgrounds. It is impossible to group African countries into regions for an analysis of economic or political developments, as for instance is possible in Asia. Neighbouring countries within a region can have radically opposed political systems (for example, Togo and Benin) or widely diverging patterns of economic development or performance (for instance, Botswana and Zambia).

A major underlying reason for the persistent attempts to find an acceptable regional categorization for countries that display similar political or economic problems or patterns of development is the fact that remedial strategies most often can be successful, or cost-efficient, only when they are implemented at a (sub-) regional level. Most African countries, however, were colonized individually. Even within those colonized by the same power, each colonial government pursued a different economic policy. Kenya, for example, was differently developed as a colony from the neighbouring British colony of Uganda. Similar divergences can be observed in Central and West African colonial history. Moreover, after attaining independence, most countries have continued to act on their own.

A cautious multi-level and holistic approach is necessary in the study of Africa. Where a shared common background and geographical access to common resources, or lack of access to certain factors, produces common political and economic regimes, similarities should be identified. Where similar political and economic trends are identifiable irrespective of colonial background, their causes should be investigated, and used to identify possible future trends. The only reliable method which one could easily trust without too many risks is the historical method, and it is this method that we shall rely on most.

Political development

It is difficult to understand the current political situation without reflecting on the past. Most studies concentrate on political reforms, while the first important question is what caused the problems that are now being redressed. Both general and specific case studies (Ergas 1987; Rothchild and Chazan 1988; Turner and Young 1985) mostly limit the period under review in their studies to the emergence of the post-colonial state and end up with the deterioration of this state into a 'vampire' or 'prebendal' state. The deeper historical roots are rarely addressed even though the roots of African political decay should be traced first within the decolonization process and only then in the post-colonial context.

Common trends in political decay

As many authors have noted, African politics began with a lot of hope. The hope of independence and the capability of people to govern themselves has been crucial in the mobilization process. The first free elections were characterized by long queues, and parliaments were respected in those early days. But elections became more and more meaningless even in countries which did not experience direct dictatorship.

Voting in elections declined over the years until the average percentage of voters dwindled to 20 per cent in many countries (Hayward 1987). The declining voter turnout was a first sign that the political process had become either meaningless or the restricted domain of vested dominant interests. Poverty also squeezed the majority of urban people out of the political process as they had to devote increasingly more time and attention to the search for a livelihood.

The second sign of political deterioration was that most leaders, irrespective of whether they came to power through ballots or bullets, soon acquired the legislative power either to pass decrees or to block parliamentary decisions and bills. Thus, the locus of decision making in the majority of African countries shifted away from the elected assemblies to the arena of closed circuits, state commissions, cabinet secretariats and presidential advisory bodies. At the ministerial level, principles of collective responsibility were gradually abandoned in favour of personal answerability to the president and parliamentary compliance with presidential prerogatives (Collier 1982; Jackson 1982).

The third symptom of political decay and the advance of authoritarianism was the way in which the state began using its power to control production and distribution. In most African countries a large public sector was quickly established, not only as a bulwark against the dissipation of state influence and possible demands for accountability – likely to arise in an economy that developed a sizeable autonomous dynamic private sector – but also as a source of accumulation and as an instrument of patronage (through employment, recruitment of political followers and a controlled welfare system of benefits and services to loyal workers). This development went hand-in-hand with the annexation of all popular movements to the state apparatus in order to ensure that all political processes were linked to the official machinery. As one author concluded, authoritarianism can only succeed if it is built into the systems of production and decision making (Thomas 1984: 83–6).

Thus, African states designed labour regimes which were corporatist in nature. A common characteristic of these regimes was the licensing of political rights, achieved through the incorporation of all mass movements into the official machinery of the nation state. Trade unions, cooperative movements, youth bodies, chambers of commerce, religious bodies and other similar organizations in Ghana, Congo, Ethiopia, Tanzania and Zambia, for example, were only allowed to operate if they were registered under the official political parties of those countries.

In the organization of production, these bodies were all dependent on a large public sector to which other sectors were subordinated. In the regulation of distribution, they relied on rigid price and wage policies. Bargaining processes were organized on the principle of state mediation. In the case of peasants the intermediaries which fixed prices and marketed produce were the crop authorities. In the case of formal-sector workers, distribution was regulated through rigid wages boards, ministerial labour tribunals, cabinet secretariats and presidential decrees.

Such labour regimes held few growth-conducive incentives for producers. While attempts were made to reduce existing income disparities between groups, little effort was made to increase incomes for any or all groups. Distributional priorities prevailed over growth considerations. To further the distribution policies, the social welfare function of the state was centralized in many if not all regimes. Since the nerve-centre of political activity was the urban sector, the primary locus of the welfare function became the public sector. The instrument of intervention was employment, and wages policies and compulsory arbitration structures became the major distributive mechanisms.

A fourth symptom of political decay in Africa has been the concentration of power. Apart from the annexation of enterprise systems and social and political movements to the state, the state itself became a consolidated unit of power. Sometimes a complete reversal of the concept of the separation of powers was attained, not only by ensuring that the presidency, party and parliament were controlled by one person, but also by making sure that the judiciary and the civil service were either nonentities or part of the technocracy.

State terror, the fifth symptom of Africa's political decay, has become a persistent feature of authoritarian regimes. The abuse of citizens through detention and torture, cruel degrading treatment of offenders and suspected offenders, and collective punishment have become characteristics of African state terror. The judicial systems have been allowed to decline, and people have been known to remain in custody without trial for years or to be sentenced without trial. Mass trials are organized in some countries or trials are held hastily to make space in remand prisons for new suspects. In many countries the invasion of privacy in homes and offices is sanctioned by law and freedom of expression or political participation has been restricted for decades. Discrimination on ethnic, religious and political grounds is rife in many states.

The abuse of organizational and participatory rights has affected trade unions disproportionately. The list of abuses of labour rights inflicted on the unions by African governments is long. The arbitrary reorganization or dissolution of unions, unlawful detention of union leaders, outlawing of lawful strike activities, suspension of collective bargaining and its replacement by presidential wage-setting practices, dismissal of striking workers and the imposition of severe sentences on labour organizers are but a few examples (ICFTU annual reports).

The historical roots of authoritarianism

Some of Africa's political movements were already authoritarian and undemocratic prior to independence. In most instances the populist parties allied to the peasants and workers found themselves competing for power with middle-class elitist parties that allied themselves with the colonial authorities. Most populist parties could not understand why fellow Africans were organizing against them and allying themselves with the colonial administration. Their lack of clarity about the world system and class alliances forced nationalist movements to adopt authoritarian tactics of organization and mobilization. Consequently they used youth wings to harass, boo and jeer opponents. In some cases they burned and destroyed the property of their opponents. These practices were very common in Kenya, Ghana, Malawi, Swaziland and Tanzania.

In some countries nationalist movements were put on the defensive by the colonial regimes. In Angola, Guinea Bissau, Cape Verde, Mozambique, South Africa and Zimbabwe the nationalist movements were outlawed and had no choice but to take up arms. Due to intimidation and penetration, they were forced to adopt tough codes of discipline and good conduct, to screen membership and to organize on rigorous lines of loyalty and obedience. Such norms, though indispensable to military discipline and cohesion, are not conducive to party democracy. The bases of participatory democracy and acceptance of the rights of others to organize were therefore easily undermined in these countries by this culture of military discipline. It is ironic that some of the movements once kept out by earlier regimes now find it difficult to tolerate political dissidence.

In most African countries, however, the independence parties initially enjoyed a lot of support and popularity. They were regarded as liberators and their leaders acquired a 'father of the nation' image, were invited to rule for life and given a mandate to outlaw the opposition. This was the case in countries such as the Central African Republic, Gabon, Ghana, Kenya, Malawi, Tanzania and Zambia. The leaders were quick to capitalize on this goodwill by installing one-party systems, centralizing authority, weakening accountability and in some cases declaring themselves leaders for life. Even when the euphoria of Independence began to wear off, they continued to cherish their father-of-the-nation image and, in some cases, even changed the names of their parties to give them a liberation orientation. An example is Tanzania where in 1977 TANU (Tanganyika African National Union) dissolved itself and adopted the name Chama Cha Mapinduzi (Party for Revolution – CCM).

Authoritarianism was also consolidated by many other factors, the first of which was populism. Populist regimes in Cameroon, Congo, Ethiopia, Guinea Bissau, Somalia, Sudan, Tanzania, Zambia and Zimbabwe concentrated on retaining legitimacy and mobilizing mass support. Without offering alternatives to the poor, they sought to please the masses by controlling or taking away from the rich. This led to a wave of nationalizations of private property including private houses, the outlawing of private trading in rural areas (Congo, Ethiopia, Tanzania), the taking over of private schools, villagization and land confiscation, among other measures. All these actions were taken to secure the support of the masses for the continuation in power of the ruling parties.

Related to this was an attempt by populist regimes to prevent the emergence of strong social groupings. In Benin, Congo, Ethiopia, Ghana, Tanzania, Togo and Zambia for example, all social movements were annexed to the official state and party machinery. Social competition was channelled and regulated, while professional organizations were either weakened or completely outlawed. In all these countries popular participation was allowed only through the established machinery at village, community or enterprise level. Such a system could only produce undercurrents of resentment and protest. It became necessary then to have a big, strong and sophisticated security system under which the majority of people were spying on each other. The less popular the regimes became, the more their dependence on intelligence and security services increased.

In populist and outrightly repressive regimes, the factors that led to authoritarianism and state terror were similar. The main motive was legitimacy and continued control over power, production and distribution processes. This could be secured through total control of the population and the illegitimization of the opposition. The explanations for terror and repression differed between countries. While the populist regimes claimed that control was necessary to prevent the emergence of capitalism, which was likened to colonialism, outrightly repressive regimes claimed that terror and authoritarianism were necessary to prevent the rise of communism. While the populists claimed to be socialists and the others claimed to be capitalists, both were nothing more than repressive, undemocratic, unparticipatory and unaccountable regimes.

Emerging political systems

The political change that swept over Africa in the late 1980s and early 1990s took two major forms. In a number of francophone countries, national assemblies were constituted, bringing together social and political groups, including trade unions, to discuss how to proceed. Benin was the first to adopt this style. Here, a national conference led to a transitional government and multiparty elections. In other cases the ruling elite managed to use this national gathering to stall progress, as happened in Togo, Gabon, the Côte d'Ivoire, Niger and Zaire. In the words of one observer: 'The entrenched authoritarian regimes easily find time and space to frustrate the planned meeting and derail the process' (Medhanie 1992: 6).

A different route was adopted in a number of anglophone countries. Multiparty politics were allowed, albeit sometimes hesitantly (Kenya, Malawi, Zambia). Subsequently, elections were called, sometimes overnight (Kenya), sometimes announced in advance (Zambia). This approach was not exclusively confined to the anglophone African countries; elections were held in Angola, Mauritania, Cameroon, Côte d'Ivoire and Cape Verde. Mali had multiparty elections in 1992 won by the opposition Alliance for Democracy in Mali. However, in most cases, opposition parties complained about poor access to the state-controlled media and the lack of preparatory time to build a strong organization.

In order to decide whether Africa's political systems are changing or not, one has to formulate clear quantitative and qualitative indicators. Quantitatively, the mere fact that in Angola 11 parties contested the election in 1992, that in Tanzania there are 16 parties awaiting the elections in 1995, and that in Kenya seven major parties participated in the December 1992 elections, all show that change is taking place. Equally significant is the fact that political parties have come into existence in former military regimes such as Benin, Burkina Faso, Congo and Zaire.

From a qualitative standpoint, a few questions arise. For instance, why did the United Independence Party and its leader Kenneth Kaunda of Zambia lose the elections? The return of Jerry Rawlings in Ghana by a landslide victory in 1992 surprised everyone – the opposition, the observers who had certified the elections as 'fair' and 'free', and Rawlings himself who had expected to win but not by such a large margin. Equally surprising was the return of Daniel Arap Moi and KANU in Kenya, after 15 cabinet ministers lost their parliamentary seats and the party lost many constituencies in the dominantly Kikuyu Central Province. The decision of UNITA in Angola to go back to full-scale civil war in December 1992 after a free and fair election in which its rival, the MPLA, was returned to power, shows how frustration could lead to irrational action when expectations are not met.

The emerging political trends in Africa are a continuation of African history. Repression was an economic and political factor. It was, and still is, supported by economic backwardness which provides the opportunity for dominant forces to control information, shape popular outlook and get the population to trust the elite. When 'their leaders' come back and apologize for past wrongs and make promises, especially when elections are preceded by infrastructural projects in key areas, the people are induced to give them another chance. Among the rural people the saying 'Better the devil you know' still works. Most politicians in the old parties have retained their rural roots and are promoted by the rural elite who have benefited from the politicians' favour. Hence they are popular in rural areas and less trusted in the urban areas.

In Zambia, the situation was different. The victory of the Movement for Multiparty Democracy (MMD) in 1991 was possible mainly because Kaunda and the UNIP had neglected the rural areas in favour of the urban areas. It was in the urban areas that all the best schools, hospitals, dispensaries, water and other facilities existed. Life in urban areas was highly subsidized. It was the urban people who kept UNIP in power. When the state was unable to keep the urban welfare system running, and when in 1988 Kaunda initiated plans to repatriate the urban unemployed, the tide turned against the government. The MMD succeeded mainly because it took control of the urban areas and at the same time mobilized the rural areas ignored by the government.

The importance of the rural sector in current African politics was shown in Ghana. Beginning in 1989, Jerry Rawlings began a massive plan of rehabilitating rural infrastructure – roads, schools and trading centres. He also liberalized primary-commodity marketing systems, enabling peasants to sell their cocoa to many competing buyers. By the time the elections came round, the peasants had been won over by the state and they voted for the National Democratic Congress and Rawlings. A similar development occurred in Kenya. In the Rift Valley, the members of Moi's tribe, Kalenjin, were categorically told that voting for the opposition would mean voting for a takeover of their land. The elections were preceded by intimidation of Kikuyus living in the region. Some who showed signs of opposing the government were killed and their property was destroyed. Seventeen KANU candidates were returned unopposed in the region.

In Tanzania, while the opposition has succeeded in attracting membership in urban areas, the ruling party, CCM, has increased its membership by 20 per cent in regions inhabited by poor and middle-income peasants, mainly central and south-eastern Tanzania. In the cash crop areas of the north and south-west, in which middle- and upper-income peasants predominate, the struggle between the CCM and the new Chama Cha Maendeleo na Demokrasi centres on the cooperative movement. The latter is struggling to form a splinter union of cooperative movements, and to mobilize all the cooperative movement leaders against the ruling party; the former is struggling to retain control over the leadership of the movement by increasing credit and rehabilitating infrastructure. Therefore, apart from the issue of the territorial union which will feature predominantly in Zanzibar, the 1995 elections in Tanzania will be won by the party or parties that have a strong influence in the rural areas.

Most of the current regimes in Africa came to power prior to the implementation of structural adjustment programmes. Some were in power when the economic climate was at its most favourable and managed to deliver some basic necessities – health, water, education and infrastructure. Most of the new parties lack past achievements or a credible inward-looking and less repressive agenda. Hence the old populist parties which oppose privatization and structural adjustment stand a bigger chance than the parties which come into existence as a product of structural adjustment programmes and IMF-World Bank conditionalities. The new parties cannot stand on old programmes that are monopolized by old parties, and cannot stand out starkly as parties for structural adjustment which is becoming increasingly unpopular among workers and peasants in Africa.

Finally, the IMF and World Bank recovery programmes are strengthening right-wing political groups. As trade liberalization seems to benefit especially the well-to-do (most of whom are non-nationals), restlessness abounds and people begin wondering if they are in the process of being recolonized. Radical nationalist parties have emerged in Tanzania, Uganda and Zambia, whose programmes aim to ensure that national wealth remains predominantly in the hands of nationals. Such groups mobilize support easily as they note that privatization and trade liberalization are instruments of alienation. Such developments are unplanned consequences of economic and political reforms.

The future topics for debate on the democratization process include the extent to which new governments are able to establish a real transformation of political practice (including bringing about widespread participation of the people); the impact of structural adjustment programmes and policies on the development of the democratization process, and the role of the international community therein; the relationship between multiparty systems and ethnicity as well as the role of religion, the media, the armed forces and/or the police (Buijtenhuijs and Rijnierse 1993; Rijnierse 1993).

Africa's economic map

It may be belabouring the obvious, but Africa's economy has been in crisis for two decades. The outward-oriented colonial economic policy left a legacy of dependence on primary commodity exports, poorly developed infrastructure, limited linkages between the rural and urban sectors, and an education system geared towards urban-based public services. In their struggle for national identity and economic development, African countries have faced similar backgrounds and problems with different results. In this section, the causes and constraints of economic development are addressed, together with the strategies for overcoming these obstacles and the long-term problems which influence the effectiveness of recovery programmes.

Industrialization stagnated from the late seventies onwards. Output per capita in sub-Saharan Africa declined, and so did the share of industry in Gross Domestic Product (GDP). Within industry, the share of manufacturing stagnated. The conclusion has already been reached that Africa, in a symptom of its general decline, is de-industrializing (Jamal and Weeks 1993: 12–13).

The industrial growth in Africa so far has been mainly due to import-substitution industrialization (ISI), resulting until the mid-1970s in growth rates similar to those in other parts of the world. At the same time quite a number of sub-Saharan countries relied for their economic performance almost singularly on the export of primary products, unprocessed raw material, and were unable to substantially change the colonial features, and inherent restrictions, of their economies.

A bird's-eye view of the present predicament of sub-Saharan Africa shows that economic performance has been poor, especially since the beginning of the 1980s, with GDP growth rates consistently falling below population growth rates, resulting in a fall in per capita income. As the United Nations Economic Commission for Africa (UN-ECA) observed, the per capita income is now only 80 per cent of what it was in 1980; there has been a concomitant deterioration in the standards and conditions of living of the average African (Adedeji 1991: 767). The World Bank is predicting that Africa will be the only region in the world where per capita income will be falling right up to the twenty-first century (Onimode 1992: 65).

The following explanation has been given in the literature for this dramatic decline (Hesp 1989): ISI created a dependence on imported machinery, technology, spare parts and inputs. In retrospect, one can even say that over-investment took place in certain sectors, in some instances supported by donors. When a drastic decline in primary commodity prices set in around 1980, export earnings were sharply reduced. At the same time, the prices of imported inputs increased. The problem was compounded by the fact that foreign debts, the majority of which had their origins in the oil crises of the 1970s, also matured at this time. The overall result was a shortage of foreign currency. Industry was no longer able to acquire all the necessary imports, aggravating the decline in earnings. Consequently, domestic markets contracted because of a decline in income in the monetized sector.

A vicious circle began in which 'natural disasters, low levels of productivity, low capacity for mobilization of domestic resources, particularly human resources, and high dependence on imports' (Adedeji 1991: 767) reinforced each other. However, as the executive secretary of the UN-ECA concluded:

The most devastating of the factors [responsible for the poor performance of the African economy] are the collapse in the commodity market
and the inexorable rise in the prices of imported manufactured goods.
(Adedeji 1991: 767)

The debt burden has been identified as a major impediment to
growth. Total debt stood at US$280 billion in 1991 (Grant 1992: 51).
From 1986 to 1988 the debt burden grew faster than output and exports.
The debt service obligations have been estimated to range, depending
on the definition used, from US$15 billion to US$25 billion annually.
Although the total African debt is only about 12 per cent of total Third
World debt, the small size of African economies and their low export
earnings make the resulting debt service ratios, which in some cases
reach 50 per cent, a crippling burden. Moreover, the ratios are highest
for the poorest countries.

Manufacturing is generally important in the industrialization
process. Comparatively, however, the contribution of industry and
manufacturing to GDP is small in sub-Saharan Africa: in 1988 industry
as a whole contributed 25 per cent to GDP, while the manufacturing
share was only 10 per cent. For low-income countries globally, these
figures are 35 per cent and 24 per cent respectively, and for upper
middle-income countries 40 per cent and 25 per cent respectively
(Riddell 1990: 5). The low level of manufacturing in Africa can also
be seen in the figures for manufacturing value added (MVA):
sub-Saharan countries contributed only 3.6 per cent of total MVA in
developing countries (and only 0.76 per cent to global MVA) (Riddell
1990: 11).

There is a wide variation within Africa in the contribution of the
manufacturing sector to GDP or MVA. Only seven African countries
together accounted for some 66 per cent of the total MVA for
sub-Saharan Africa. These were Nigeria (which alone accounted for
28 per cent), Cameroon, Côte d'Ivoire, Ghana, Kenya, Zambia and
Zimbabwe; each of these countries produced MVA of US$500 million
or more in 1985. A middle group of 15 countries produced between
US$100 million and US$500 million in 1985. These were Angola,
Burkina Faso, Congo, Ethiopia, Gabon, Madagascar, Malawi,
Mauritius, Mozambique, Rwanda, Senegal, Somalia, Sudan, Uganda
and Tanzania. Together these 15 countries contributed 28 per cent of
total MVA in sub-Saharan Africa, equalling the contribution of
Nigeria. The other 23 countries produced MVA of less than US$100
million, together contributing a mere 7 per cent of total MVA for
sub-Saharan Africa (Riddell 1990: 16).

Manufacturing shows a concentration in food, beverages and textiles, accounting for almost 50 per cent of the total. Riddell (1990: 22) concludes that this

> dominance of consumer rather than intermediate or capital-oriented manufacture would suggest not only that manufacturing is relatively simple in technique but also that there has been little structural change in the post-independence period.

An important feature of the manufacturing sector is the preponderance of state-owned enterprises. For instance, in Tanzania the number of public enterprises increased from 80 in 1967 to 400 in 1981. In Kenya the number grew from 20 in 1963 to 60 in 1979, while Ghana experienced a rapid increase immediately after independence to reach over 100 in the early 1960s. The share of public enterprises in the GDP of African countries is almost twice that in developing countries generally (Herbst 1990: 950). Moreover, this sector is characterized by relatively high overemployment.

The prospects for recovery of industrial production are poor. According to Riddell (1990: 49), this is because the assumptions in the structural adjustment policies supported by the IMF and World Bank are too optimistic regarding the earnings accruing from export of relevant primary products. In other words, the assumptions made for alleviation of the foreign exchange constraints are too optimistic. In a detailed analysis of the textile sector in Africa (next to food and agriculture, the second-largest of the manufacturing sectors in the continent), de Valk (1992: 153) notes that technological problems (antiquated machinery), human-resource problems, including poor management skills, inferior quality performance and the limitations of the small domestic market are, among others, constraints facing African industrialization.

In an attempt to launch economic recovery, the IMF and World Bank have introduced stabilization and adjustment programmes aimed at the demand and supply side of the economy respectively. The initial programmes, often referred to as orthodox, purported to bring about structural change through the use of price policies, thereby ignoring structural constraints to industrial production. Of late, World Bank programmes do focus on constraints such as physical infrastructure, information flows and water supply, but scepticism has been voiced about the impact of these programmes on the existing manufacturing base (Stein 1992).

Often the acceptance of structural adjustment programmes is a precondition for further credit. In general, such programmes contain measures which can be grouped as follows: stimulation of production for export and productivity, including currency devaluation; reduction of government expenditures, including cost recovery measures, removal of subsidies and retrenchment of civil servants and public-sector employees; and liberalization of (internal) trade.

Structural adjustment programmes have been criticized for a number of reasons (Mosley and Weeks 1993; Riddell 1992; Stein 1992). The policy instruments of the traditional programmes are mainly exchange rate adjustment (resulting in most cases in repeated currency devaluations), increases in interest rates, trade liberalization, wage freezes, control of money supply and domestic credit, and reductions in government expenditure, particularly expenditure in the social sector, namely education, health and social welfare. The UN-ECA views these as rather overemphasizing the 'pursuit of fiscal, trade and price balances as ends in themselves and as virtual complete sets of means to production increases' (Adedeji 1991: 780). In addition, in their focus on monetary policies, orthodox structural adjustment programmes have almost completely ignored the human factor. As a result of massive retrenchment, budget squeezes and cuts in subsidies, unemployment at all levels has risen sharply. The privatization of many public enterprises has also resulted in job losses (Diejomaoh 1993). Moreover, Green (1989: 35–6) cites evidence showing that private consumption declined, daily calorie supply per capita dropped, health care was cut back as shown by the decrease in the health budget as percentage of GDP, life expectancy fell, and morbidity and infant mortality increased. Describing the situation regarding education and the effects of the crisis on the formation of human skills at the beginning of the 1990s, Vandermoortele (1991: 83) concludes that Africa suffered 'social overkill'.

Structural adjustment programmes have had a disproportionate impact on women (Diejomaoh 1993: 16). Women have borne a larger share of the costs of the decrease in social services. As Elson argues, women suffer most from the general decline in the provision of health and education services because the responsibility to make up for this is placed on their shoulders:

> If fewer of the services [in health and education] required for the sustenance of human resources are provided by the public sector, then women have to make up for some of the shortfall. (Elson 1991: 177)

In the rural areas, moreover, the incentives to produce for export have the effect of increasing the workload for women in food production, since men concentrate more on export-oriented activities. To add to the problem, the profitability of food production is going down because of the rising cost of inputs.

On average, real wages declined by 25 per cent between 1980 and 1985, with Somalia's 84 per cent and Tanzania's 64 per cent being the worst. In the second half of the 1980s, the average decline in real wages went as high as 50 per cent (Onimode 1992: 64). It is important to note that real wages have dropped more rapidly than income per capita. This means that wage earners have borne the brunt of the economic crisis. Real earnings have fallen to such low levels that wages have to be supplemented with income from other sources, and the phenomenon of secondary and even tertiary employment has become quite common (see Mihyo 1990 for a case study of Tanzania). Several observers have noted that the more skilled and higher-paid employees have suffered a proportionally greater reduction in their incomes (Ghai 1989: 220; Jamal and Weeks 1993: 119), compressing the wage structure (Vandermoortele 1991: 86).

It is a deliberate policy of orthodox structural adjustment programmes not to allow wages to be adjusted in line with the hefty devaluations. The argument is that wage costs need to be reduced because they are an important constraint in the promotion of industrial/manufactured exports. However, de Valk (1992: 347) shows for the textile sector that labour costs in sub-Saharan African countries are considerably lower than those in the major textile exporting countries. Hourly wages in 1990 in Taiwan were 15 times higher than in Nigeria or Tanzania, in Hong Kong they were ten times higher and even in Morocco they were four times higher. This makes it difficult to maintain that wages are the constraining factor.

In May 1986, the UN-ECA and the Organization of African Unity organized a meeting to address the continent's economic crisis. They came out with a paper entitled 'Africa's Submission to the Special Session of the UN General Assembly on Africa's Economic and Social Crisis'. In 1987 the UN-ECA organized an international conference on 'The Challenge of Economic Recovery and Accelerated Development'. Here the conclusion was reached that the traditional structural adjustment programmes

> have separated the pursuit of short-term objectives from the long-term transformational goals. They constitute the very antithesis of achieving these long-term development objectives... What we need is a complete refocus on domestic development and the total integration of short-term objectives with medium- and long-term development goals... It will logically and inevitably oblige all concerned...to put all the emphasis on Africa's domestic and intra-regional market... It will also compel all concerned to devote energy and resources on how to engineer a fundamental restructuring of the African economies instead of perpetuating the neo-colonial monocultural export production system at a time when the external demand prospects are dismal. (Adedeji 1991: 780–81)

Consequently, the African Alternative Framework — Structural Adjustment Programme (AAF-SAP) insists on a long-term development objective for which four strategies are identified: a focus on human-centred and self-sustaining development; transformation of Africa from an exchange economy to a production economy through the development of production activities; popular participation and accountability in public affairs in order to democratize the developmental process; and regional co-operation and integration (Onimode 1992: 79). To achieve this, a framework of policy measures is proposed which includes:

- land reform;
- the use of 25 per cent of total public investment in agriculture;
- increased foreign exchange allocation to vital imports;
- the introduction of a differential system of interest rates, including subsidized rates for borrowers in the rural areas;
- rehabilitation of infrastructure, also to boost capacity utilization;
- the promotion of small-scale industries to strengthen domestic production at grassroots level (Onimode 1992: 86–7).

The labour markets

Before a description and analysis is provided of African labour markets, it is essential to recall that the continent has been and continues to be ravaged by a number of wars, which have had and continue to have substantial impacts on the labour markets, national and international: the old and new conflicts in the Horn of Africa with turmoil and destruction in Ethiopia, Somalia and Sudan; internal wars in Burundi, Liberia and Rwanda; and destabilization and internal wars in Southern Africa affecting Angola, Malawi, Mozambique, South Africa and Zimbabwe.

Not only are the effects devastating in terms of human suffering and loss of human resources, loss of agricultural production including food, destruction of infrastructure, capacity disutilization and de-industrialization, the impact also transcends national frontiers. On the one hand, major flows of refugees to neighbouring countries have been created, placing an additional burden on already precarious economic and ecological balances. Africa today has nearly half the world's refugees, especially from Liberia, Mozambique, the countries in the Horn of Africa, Sudan and Rwanda. On the other hand, these wars have upset migratory flows which have been characteristic of the African labour markets for a very long time.

Migration

Data on international migration within Africa are scarce and unreliable. Zeleza (1989: 40) estimates the total number of migrant workers in Africa in the middle of the 1980s at five to six million.

Migration is seasonal and cyclical and is characterized by a dominance of migrants from neighbouring countries. Cyclical migration has a long-standing history and is facilitated by cultural links and proximity.

Apart from South Africa, the major countries that are attractive for migrant workers are the richer oil-exporting ones: Congo, Gabon, Côte d'Ivoire, Nigeria, Zaire (Adepoju 1991: 45). Other important recipient countries are Zaire, Kenya, Uganda, Zambia and Zimbabwe. Mines and plantation agriculture are the main destinations. The major sending countries are Burkina Faso, Togo and Mali in West Africa; Malawi, Lesotho, Botswana and Swaziland in Southern Africa; and Cameroon, Rwanda, Central African Republic and Angola in Central Africa. Lesotho is the top sending country, with 51 per cent of its adult males in South Africa, and deriving half of its foreign exchange from remittances (Adepoju 1991: 49, 53). South Africa allows only temporary migration and family migration is restricted, thus ensuring that the migrant workers will not settle. Migrant labour was further restricted in the late seventies with only experienced workers being admitted to the mines, and from 1977 labour from the newly created homelands was favoured.

Adepoju links the characteristics of the migrants to the nature of their migration. Refugees fleeing from famine and/or war are usually older persons, women and children; migrants to South Africa and seasonal migrants in West Africa are predominantly male. In general, he concludes:

> Migrants within Africa include a high proportion of young adult males of working age who often have lower levels of schooling than the population they join. (Adepoju 1991: 50)

This concentration in the non-skilled category makes the migrants extra vulnerable to retrenchment during implementation of structural adjustment programmes (Gozo and Aboagye 1986: 370).

Many attempts have been made to contain these migratory flows. In West Africa, Ghana expelled Nigerians in 1969 and Nigeria closed its borders to foreigners in 1983 and 1985, which resulted in the forced return of many Ghanaians. In Southern Africa, Zimbabwe tried formally to prevent labour migration to South Africa, while Mozambique incorporated measures to regulate migration in the Nkomati Accord. At the same time, the downward trend in South

African mining and industry, and changes in management strategies, led to a drastic decline in job openings for migrants. As Tahane (1991: 69) puts it: 'South Africa will have to create more jobs for its own people, thereby decreasing the number of foreign workers it can absorb'. In general, labour-importing countries are posing more and more restrictions on migrant workers, restrictions which are not only motivated by political objectives but increasingly also by economic motives in view of the worsening employment situation as a result of the retrenchment which is part of structural adjustment. This led Zeleza to conclude that

> migrant workers in Africa faced bleak prospects as desperate governments brazenly expelled workers from neighbouring countries, while at the same time they were falling over themselves to attract foreign capitalists. (Zeleza 1989: 40)

The earnings which migrants send home are one of the benefits to the sending countries. In Southern Africa remittances form the major source of government revenue in Lesotho, while for Malawi, Swaziland and Botswana the remittances are substantial (Tahane 1991: 81). Migration also constitutes an enormous social cost for the sending country which bears the costs of the reproduction of labour and has to receive back the migrants, usually old or sick because of poor working conditions, once their productive years are over. Migration has an important impact on food and agricultural production in the sending country, a burden which falls mainly on the shoulders of women.

Migration to countries outside Africa has a totally different character and can be best described as a brain drain. An ILO/UN-ECA estimate puts the number of Africans with middle-level and high skills who had left the continent by 1987 at 70,000, representing almost 30 per cent of Africa's skilled human resources (Zeleza 1989: 41).

Despite the unprecedented fall in urban real wages and the narrowing of the income gap between the urban wage worker and peasants, rural–urban migration has continued unabated (Jamal and Weeks 1993). Jamal argues away this paradox by pointing out that rural–urban migration has become part of the survival strategy of the extended family (Jamal 1993: 27). Although urbanization in Africa has not been on the same scale as in Asia or Latin America (no African city is among the ten largest in the world), the dramatic growth in the size of cities like Lagos, Abidjan, Nairobi and Harare indicates an alarming trend in rural–urban migration. In the past two decades, African cities have grown by 6 to 7 per cent annually and during the 1980s the migration into towns doubled. While in 1950 sub-Saharan Africa had no city with more than one million inhabitants (and Africa as a whole had only one, Cairo), in 1991 this number had risen to 19. At the end of the twentieth-century there will be sixty. It has been estimated that in 1990 31 per cent of the population was urban based, of which 42 per cent lived in urban conglomerates of more than 500,000 inhabitants. In 1960, 15 per cent of the total population was urban, while for the year 2000 the figure is expected to be 38 per cent. In comparison, the figures for Latin America, including the Caribbean, are 72 per cent in 1990 and 76 per cent in the year 2000.

The informal sector
Definitional problems regarding this sector have dominated the debate since the publication of the report of the ILO Employment Mission to Kenya in 1972. The issues have included: the homogeneity or heterogeneity of the informal sector; and the access to or articulation of, and intricate linkages between, the formal and informal sectors. Two characteristics have emerged for identifying the informal enterprise: its small size and the extent to which an enterprise avoids official regulation and taxes. The micro-size usually coincides with the avoidance of regulation, the latter feature making policy design difficult. Lubell (1991: 13) concludes that in particular the restrictive effect of counter-productive regulations has been identified as the main policy constraint on informal-sector activity. He also observes, however, that for sub-Saharan Africa these restrictions are generally more moderate than for countries in Latin America. Moreover, the regulations are less prominent in anglophone Africa than in francophone Africa.

Size
As outlined above, sub-Saharan Africa has experienced rapid urban growth. This growth has been caused by such factors as better prospects for jobs and access to education and medical treatment. Many migrants to the cities have discovered, however, that their prospects have not improved and that unemployment and underemployment are rampant. Entry into the informal sector is easier for the well-established urban dweller than for the recently arrived rural migrant, as Brand found in Harare (Brand 1986). This would seem to give an advantage to the recently retrenched job seeker, although with the saturation of the informal sector this would seem to be a rather marginal gain.

Exact, let alone accurate, data on the size of the informal sector are not available. For one, the distinction between the urban and rural informal sectors is not reflected in the statistical literature, which treats the phenomenon mostly as purely urban. However, as the Zimbabwe case study in this book and a study on the second economy in Tanzania (Maliyamkono and Bagachwa 1990) make clear, this perspective needs revision.

Furthermore, as an extensive ILO literature survey concludes, research on the informal sector has focused almost exclusively on production and repair services and, to a lesser degree, on trade. This ignores the important contribution of the informal sector to transport and construction in Africa.

It has been estimated that the informal sector provides employment for a large proportion of the urban labour force: an ILO/JASPA study published in 1985 estimates that the sector accounts for 60 per cent of the urban labour force, and that it might contribute between one-quarter and one-third of urban incomes. In West Africa, the informal sector accounts for 50 per cent of the labour force in Lagos, 50 per cent to 60 per cent in Kumasi, and 73 per cent in Ouagadougou (Trager 1987). Between 1980 and 1985 the modern sector in sub-Saharan Africa

> absorbed a mere six per cent of new labour force recruits, whereas almost three-quarters of them were absorbed in the informal sector. (Vandermoortele 1991: 99)

These figures would seem to put sub-Saharan Africa well above the average for developing countries.

Special characteristics: education, income, women

The traditional apprenticeship system is particularly significant for goods production in the informal sector. The on-the-job training provided by artisans for payment in cash or kind is often the only education/training to which children from poor families have access. Informal colleges have sprung up in the absence of formal training institutions. It has been estimated that up to three-quarters of those hired in the informal sector are apprentices without a regular wage (ILO/WEP 1991). After completion of the apprenticeship period, few continue as wage earners in the informal sector since it is more remunerative to set up their own small workshops.

As far as income is concerned, studies in sub-Saharan Africa confirm the general, global trend: earnings of heads of informal enterprises are higher than the official minimum wage, even sometimes higher than the average wage in the formal sector. However, the wages of hired workers are usually lower than in the formal sector, while apprentices often have no wage at all. Income distribution has clearly tilted away from wage earners in favour of the urban entrepreneur (Jamal and Weeks 1993: 123). Moreover:

Wages have fallen in relation to both urban incomes and farm prices, and in the context of heavily eroded wages these trends signify increasing overall inequality. (Jamal 1993: 35)

Women in the informal sector are concentrated on the services side: trade, tailoring and food preparation on pavement stalls. With a few exceptions, notably in West Africa, the women are the poorest in the informal sector, and concentrated in low-productivity activities. One study lists as explanations for this the lower education levels of women, discriminatory legal structures regarding property which restrict their access to credit and labour-market discrimination (ILO/WEP 1991: 45).

Summarizing the impact of structural adjustment

African labour markets have been influenced in a number of ways by the structural adjustment measures: urban formal-sector employment was dramatically reduced; urban wages fell sharply, and, moreover, the wage structure was drastically compressed; and the capacity of the informal sector to absorb the growing number of expelled people from the formal sector slowed down. The informal sector became saturated.

With the public sector in Africa traditionally being the predominant wage-employer, responsible for over 50 per cent of non-agricultural employment, the loss in this sector had a severe impact on modern-sector wage-employment levels. Internationally, Africa had the highest share of public-sector employees in the non-agricultural sector, with 54 per cent, while Asia had 36 per cent, Latin America 27 per cent and OECD countries 24 per cent (Vandermoortele 1991: 92). Among African countries, Tanzania with 78 per cent, Zambia with 80 per cent, Ghana with 82 per cent and Benin with 87 per cent were at the top (Diejomaoh 1993: 2). Several waves of retrenchment rolled over the continent in the 1980s resulting in some 20 per cent of the total employment in this sector being lost through layoffs; the latest wave was initiated in the early 1990s to lay off another 25 per cent to 30 per cent of the labour force (Diejomaoh 1993: 9). Unemployment rates are expected to range between 15 per cent and 30 per cent of the urban labour force (*ibid*; also Vandermoortele 1991: 91). Vandermoortele (1991: 94–8) lists three characteristics of the urban unemployed: their relative young age; their high educational level; and the particular vulnerability of women to unemployment, with a rate twice as high as for men.

While the real wages of urban workers have been reduced drastically, wage figures have to be treated with caution. In view of the importance of non-wage allowances and benefits, Vandermoortele rightly states that wages and salaries only provide an approximation of total earnings. Moreover, family income is derived increasingly from an ever-greater variety of sources: formal- and informal-sector wages, entrepreneurial income and farming proceeds, both urban and rural. Nevertheless, since these other sources have also come under pressure, wage trends do give an indication of total earnings (Vandermoortele 1991: 85). In the first five years of the 1980s real wages fell on average by 25 to 30 per cent. In the period 1975–85 government salaries in a selection of 14 African countries fell by 50 per cent for the lowest-paid workers, and by 60 per cent for the highest-paid ones (Jamal and Weeks 1993: 121). This differentiation points to a compression of the wage structure, which is also indicated by the fact that the difference between the average and minimum wage diminished markedly (by 15 per cent) in the first half of the 1980s (Vandermoortele 1991: 87).

Structural adjustment measures have also affected the division within the urban labour markets between the formal and informal sectors. Urban labour markets have fused, making it no longer possible to maintain a dichotomous view of them as having a high-wage modern sector and a low-wage traditional/informal sector (Vandermoortele 1991: 89). Some observers have even concluded that a wage-earning class has ceased to exist as a distinct entity in Africa. For one, the winding up or privatization of parastatal companies has retrenched many who had no alternative but to look for gainful activity in the informal sector, where the absorbtive capacity is quickly being reached. For a good number of former urban wage-workers this has meant intensifying already long-standing activities to augment the insufficient single-sourced income.

> Urban households now extend their outreach over the whole gamut of economic activities to survive, from wage labour to informal sector to even subsistence farming. (Jamal and Weeks 1993: 122)

The last activity is also referred to as urban agriculture.

Labour-force characteristics

Population growth rates in sub-Saharan Africa are generally high, with Kenya and Côte d'Ivoire having the world's largest growth rate of just under 4.5 per cent per annum. The projected growth rate is 3.1 per cent for sub-Saharan Africa as a whole. However, some researchers have predicted that as a result of AIDS the growth rate might well be restricted to one per cent per year, and some have even suggested an actual decline by the year 2010. By 1990, an estimated 300,000 people in Africa had died from AIDS and some have forecast two million AIDS-related deaths during the 1990s. By mid-1992 the total of HIV-infected adults was conservatively put at 'more than 6.5 million'

(*Current* 1992: 8). In Africa, AIDS is almost as prevalent among women as among men. Projections are that AIDS will kill between 1.5 and 2.9 million women of reproductive age in Africa by the year 2000 (Sanders and Sambo 1991: 162). As Sanders and Sambo argue, the decline in formal employment caused by structural adjustment programmes has led many to look for alternative sources of income, which for women has often meant resorting to prostitution', exposing them to grave risks (1991: 163). Another combined impact of structural adjustment and AIDS is that the (especially urban) health sector is burdened by the increasing demands for the treatment of HIV/AIDS patients while government spending on health is diminishing.

The population in the 15 to 64 age group has reached just over 50 per cent of total population, or 251 million people. The total labour force in sub-Saharan Africa has been estimated at 198 million, of whom 37.6 per cent are female. The percentage of the labour force in agriculture dropped between 1965 and 1989, but only from 79 per cent to 67.6 per cent. The industrial labour force in sub-Saharan Africa also declined in the same period from 8.1 per cent to 7.7 per cent while the labour force in services increased from 12.9 per cent to 24.7 per cent.

Internal labour markets have also undergone a further segmentation process. First, in addition to the dichotomy between permanent workers and casual workers, a further stratification has emerged between higher-skilled and lower-skilled workers, which is again buttressed by structural adjustment strategies. More often than not, this development, as in Zimbabwe, has been supported actively by the national government because of the weakening effect it has on the organizational capabilities of the trade union movement. Second, the introduction of a large variety of employment contracts at the enterprise level through subcontracting and farming out of substantial parts of the production process has added new dimensions to the already staggered internal labour markets.

The impact of these trends on the role and functions of trade unions will be analysed in the following sections.

Future trends for the trade unions

The major changes in the African economic and political landscapes have had many consequences for the trade union movement: the economic crisis and the changes in labour markets eroded the traditional membership base of the unions, while the structural adjustment programmes struck out legislative provisions favourable to labour, in providing job security, participatory rights or guaranteed collective bargaining rights. Moreover, new industrialization policies are aimed particularly at small-scale enterprises, which because of their paternalistic labour relations are a difficult recruiting ground for trade unions. The political crisis found many a trade union with close ties with the ruling political party when workers were looking for alternatives.

The impact of the crisis on the trade unions

Trade union history throughout the continent is varied and so is the trade union structure, reflecting in some instances the colonial past and tutelage. There are divergent trends in trade union membership, diverse across countries as well as across economic sectors. In Southern Africa there has been an upsurge in both private and public sectors in a number of countries (Botswana, Zimbabwe and South Africa). This part of Africa is an exceptional case, however. Botswana has been one of the most successful countries in recent years, a development which was helped by substantial relocation of South African interests in a proactive bid to circumvent possible anti-apartheid sanctions. As the country study of Zimbabwe shows (see Chapter 10), economic progress has ground to a halt. And while the transition in South Africa will herald a new political era, it is unlikely that economic developments will be able to fulfil the expectations of many. Elsewhere in Africa, trade union membership has been dwindling since the late 1980s.

The reasons for the decline in trade union strength have already been alluded to briefly. Some of these are internal to the trade unions, others external. Internal factors are: insufficient attention to democratic structures within the trade unions; too close an alignment with, and sometimes dependence on, the political elite; weak autonomous organizational and financial strength; male dominance; and an almost exclusive focus on the formal, often urban, sector of the economy. A further analysis of these internal factors is provided below (see pp. 193–4). First, though, it might be a good idea to recall the external factors beyond the control of trade unions which have also played a role in their decline.

As stated above, waged and salaried workers are impoverished throughout the continent. Real incomes dropped as a result of rising inflation, sudden and often massive devaluations, and the withdrawal of price controls and food subsidies. It has also been noted that a decline of 50 per cent in the real wage was recorded in the second-half of the 1980s.

Structural adjustment programmes introduced dramatic retrenchment in the public and private sectors alike. At the risk of repetition, a few examples might help the reader to grasp the magnitude of the problem. In Ghana it has been estimated that up to 90,000 workers have lost or will lose their jobs (Zeleza 1989: 36). In Côte d'Ivoire, 30,000 workers in 36 state-owned enterprises were affected by the adjustment programme (Gozo and Aboagye 1986: 370). In Kenya, 149,000 were retrenched, excluding the Teacher Service Commission, while the figures for Nigeria and Zimbabwe are 156,550 and 123,000 respectively (Diejomoah 1993: 10). In the private sector, too, structural adjustment took its toll. For instance, Zambia Consolidated Copper Mines announced in 1986 that 20,000 miners would be declared redundant within five years (Zeleza 1989: 36). For Africa as a whole, one estimate states that structural adjustment measures directly led to the loss of some 3.6 million to 4 million permanent jobs between 1985 and mid-1987 (Zeleza 1989: 36). With cuts of this size, the traditional recruitment grounds of the trade union have almost vanished.

The deconstruction of the large enterprises and the attempts to revive the private sector will require a change in approach by the trade unions. No longer can they rely on the government for improvement in wages and working conditions. Corporatist tendencies as they existed in francophone Africa will increasingly come under pressure as adjustment programmes unfold, limiting the possibility for governments to distribute patronage (Herbst 1990: 952).

An important element in all the recovery programmes – the traditional/orthodox structural adjustment programmes as well as the ones presented within the AAF–SAP – is a focus on the stimulation of small-scale enterprises. If, indeed, these are to substitute for the loss of the large-scale enterprises, then trade unions will have to reorient themselves from the concentration on urban wage-workers in large establishments.

Given the nature of the onslaught on the position of the workers, it is small wonder that unions could do little to prevent the fall in living standards of their members. In addition, as a result of the liberalization policies associated with many structural adjustment programmes, labour legislation was changed: relaxed where it protected organized labour (for example, in the definition of unfair labour practices, including dismissals), and made more stringent where it provided favourable conditions for organized labour (for example, in the definition of the collective bargaining agent).

Trade unions and democratic change
Despite their declining membership, trade unions in various countries still had enough political clout to play an important role in democratic transitions. In Benin, Congo, Mali, Niger and Zambia trade unions

were in the forefront of the struggle for more democratic governance. In South Africa the trade unions played an extremely important role in building pressure for change. At the other end of the spectrum, one finds countries like Zaire where the single ruling party and the union still maintain close ties.

Between these two extremes a fluid situation is to be found. Most unions have opted for a more autonomous position from the political party, and many formal affiliations between union and party have been severed. Cameroon and Tanzania are cases in point. Sometimes this has led to a sudden and dramatic reduction in the financial resources of the trade union because the party stopped its subsidies in both money and kind (for example, free offices and vehicles). Because of this financial tie, in some countries, for example, Mauritania, the relationship between the ruling party and the trade unions is not severed but subject to heated debate. In other countries such as Togo, Chad and Cape Verde, new unions have emerged to challenge the position and strategies of the old guard. These developments have meant that unions have become weaker at the national level, especially in the francophone countries.

In some of these cases, however, the change is not unambiguous. In some instances political leaders of the old guard have reserved for themselves positions within the now autonomous trade union, possibly with the objective of once again using the trade union movement as a springboard for furthering their political agendas. Tanzania is a case in point.

Whatever the position of the trade union has been in these political transitions, in many countries the political elite ruled that the concept of 'one industry-one union' should no longer apply. Moreover, check-off systems, in the past often granted to trade unions as a reward for political support, were withdrawn or are under threat. Both these measures put the trade unions in a precarious organizational position, especially where the initiative has come from the side of the state, and where it has caught the unions unaware.

In the latter case, this imposed autonomy seems to have had a paralysing effect. For others it has proved to be a source of inspiration in the search for new and innovative ways of worker mobilization, in which wider issues than strictly workplace-related ones are addressed on behalf of a broader constituency than traditionally catered for, and in a number of ways, not only through collective bargaining.

Concluding observations

A multifaceted trend is emerging: the internal strengthening of the organization by making full use of the resources at hand, and the simultaneous opening up towards new issues, new members and constituencies, and new strategies.

Measures directed at the internal organization entail a search for ways to improve the reach to traditional constituencies, or what is left of them, and involve rank-and-file members in a more meaningful way. Also required is a recognition of the need to involve women workers more actively in trade union affairs, including governance. This can be done through either autonomous women's sections or integrated empowerment initiatives. There are indications that active cooperation with local NGOs operating in this same field are fruitful (Klugman 1989; Shettima 1989).

Another way to strengthen the organization is by critically reviewing the internal governance of the union. The moves towards a more democratic governance in the wider society have also had an impact on the internal administration of the trade unions themselves. Trade unions in South Africa and Zimbabwe have realized, for example, that democratic internal structures providing for accountability and the active participation of members in the governing of the unions at all levels are a major source of strength. Decentralization drives have accompanied this process. Pressure from the rank-and-file, either in the form of verbal criticism or by members voting with their feet, will add further to this opening up of structures which hitherto have been rather closed. The August 1994 events in Nigeria, where the member unions of the Nigerian Labour Congress (particularly in the petroleum sector, like the National Union of Petroleum and Natural Gas Workers) called a general strike in defiance of their umbrella organization, illustrate the vigour of this development.

The externally geared strategies are multipronged. The fusion of urban labour markets and the closing of the urban–rural gap call for new approaches. To make up for the loss in the modern sector, trade unions will have to open up towards workers in the informal sector and in the rural areas. This will involve different strategies and different tactics. Not only will trade unions have to address different kinds of workers than those who have formed their traditional constituency, but they will also have to address issues of a broader nature in order to attract the non-waged worker while remaining meaningful to the wage-worker who now has to survive on a multiplicity of income sources each with its specific problems. In the South African context, this has been dubbed political or social movement unionism which 'attempts to link production issues to wider political issues' (Lambert and Webster 1988: 21). In this conceptualization, political issues include community issues.

The democratization process has a further dimension. Not only do changes in the wider polity have an impact on the internal governance of the trade unions; these two developments will also reinforce, and in turn be fed by, the drive towards industrial democracy. This means that trade unions will have to come to grips with forms of collective action which are supplementary to traditional collective bargaining with its confrontational nature. Developments in South Africa have moved in this direction. Realizing the need for restructuring in the manufacturing sector, unions now seem willing to accept responsibility for improvements in efficiency and productivity in exchange for a greater say in decision making (see also Maller 1992). As the acting General Secretary of the National Union of Mineworkers stated:

> For us the struggle for greater control over the production process is starting with participation... We are now talking about one of the most critical areas itself, the workplace and participation in decisions made at the workplace...we are beginning to challenge management's prerogative in decision-making over what they believed was their exclusive right... By engaging with employers you begin to understand their psychology and perspective. Not everything an employer says is necessarily wrong. You've got to assess it. So you participate in order to achieve control. It's a process. (von Holdt 1991: 21)

This kind of approach has subsequently been labelled 'strategic unionism', for which it is deemed necessary for the trade union movement to build alliances and coalitions with labour-supporting organizations within the political and academic fields (von Holdt 1992: 33).

The current economic and political transformations also imply a different arena of operation. There is clearly the need for broader strategies. On the one hand, unions have to defend the interests of their members, interests which are becoming more and more heterogeneous as a result of a further widening of the gap in skills as well as of a differentiation in the nature of employment contracts (through subcontracting and casualization). On the other hand, the interests of groups of working people outside the formal, waged sector are coming increasingly into the orbit of the trade unions: women workers, informal-sector workers, the self-employed, rural workers and smallholders.

Strategies which recognize this differentiation in interests and constituencies will include the building of alliances with other groupings in civic society that articulate these concerns, including consumer, human rights, student and women's groups. They will also involve strategic alliances with training and research institutions that can provide the necessary depth of analysis to build viable and above all sustainable bridges. Such a multiple strategic approach would seem to make it possible for a new form of trade union to regain a meaningful position for working men and women.

References

Adedeji, A. (1991) 'Will Africa Ever Get Out of its Economic Doldrums?', in A. Adedeji, O. Teriba and P. Bugembe (eds) *The Challenge of African Economic Recovery and Development*, pp. 763–82. Frank Cass, London.

Adepoju, A. (1991) 'Binational Communities and Labor Circulation in Sub-Saharan Africa', in D. Papademetriou and Ph. Martin (eds) *The Unsettled Relationship: Labor Migration and Economic Development*, pp. 45–64. Greenwood Press, New York.

Brand, V. (1986) 'One Dollar Workplaces: A Study of Informal-Sector Activities in Magaba, Harare', *Journal of Social Development in Africa* Vol. 1, No. 2.

Buijtenhuijs, R. and E. Rijnierse (1993) *Democratisation in Sub-Saharan Africa (1989–1992): An Overview of the Literature*. Research Report No. 51. African Studies Centre, Leiden.

Callagy, T. (1987) 'The State as a Lame Leviathan: The Patrimonial–Administrative State in Africa', in Z. Ergas (ed.) *The African State in Transition*, pp. 87–116. MacMillan, London.

Collier, R.B. (1982) *Regimes in Tropical Africa: Changing Forms of Supremacy 1945–1975*. University of California Press, Berkeley.

Current (1992) *Current and Future Dimensions of the HIV/AIDS Pandemic*. WHO, Rome.

Diejomaoh, V.P. (1993) 'Effects of Structural Adjustment Programmes on Labour Markets in Africa: The Challenge of Public Sector Retrenchment and Redeployment Programmes', Paper prepared for the OATUU/ILO Conference on *Structural Adjustment and African Trade Unions*, Cairo (16–18 April).

Elson, D. (1991) *Male Bias in the Development Process*. Manchester University Press, Manchester.

Ergas, Z. (1987) (ed.) *The African State in Transition*. MacMillan, London.

Ghai, Dh. (1989) 'Economic Growth, Structural Change and Labour Absorption in Africa, 1960–1985', in B. Salomé (ed.) *Fighting Urban Unemployment*, pp. 201–44. OECD, Paris.

Gozo, K. and A. Aboagye (1986) 'The Impact of Recession in African Countries: Stabilization Programmes and Employment', in *The Challenge of Employment and Basic Needs in Africa*, pp. 364–74. Oxford University Press, Nairobi.

Grant, J.P. (1992) *The State of the World's Children 1992*. Oxford University Press for UNICEF, Oxford.

Green, R. (1989) 'The Broken Pot: The Social Fabric, Economic Disaster and Adjustment in Africa', in B. Onimode (ed.) *The IMF, the World Bank and the African Debt*, pp. 31–55. Zed Books, London.

Hayward, F.M. (1987) (ed.) *Elections in Independent Africa*. Westview, Boulder.

Herbst, J. (1990) 'The Structural Adjustment of Politics in Africa', *World Development* Vol. 18, No.7: 949–58.

Hesp, P. (1989) 'Manufacturing in Sub-Saharan Africa: Which Way Out of the Crisis?', *Journal für Entwicklungspolitik* 3: 3–8.

Holdt, K. von (1991) 'Productivity: "Participating to Achieve Control"', *South African Labour Bulletin* Vol. 16, No. 2: 18–23.

——— (1992) 'What is the Future of Labour?', *South African Labour Bulletin* Vol. 16, No. 8: 30–37.

Hyden, B. (1983) *No Short Cuts to Progress*. Heinemann, London.

ICFTU (various years) *Annual Survey on Violations of Trade Union Rights*. ICFTU, Brussels.

ILO/JASPA (1985) *Informal Sector in Africa*. ILO/JASPA, Addis Ababa.

ILO/WEP (1991) *The Urban Informal Sector in Africa: In Retrospect and Prospect: An Annotated Bibliography*. International Labour Bibliography No. 10. ILO, Geneva.

Jackson, J. and C. Roseberg (1982) *Personal Rule in Black Africa: Prince, Autocrat, Prophet, Tyrant*. University of California Press, Berkeley.

Jamal, V. (1993) 'Adjustment Programmes and Adjustment: Confronting the New Parameters of African Economies', Paper presented at the *Rural Development Studies Research Seminar*. Institute of Social Studies, The Hague (17 November).

Jamal, V. and J. Weeks (1993) *Africa Misunderstood: Or Whatever Happened to the Rural–Urban Gap?* Macmillan (for the ILO), Basingstoke.

Kilson, Mo. (1963) 'Authoritarian and Single-party Tendencies in African Politics', *World Politics*, Vol. 15, No. 2: 262–94.

Klugman, B. (1989) 'Women Workers in the Unions', *South African Labour Bulletin* Vol. 14, No. 4: 13–36.

Lambert, R. and E. Webster (1988) 'The Re-Emergence of Political Unionism in Contemporary South Africa?', in W. Cobbett and R. Cohen (eds) *Popular Struggles in South Africa*, pp. 20–41. Review of African Political Economy in association with James Currey, London.

Lubell, H. (1991) *The Informal Sector in the 1980s and 1990s*. OECD Development Centre, Paris.

Maliyamkono, T.L. and M.S.D. Bagachwa (1990) *The Second Economy in Tanzania*. James Currey, London.

Maller, J. (1992) *Conflict and Co-operation: Case Studies in Worker Participation*. Ravan Press, Johannesburg.

Medhanie, T. (1992) 'The Democratisation Process, its Socio-Economic Base, and the Role of the ACP/EEC Economic and Social Interest Groups', report prepared for the Sixteenth Annual Meeting of ACP/EEC Representatives of Economic and Social Interest Groups, Mimeo. University of Bremen, Bremen.

Mihyo, P.B. (1990) 'The Economic Crisis, Recovery Programmes and Labour in Tanzania', *Labour, Capital and Society* 23: 70–99.

Mlimuka, A. and P.A.J.M. Kabudi (1985) 'The State and the Party', in I.G. Shivji (ed.) *The State and the Working People in Tanzania*. Codesria, Dakar.

Moi, D.T.A. (1986) *Kenya African Nationalism: Nyayo Philosophy and Principles*. MacMillan, London.

Mosley, P. and J. Weeks (1993) 'Has Recovery Begun? "Africa's Adjustment in the 1980s" Revisited', *World Development* 21: 1583–606.

Onimode, B. (1992) *A Future for Africa: Beyond the Politics of Adjustment*. Earthscan, London.

Riddell, J.B. (1992) 'Things Fall Apart Again: Structural Adjustment Programmes in Sub-Saharan Africa', *Journal of Modern African Studies* 30: 53–68.

Riddell, R.C. (1990) *Manufacturing Africa: Performance and Prospects of Seven Countries in Sub-Saharan Africa*. James Currey, London.

Rijnierse, E. (1993) 'Democratisation in Sub-Saharan Africa?', *Third World Quarterly* 14: 647–64.

Rothchild, D. (1987) 'Hegemony and State Softness: Some Variations in Elite Response', in Z. Ergas (ed.) *The African State in Transition*. MacMillan, London.

Rothchild, D. and N. Chazan (1988) (ed.) *The Precarious Balance: State and Society in Africa*. Westview, Boulder.

Sanders, D. and A. Sambo (1991) 'AIDS in Africa: The Implications of Economic Recessions and Structural Adjustment', *Health Policy and Planning* 6: 157–65.

Shettima, K.A. (1989) 'Women's Movement and Visions: The Nigeria Labour Congress Women's Wing', *Africa Development* Vol. 14, No. 3: 81–98.

Stein, H. (1992) 'Deindustrialization, Adjustment, the World Bank and the IMF in Africa', *World Development* 20: 83–95.

Tahane, T. (1991) 'International Migration in Southern Africa', in D. Papademetriou and Ph. Martin (eds) *The Unsettled Relationship: Labor Migration and Economic Development*, pp. 65–87. Greenwood Press, New York.

Thomas, C.Y. (1984) *The Rise of the Authoritarian State in Peripheral Societies*. Monthly Review, New York.

Trager, L. (1987) 'A Re-Examination of the Urban Informal Sector in West Africa', *Canadian Journal of African Studies* 21: 238–57.

Turner, T. and C. Young (1985) *The Rise and Decline of the Zairian State*. University of Wisconsin Press, Madison.

Valk, P. de (1992) 'A General Framework for Evaluating the Performance of Textile Enterprises in LDCs', Ph.D. Dissertation. Free University, Amsterdam.

Vandermoortele, J. (1991) 'Labour Market Informalisation in Sub-Saharan Africa', in G. Standing and V. Tokman (eds) *Towards Social Adjustment: Labour Market Issues in Structural Adjustment*, pp. 81–113. ILO, Geneva.

Zeleza, T. (1989) 'The Global Dimensions of Africa's Crisis: Debts, Structural Adjustment and Workers', *Transafrican Journal of History* 18: 1–53.

9. Against Overwhelming Odds: The Zambian Trade Union Movement

Paschal Mihyo

Introduction

The Zambian trade union movement has long been one of the strongest in Africa. Firmly based in the mining area of the Copperbelt, it began by effectively voicing the economic concerns of its members and then evolved into a political opposition. The turning point came in 1973 when President Kenneth Kaunda declared a one-party state ruled by the United National Independence Party (UNIP). The Zambia Congress of Trade Unions (ZCTU) resisted attempts by UNIP first to control it and then to transform it into a wing of the party. From a position of little popular acclaim in the 1970s, the ZCTU developed in the early 1980s into the unofficial national opposition:

> The ZCTU has emerged as a viable *de facto* opposition party. Although in the main still concerned with working conditions and wages, the ZCTU has increasingly pronounced on and often criticized general political matters. (Woldring, in Hamalengwa 1992: 113)

This high-profile political role made the trade unions a major player in the bid for power made by the Movement for Multi-Party Democracy (MMD) in the 1991 elections. Frederick Chiluba, a former chairman-general of the ZCTU and the MMD's most outspoken protagonist, was elected the second president of Zambia, defeating Kaunda by a landslide.

This chapter presents an analytical overview of the role of labour in the events leading to this dramatic development. It also addresses the strategic dilemmas faced by, and options open to, a trade union movement whose leadership has become part of a *de facto* coalition government. Beginning with a short socio-economic background to provide the context, the chapter evaluates the Kaunda administration's development policies, examines the role of the labour movement in the democratization process and, finally, delineates the dilemmas facing trade unions under the new regime.

Socio-economic background

The Zambian economy has been going through a deep crisis since the second half of the 1970s when Gross Domestic Product (GDP) per capita dropped by more than 50 per cent. The 1980s saw a real GDP growth rate of only 0.8 per cent, resulting in GDP per capita of US$390 in 1990 (Simutanyi 1993: 7).

The economy is dominated by copper mining, which for a long time contributed over 90 per cent of government revenues. Mining is the largest employer, although recently its contribution to employment has been reduced by sharp falls in mineral dividends and prices. International copper prices plummeted steeply in the 1980s, halving Zambian terms of trade between 1977 and 1988 (Jamal and Weeks 1993: 84). Copper production fell as well, reaching its lowest level in the mid-1980s. Mining's contribution to GDP halved between 1986 and 1990, reaching 9 per cent (Republic of Zambia 1991: 64). The result was a severe shortage of foreign exchange, affecting adversely the import-dependent manufacturing and agricultural sectors.

The consequence of the country's dependence on mining has been the neglect of the rural sector. The rate of urbanization is significantly higher in Zambia, at 51 per cent, than in neighbouring countries: for example, it is 30 per cent in Zimbabwe and 15 per cent in Tanzania (Loxley 1990: 10; Rakner 1992: ix). However, over 66 per cent of the population of Zambia depends on the rural sector.

Since colonial times the rural sector has suffered from low investment allocations, low producer prices, poor social services, very poor infrastructure and lack of agricultural extension services. This has resulted in the over-exploitation of natural resources in rural areas; rural–urban migration in search of better social services and employment; rapid urbanization and consequent housing and social-service problems in urban areas; rising unemployment in urban areas; and overemployment in public services.

The neglect of the rural sector is reflected in the low contribution of agriculture to GDP over the three decades of Zambia's independence. In the seventies this contribution was estimated at an annual average of 13 per cent, from which it has picked up, to reach 18 per cent in 1990 (Republic of Zambia 1991: 64). The largest contribution has come from large-scale commercial farms concentrated along the railway line provinces. Agricultural production per capita has been declining since 1977 (Jamal and Weeks 1993: 83) while the manufacturing sector has seen its contribution to GDP rise from 22.9 per cent in 1985 to 31.9 per cent in 1990 (Republic of Zambia 1991:64).

The majority of the economically active population lives in the rural areas. The Labour Force Survey of 1986 found that out of a population of almost four million people aged 12 and above, 71.3 per cent were economically active, of whom only 28 per cent were in the urban areas. It was estimated that 52.4 per cent of the labour force was male and 47.6 per cent female. Of the people in formal employment, 55.1 per cent were male and 44.9 per cent female. Zambia has a relatively young labour force, with 30.2 per cent aged between 12 and 24, of whom 82.6 per cent live in the rural areas.

In the first two decades after Independence, a fairly large proportion of the labour force, 30 per cent, was employed in the formal sector, which is unusual in Africa (Jamal and Weeks 1993: 75). In the late 1980s, however, Zambia lost this distinction as retrenchments, especially in the public sector, reduced formal-sector employment, which reached just under 10 per cent of the labour force by 1990 (Rakner 1992: ix). The services sector became the absolute leader in employment, with 47.1 per cent of the workforce in 1988. Mining was second, with 15.2 per cent, followed by manufacturing with 13.9 per cent and agriculture with 10.2 per cent (Loxley 1990: 9). Employment is rather stagnant in agriculture, decreasing in mining, gradually increasing in manufacturing and booming in services.

The Labour Force Survey of 1986 estimated unemployment at 13 per cent. Predictably, most of the female respondents were found to be engaged in unpaid, unassessed and unevaluated housework (Munachongwa 1990). Asked why they did not have regular paid jobs, most said they had no access to business, finance, raw materials, equipment, business information or skills. In urban areas of Zambia, most of the women are in lower-level, low-paid jobs and have longer working hours than men. There are fewer retraining programmes in low-category jobs.

Formal-sector wages rose steeply immediately after Independence, mainly in an attempt to correct the racial wage disparities in mining. Between 1965 and 1970 minimum wages rose by two-thirds in real terms (see also World Bank 1987).

However, as Jamal and Weeks (1993: 75–82) rightly point out, this has not led to the formation of an urban labour aristocracy. In the early 1980s Zambia began to experience the erosion of wages so typical of sub-Saharan Africa. Between 1980 and 1985 the real minimum wage dropped by 25 per cent while the Consumer Price Index rose astronomically from 100 in 1980 to 883 in 1988 (Jamal and Weeks 1993: 81). Low- and middle-income earners were particularly affected as their real incomes declined by an average of 55 per cent over this period (Simutanyi 1993: 10). Since then, inflation has reached double-digit levels: 120.2 per cent in 1989 and 129 per cent in 1990 for low-income groups (Simutanyi 1993: 15).

The policies that led to this state of affairs are the subject of the next section.

The Kaunda regime and its development policies

Zambia was ruled by one party, UNIP, and one president, Kenneth Kaunda, for 27 years under a state of emergency. The president was the sole source of authority and wielded wide administrative powers, including the powers: to impose collective punishment on groups of people or communities; detain people without trial; change the domicile of people within Zambia; declare war without calling the national assembly; and appoint or sack public servants. The president was the top executive of both the government and of the sole ruling party, whose machinery and institutions were politically stronger than those of the government.

A small group of politicians monopolized key decision making in the party and the government. Dissidents were marginalized and kept under surveillance. The one-party system in Zambia promised more than it delivered. While claiming to operate in the interests of workers and peasants, in reality it made their lives worse.

Education was used to popularize the state ideology of humanism and to promote the party and President Kaunda as liberators of Zambia. State power was also used to reward loyalty and punish dissidence. In the public services and enterprises, those who cooperated could be assured of easier access to health, transport, subsidized meals, loans, allowances, imprests and other benefits. These enterprises established institutions such as paramilitary brigades, workers' education departments, cultural groups and political party branches, which were funded directly by the state and the members of which were assured of privileges and material benefits.

Incorporation was also attained in more subtle ways. Takeover and subordination of local organizations and traditional institutions was one of the means used to keep the population under control. Development associations, cooperatives and local authorities were annexed to the state. Leaders, especially of cooperatives and in some cases trade unions, were coopted as party secretaries or members of boards of directors. Where incorporation was difficult, as in the case of the Zambia Congress of Trade Unions, these organizations were made dependent on the state for their existence or legitimacy.

Trade unions, for example, were subjected to controls over registration, acquisition of foreign funds, travel outside the country, international affiliation, recruitment of outside consultants and holding of conferences. Mobilization of finances by means of a check-off system was controlled through employers, most of whom were public enterprises.

Other organizations such as cooperatives were controlled through registration, incorporation within the government departmental structures, appointment of district and provincial leaders, state audits and supervision of expenditure, price and levy regulations, and procedures governing the right of the state to divide, amalgamate, dissolve and suspend registration without consultation or arbitration. As far back as 1975, the government began to form workers' councils controlled by enterprise party branches and state-appointed managers to weaken the trade unions.

Because the nerve centre of political and social action in Zambia was in the urban areas, the government's investment and resource allocation policies favoured these areas over rural ones. The post-colonial government continued the colonial neglect of the smallholder agricultural subsistence sector, and as a result the country became dependent on imports for agricultural products including food, and inputs for the manufacturing and mining sectors.

Poverty increased among peasants and they were deprived of basic social amenities such as health services, water, food and education (Good 1989: 40; ILO/JASPA 1981). Lack of infrastructure made it difficult for rural producers to gain access to urban markets and to purchase basic necessities produced in towns and cities. High transport costs made agricultural products more expensive in the rural areas and urban products more costly in rural areas. While urban areas were well stocked with food and other basic needs, rural areas experienced acute shortages and therefore even higher prices than caused by transport costs.

The regime failed to develop a dynamic policy of rural transformation through small-scale industrialization, support for careful utilization of natural resources and the provision of agricultural extension services. Off-farm income activities were not promoted and rural employment-generation issues remained unaddressed. As a result, young Zambians migrated to towns in search of jobs.

As long as aid and earnings from minerals sustained the populist urban-welfare infrastructure, the government could afford to ignore the migration. However, falling copper prices, combined with droughts and a sharp rise in fuel prices, turned the balance in the late 1970s. The immediate reaction of the government was to try to control the influx into urban areas, and in 1980 it tried unsuccessfully to introduce a pass system. In 1985 it passed laws restricting movement, but those also failed.

The government's second line of attack was withdrawal of the subsidies which had made food cheap in the cities. In 1985 measures to remove the subsidies, introduce school fees and devalue the Zambian kwacha were announced. As devaluation led to a rapid rise in inflation, these measures affected sections of the population that had until then been loyal to the government because it had ensured their relative comfort.[1]

The 1985–86 reforms did not address the key issues. The rural sector remained stagnant and Zambia's historical dependence on copper exports and imported food and consumer products continued. Moreover, the reforms were not based on consultation, their goals were not clarified and their implementation was not consistent. Food subsidies were removed in 1986, partially restored in 1987, and again removed in 1990. The export-earnings retention scheme, under which exporters could retain 50 per cent of export earnings in foreign exchange, was introduced in 1984 but then abruptly and without any explanation cancelled in 1986.

The way the reforms were implemented was an indication of the two conflicting pressures on the Kaunda regime: from urban people, mainly workers, and their unions, who had supported the government and kept it in power for more than two-and-a-half decades; and from international donors. These two groups had different expectations from the government. The urban population wanted continued featherbedding of wages, subsidized food and inexpensive social services, while the donors expected economic reforms leading to structural adjustment. When the government began reversing its policy on subsidies, retention policy and devaluation, donors withdrew their aid. The International Monetary Fund (IMF), for example, withdrew its commitment of US$550 million.

Caught between these two poles, Kaunda tried to organize demonstrations against the IMF; but the bonds between labour, urban youths, university students and UNIP were already cracking. In 1985 the government had passed laws restricting the rights of the unemployed to move within or into urban areas. The same year it banned strikes and removed the check-off system in order to starve the unions of the funds needed to mobilize workers against structural adjustment policies. Therefore, when the government tried to organize demonstrations against the IMF and other lenders, it met with a lukewarm response.

In December 1987, workers began organizing anti-government protests, beginning in the Copperbelt. On the eve of New Year 1987/8, 15 people were killed in clashes with the police in the Copperbelt. In

March 1988 teachers, nurses and medical officers went on strike in defiance of a government ban. An earlier strike by teachers in December 1986 had been condemned by Kaunda as reactionary and anti-people.

In July 1987, with retrenchment causing many job losses, Kaunda gave an ultimatum to all unemployed people to return to the rural areas. However, even if the government had the will to drive the unemployed back to the rural areas, it had no money to resettle them. As UNIP and Kaunda lost the support of their domestic allies, including the unions, they became increasingly dependent on the military, and on 21 July 1987 the Minister for Defence promised a ruthless fight against the government's opponents.

In June 1990, the government announced a 100 per cent rise in the price of maizemeal. This led to three days of rioting in Lusaka, headed by the unions and university students. There followed an attempted coup, which Kaunda survived because of inter-factional rivalries in the army. After the coup attempt, Kaunda loosened his political control and called a general election through which he was swept out of power on 25 October 1991.

The labour movement and democratization

The legalization of one-party rule in 1972 sparked a confrontation between the ZCTU and the Kaunda government. In 1974 the congress elected a leadership, under Frederick Chiluba, that promised to defend its autonomy. The new leaders immediately took steps to strengthen democracy and accountability within the ZCTU and its affiliated unions. All members were given the right to stand for leadership posts, votes had to be cast by secret ballot and no committee had a right to screen aspirants for leadership.

Having established the basis for democracy within the labour movement, the ZCTU leaders began demanding democracy in local and national representative bodies. When in 1980 the government abolished free and multiparty procedures in local-government elections, the move was opposed by the ZCTU (Simutanyi 1991: 14). The government integrated the mine-township councils with the newly formed district councils which would be controlled by UNIP. In response, the Mineworkers' Union of Zambia declared a dispute and organized a strike and demonstration for one week. UNIP reacted by expelling all senior union leaders from its membership (Simutanyi 1991: 15), thus making it impossible for them to continue as union leaders. However, the workers went on strike until the party agreed that the expelled leaders could continue to head their unions.

After this defeat, the government attempted to take control of the unions by sponsoring pro-government candidates in union elections. Most of these candidates were rejected and subsequently given senior cabinet and party posts. Union members remained vigilant against government influence, and votes of no confidence were regularly declared against suspected party protégés. Leaders who accepted party posts while still holding office were removed. Even as late as October 1990, union leaders who agreed to sit on the Constitutional Commission to draft a multiparty constitution were removed from ZCTU leadership (Simutanyi 1991: 19).

Intimidation, surveillance and detention were also used by the government to frighten and silence ZCTU leaders. On several occasions in 1980 and 1986, ZCTU leaders were arrested, detained and released without being charged. The government's signing of an agreement with the IMF in 1983 seems to have been taken by the unions as a declaration of war. The ZCTU moved to the political forefront by targeting the economy and the wages and incomes policy. The sudden price rises in 1985 were painted as a failure of the ruling party's ideology of humanism since they had the effect of widening the incomes gap (Lungu 1986: 402). The research and information sections of the ZCTU kept the leaders fully informed about trends in the economy, making it difficult for the government to undermine the credibility of their public statements (Lungu 1986: 404). Such was the success of the unions that President Kaunda warned during a visit to the Copperbelt in 1984 that the region had become a hotbed of politics (Lungu 1986: 404).

One of the main strengths of the labour movement lay in its democratic organizational structure. This was demonstrated when the government banned the check-off system in 1985, and the workers began voluntarily paying their fees directly to their unions because they viewed the leadership as accountable to them and free from corruption.

The ZCTU avoided a head-on collision with the government until 1986 when the withdrawal of food subsidies led to workers being called out. This happened again in 1990 when food prices were doubled. Following the June 1990 riots, the MMD was launched with Chiluba, the ZCTU chairman, as the vice-chairman in charge of administration and organization. ZCTU district committees became MMD committees and district and regional trade union leaders mobilized extensively for the MMD. This made the victory of the MMD in the October 1991 elections an almost foregone conclusion.

The ZCTU seems to have had its political role thrust upon it. Rakner (1992: 59) points out that while the ZCTU consistently took the lead in the struggle against the government, it had no intention of replacing UNIP or of becoming a political party. She quotes Alec Chirwa, secretary-general of ZCTU, as saying in September 1991 that the unions would return to their traditional role as soon as another political party replaced UNIP.

Rakner cautions against viewing the ZCTU and MMD as merely two aspects of one entity or regarding the Zambian experience as being replicable by unions elsewhere in Africa. The unsuccessful attempt by Chakufwa Chihana to win enough seats to form a government in Malawi shows that the victory of the MMD was due to more than the combination of an unpopular government and mobilization of workers.

Rakner attributes the achievement of the ZCTU to three main factors:

- a long history of struggle against undemocratic policies and tendencies;
- the mobilization by the ZCTU leaders of other basic organizations and social movements;
- and the extensive network of trade union committees in various sectors and provinces of Zambia which could be used to campaign for multiparty democracy and the MMD (Rakner 1992: 57–69).

Other factors also came into play. Timing was crucial. Although the ZCTU had openly fought for democracy, it did not commit itself to the fight to restore multiparty democracy until 30 December 1989, when at the ZCTU General Council Chiluba declared that Africa had to get rid of one-party democracy since the nations that had founded the concept had abandoned it in Eastern Europe.

A second important factor was the opening of the multiparty debate within the ranks of the ruling party by the ZCTU. At the UNIP national convention in March 1990, the ZCTU tabled a policy paper calling for multiparty politics in Zambia. Although this was rejected by the convention, it placed the issue on the table.

Another factor contributing to the electoral success was cross-social participation in the protests. When the price of maizemeal was doubled in 1990, the government expected protests on the university campus as had occurred in 1988 and 1989, but the riots began mainly in the inner-city quarters of Lusaka and spread to the city centre, with the students joining the compound dwellers.[2] The alliance of students, unions and the unemployed took the government by surprise. A suspicion that soldiers from the junior ranks had helped to plan the riots seemed to be borne out by the coup attempt that followed immediately. At the end of June 1990, a national interim committee was formed to press for multiparty democracy and the ZCTU was asked by the other groups to lead the campaign. On 17 July 1990, Kaunda and UNIP reluctantly lifted the ban on opposition parties, and the Movement for Multiparty Democracy was launched three days later.

Immediately after the formation of the MMD, the ZCTU began to create distance between the two organizations, making it possible for non-unionized sections of the population to support it as an independent party. When Chiluba was nominated to stand for the national presidency in the 1991 general elections, he resigned from the ZCTU leadership. Likewise, Arthur Wina stepped down from the position of secretary-general when he became chairman of the MMD. The distancing reassured the business community and investors that the MMD would not be a puppet of the unions after the general elections.

In 1991 the ZCTU began a campaign of strikes and politicization, with teachers taking the lead. In April 1991 secondary school teachers began an open campaign for the MMD. The National Union of Communication Workers (NUCW) joined the campaign, and its networking on behalf of the MMD so alarmed the authorities that a month before the general elections the Posts and Telecommunications management issued a circular ordering the union to restrain its members from actively participating in politics during working hours.

The 1991 strikes were not only about pay. Some were about governance. In February 1991 the Hotels and Catering Workers' Union of Zambia accused the Minister of Tourism of concentrating on irrelevant issues instead of showing interest in the well-being of the industry. Between March and May workers at the Zambian National Savings and Credit Bank organized four sit-ins demanding the removal of the manager for alleged corruption and lack of contact with workers. In May the general secretary of the Zambia National Union of Teachers openly called for 'capable people to run the system' after 3,000 Standard VII pupils were left out of the computer in national examinations (*Times of Zambia*, May 1991).

Later that year, another wave of strikes focused on issues of efficiency, transparency, accountability and professionalism. Staff of the two Zambian universities took the lead and kept the pressure on until the general election in October 1991. Public servants also kept the government under pressure. In February 1991, eight months before the general elections, they started challenging retrenchment plans, and the unions declared an indefinite strike after negotiations failed. On 7 August, the government tried to mobilize the population against these strikes by claiming that they were politically motivated.

On 10 August, health workers went on strike and the government brought in prisoners to clean hospitals and remove corpses from wards and mortuaries. In spite of the government's attempts to isolate the health workers by painting a horrific image of the effects of the strike, the general public supported the strikers. Doctors joined the walkout after eight days, and after two weeks most hospitals had come to a standstill. Other public servants also went on strike and the dispute continued until September when the government awarded all public servants a 100 per cent salary increase backdated to 1 August 1991.

To maintain the loyalty of the police, army and security forces while the strikes were on, the government awarded them salary increases ranging from 100 per cent to 170 per cent in August 1991.

In conclusion, it can be said that the ZCTU succeeded in leading various social groups against the government because of its long history of independence and its refusal to be incorporated into government and party structures. After the MMD was formed, the ZCTU continued to work with it for democratization, with the two organizations being autonomous but closely linked. The final success of MMD is primarily attributable to the widespread industrial action by various unions, coordination by the ZCTU and the capability of the MMD itself to form an effective network of alliances between various social movements including the trade unions.

The trade unions under the MMD regime

Six of the ministers in the new MMD government were former ZCTU leaders. Most prominent among these were, of course, Chiluba himself and Newstead Zimba, former secretary-general of the ZCTU. Thus, the MMD achieved overnight what UNIP had been unable to accomplish: the decapitation of the ZCTU. It took almost a year before the vacancies were filled.

During its final months, the Kaunda government had introduced a new Industrial Relations Act which abolished the one industry–one union' policy, and the unions expected the MMD to keep its promise to revoke that. However, the MMD did not do so, causing a split in some sections of the labour movement. The government also faced a number of strikes for higher wages.

New unions are being formed among banking employees, miners, teachers, university staff, medical staff and journalists. Although the established unions favour pluralism in political life, they do not want to see this multiplicity extended to industrial organization. They consider a legislated one industry–one union rule the best guarantee for a strong labour movement. The others, however, believe that competition would strengthen the labour movement by enhancing democracy and accountability.

This dispute has given an unfavourable impression of the established unions, one that is strengthened by the ZCTU's continuing hostility towards Work Councils at the enterprise level. The councils, elected democratically but controlled by UNIP and state-appointed managers, were created in the 1970s to undermine the trade unions and so they were shunned by the ZCTU. In the new political era, the unions have failed to work out a way to involve the councils in the labour movement and instead are looking forward to their abolition through a new labour law.

In general the unions are critical of the MMD government but cooperative. The ZCTU has condemned the government's failure to introduce new legislation and is sceptical about plans to reorganize the existing social-security systems under one umbrella fund. Strikes are supported reluctantly. In 1993 the strikes that received ZCTU backing were called off because they had lost public support. In 1993 wage negotiations were settled at a maximum of 50 per cent while the unions had initially demanded 300 per cent, even though inflation was recorded at 193 per cent between April 1992 and April 1993.

The unions have accepted a place in two new fora for national-level consultation: the Permanent Tripartite Labour Consulting Council and a broadly constituted National Economic Advisory Council comprising representatives of churches, chambers of commerce, the university, cooperatives and trade unions. The participation of the unions has not prevented anti-labour changes. The right to strike, which survived the UNIP government, has been undermined, with employers now being allowed to dismiss striking workers summarily.

The union leadership is relatively new and seems to lack experience. It operates in an international environment that supports democratization but does not seem to favour strong unions or effective collective action. The alliances with church groups and students, which were forged during the last years of the Kaunda administration, fell apart after the elections. It may take a few years before the unions gather their strength again to continue their championing of democracy, equality, equity and accountability.

The coming years hold several challenges for the ZCTU. First, it has to devote more time to re-examining its power base. Traditionally it has depended on formal-sector labour and has ignored the organizational strength of the informal sector. Both the state and the ZCTU have failed to take aboard the wide network of informal-sector organizations based on the *chilemba* system. These organizations, though unregistered and informal, have played a big role in mobilizing, regulating and representing informal-sector operators. They organize credit, procurement, land and other allocation systems, and have recognized leaders and a membership structure. The ZCTU could endorse these organizations and take them under its wing. Doing so would also enable it to address issues particular to young people and women as these two groups are represented to a significant degree in the informal sector.

Also needing attention is the power-bargaining model inherited by the ZCTU from the colonial industrial relations system. This model, which has been taken for granted by unions and the state, assumes that unions will remain a united force and will be able to exert their power on the labour markets. Inflation and intra-union fragmentation have, however, reduced the capability of unions to bargain for economic gains as a united force. This changed situation calls for a new agenda of union and worker empowerment through specialized training programmes to increase the skill base of labour and after-work counselling to help workers prepare for unemployment or retirement. These schemes would significantly reduce worker dependence on the enterprise system and strengthen the position of unions.

The ZCTU has to formulate a new economic programme. Rural–urban migration, trade liberalization and labour-market reforms continue to affect the strength of the unions, and the ZCTU needs to influence state policy on resource allocation between urban and rural sectors, environmental rehabilitation and rural industrialization. Issues of technology for rural and urban non-farm and on-farm producers, which have an impact on the future of organized labour, could be made part a broad-based national agenda for unions to enable the translation of political gains into sustainable economic benefits.

As Zambia prepares for the new millennium, the ZCTU has the potential to take the lead in seeking out new avenues for widening the economic base of union power and strength.

Notes

1. The government's increasing inability to deliver welfare services as a result of the drop in copper prices and the rise in fuel prices had already alienated the unions at the beginning of the eighties, with the ZCTU president promising that the Congress would continue highlighting the problems besetting the nation 'without sweeping any dirt under the carpet' (*Times of Zambia*, 21 October 1981).

2. For more on the riots, see Omari and Mihyo 1992.

References

Good, K. (1989) 'Debt and the One-Party State in Zambia', *The Journal of Modern African Studies*, Vol 27, No.2: 297–313.

Hamalengwa, Munyonzwe (1992) *Class Struggles in Zambia and The Fall of Kenneth Kaunda*. University Press of America, Lanham.

ILO/JASPA (1981) *Narrowing the Gap: Planning for Basic Needs and Productive Employment in Zambia. Report to the Government of Zambia, by a JASPA Employment Mission.* ILO/JASPA, Addis Ababa.

Jamal, V. and J. Weeks (1993) *Africa Misunderstood or Whatever Happened to the Rural–Urban Gap.* MacMillan, London.

Loxley, J. (1990) *Structural Adjustment and Rural Labour Markets in Zambia,* WEP Research Paper 10–6/WP 10A. International Labour Office, Geneva.

Lungu, C.F. (1986) 'The Church, Labour and the Press in Zambia: The Role of Critical Observers in a One-Party State', *African Affairs* Vol 85: 385–410.

Munachongwa, M.L. (1990) 'Women and the State: Zambia's Development Policies and Their Impact on Women', in J.L. Parpart and K.A. Staudt (eds) *Women and The State in Africa.* Boulder and London: Lynne Rienner Publishers.

Omari, I.M. and P.B. Mihyo (1992) *The Roots of Student Unrest in African Universities.* Man Graphics, Nairobi.

Rakner, L. (1992) *Trade Unions in Processes of Democratization. A Study of Party Labour Relations in Zambia.* Michelsen Institute, Bergen.

Republic of Zambia (1991) *Monthly Digest of Statistics,* April/June 1991. Government Printer, Lusaka.

Simutanyi, N.R. (1991) 'Trade Unions and the Democratization Process in Zambia', Mimeo. Institute of African Studies, University of Zambia, Lusaka.

——— (1993) 'Organised Labour, Economic Crisis and Structural Adjustment in Africa: The Case of Zambia', Paper prepared for the conference 'Poverty and Developing Countries'. University of Sussex, Brighton, 8–10 September 1993.

World Bank (1987) *Zambia: Country Economic Memorandum, Economic Reforms and Development Prospects.* World Bank, Washington DC.

10. The Emergence of Civil Society: The New Place of Unions in Zimbabwe

Freek Schiphorst

Trade unions in Zimbabwe, as we know them today, are a relatively new phenomenon. Before Independence in 1980 the development of a black trade union movement was severely hampered by colonial rules and regulations. After Independence the government sought to create a societal order in which black labour was given a better deal, but at the same time organized labour was controlled. Moreover, the Zimbabwe African National Union–Patriotic Front (ZANU-PF), the ruling party, sought to subordinate the trade union movement by converting it into its labour wing in accordance with the prevailing ideology. To achieve these ends the government has intervened several times in the industrial relations system since 1980. This has made for a troubled adolescence for the nascent trade union movement.

At the same time, political and economic realities provided a difficult learning ground for the emerging labour movement. The defence of the interests of labour was a novel phenomenon to many managers and owners. The fact that ownership structures remained unaltered inspired many owners to persist in their attitudes towards labour. Not only was the trade union movement not consulted prior to the introduction of the Economic Structural Adjustment Programme (ESAP) in 1991; it also discovered that it had lost the small safeguards that existed. After an initial period of confusion, the umbrella body of the trade unions, the Zimbabwe Congress of Trade Unions (ZCTU), attempted to steer an autonomous course. This did not meet with unequivocal support from the ruling party or even from within its own ranks. However, the trade union membership on the whole welcomed the move as well as the drive towards decentralizing ZCTU activities.

The following sections will present an overview of the political background and the developments in the Zimbabwean economy from a labour perspective. Finally, the developments in the trade union situation will be analysed.

The political situation

In 1923, colonial Zimbabwe, or Southern Rhodesia as it was then known, became a self-governing colony when the British South Africa Company withdrew and the white settler population voted against a federation with South Africa. White settler interests ruled the country until formal political independence was achieved in 1980. In between, the country was part of the Central African Federation, a short-lived (1953–63) political merger of what are now Zambia, Malawi and Zimbabwe which aimed to further entrench white rule in Southern Africa. After the collapse of the federation, white politics in Southern Rhodesia hardened, culminating in the Unilateral Declaration of Independence (UDI) by the Ian Smith regime in November 1965. This led to international economic sanctions which, though frequently undermined and certainly not effective, to some extent shaped the structure of the country's economy. In the early 1970s a liberation war started, with Tanzania, Zambia and, after 1974, Mozambique being used as bases by the guerrillas. The 1979 Lancaster House Agreement marked the end of this protracted war between the forces of the Zimbabwe African People's Union (ZAPU) and the Zimbabwe African National Union (ZANU) – combined in the Patriotic Front (PF) – against the Smith regime.

The agreement included provisions for the transitional period after political independence, covering sensitive issues such as the ownership of land and guaranteed political representation for whites. In the new parliament, this meant that 20 per cent of the seats were reserved for whites. The remainder were contested in the first free elections of March 1980. Robert Mugabe's ZANU-PF won a landslide victory, securing 57 per cent of the seats. John Nkomo's PF-ZAPU obtained 20 per cent, while 3 per cent went to Bishop Abel Muzorewa's United African National Council. Although reconciliation was the catchword of the day, racial differences continued to play a role in parliamentary life. When after seven years the reservation clause in the Lancaster House Agreement for 20 white seats lapsed, the clause was abolished and the vacancies filled by presidential appointees.

If attempts at reconciliation best describe the racial politics, then national unity would be the phrase for politics in general (Moyo 1992: 22). The Patriotic Front alliance between ZANU and ZAPU was short-lived. Tension between the two parties heightened early in 1982 after arms caches allegedly belonging to PF-ZAPU were discovered. This was also the start of what was later called the 'dissident problem' in Matabeleland, the stronghold of Nkomo's party. The dissidents were brutally repressed by the Fifth Brigade of the army. Despite this massive show of force, PF-ZAPU managed to maintain most of its support and won 15 per cent of the seats in the 1985 elections, while ZANU-PF won 64 per cent. Unity talks began after the elections, resulting in the merger of the two parties into ZANU(PF) in December 1987. Soon after an executive presidency was created with Mugabe as its first incumbent with 'the omnipotent powers typically given to executive presidents in a one-party state' (Moyo 1992: 30). Subsequently, Zimbabwe's constitution was amended, abolishing the senate and enlarging the single-chamber parliament by 50 per cent to 150 members with 30 seats reserved for presidential appointees.

There was, however, some opposition to this move towards a one-party state, from within as well as outside the party. One internal dissident was Edgar Tekere. After accusing the ZANU(PF) leadership of corruption and non-adherence to its own Leadership Code throughout 1988, he became the first person to be expelled from the party in October 1988. Following anti-corruption demonstrations by students in late 1988, a special commission of inquiry named after its chair, Justice Wilson Sandura, was appointed to investigate allegations of corruption in the distribution of vehicles to ministers and members of parliament. Its public hearings drew large crowds and were covered almost verbatim by the press. In what quickly became known as the Willowgate scandal several ministers were found guilty of illegally buying and selling scarce vehicles and subsequently resigned. This first widely publicized evidence that the ZANU(PF) Leadership Code was not taken seriously by some sections of the ruling elite created fertile soil for political opposition.

This was the stage on which the Zimbabwe Unity Movement (ZUM), a new party founded by the expelled Edgar Tekere one year before the 1990 general elections, arrived. The initial response of the political elite was to give ZUM the cold shoulder, and then to ridicule it. The slogan 'ZUM will zoom itself into doom' became popular amongst ZANU(PF) supporters. However, ZUM soon attracted a substantial following, especially in urban centres and university circles, by exposing the non-democratic tendencies in ZANU(PF). In the elections, ZUM received over 17 per cent of the votes. Because of the constituency system this translated into only two parliamentary seats instead of the 21 which a proportional system of representation would have generated. One more opposition seat went to ZANU (Ndonga) led by the veteran politician Ndabaningi Sithole. ZANU(PF) secured 117 seats in addition to the 30 presidential appointees.

ZUM's creation put the spotlight on the determination of powerful factions in ZANU(PF), including the president, to introduce legislation transforming Zimbabwe into a one-party state. In the debate during the months preceding the elections, it became clear that public opinion was against this move (Mandaza and Sachikonye 1991), and the idea was abandoned after the elections.

The ZCTU was eventually forced to take a public stance on the issue. Faced with internal divisions over the question of undivided loyalty to the ruling party and the president, the ZCTU decided it could not impose a line of action on its members over an issue that had been debated so widely and with such divergence of opinion. This neutrality led some in ZANU(PF) to accuse the ZCTU of planning to become a political party. The ZCTU's secretary-general responded by stating that while the trade union movement was definitely a political force, it was certainly not a political party.

In the ensuing years ZUM disintegrated under factional struggles, and during the run-up to the 1995 elections merged with Muzorewa's party in what many saw as a marriage of convenience. More credible opposition is provided by the Forum Party of Zimbabwe, led by Enock Dumbutshena, the country's first chief justice.

All the opposition parties are mainly urban-based and voice urban grievances. In contrast, ZANU(PF) has carefully nurtured and wooed rural people, who constitute 75 per cent of the population, depicting the party as 'synonymous with their well being, prosperity and security' (Deve and Gonçalves 1994: 9).

The attacks by the ZANU(PF) leadership on the ZCTU have to be seen against this background. The only organization which could stand any chance as an opposition movement was the ZCTU, which provided a concerted voice and had started to establish branches at the district level. Even though the ZCTU repeatedly stated that it did not want to be a political party, the ruling elite feared a repetition of the events in Zambia, where a trade union leader had ousted the incumbent president. Consequently, efforts were made to try and discredit the ZCTU's leadership as well as to stimulate labour organization outside the ZCTU. They were unsuccessful.

The growing number of parties in Zimbabawe does not reflect a rich diversity of opinions on policy issues. On the contrary, Zimbabwean politics is more governed by personalities than programmatic differences, let alone ideological disputes. This is exemplified by the fact that exchanges between the parties consist almost entirely of dismissal of each other's leaders as 'tired old men' or dumped and recycled leaders.

Economic developments from a labour perspective

The formal sector

Zimbabwe is not a typical African economy. It inherited a large formal sector with an advanced and diversified manufacturing sector from its colonial past (Riddell 1992: 226). Manufacturing has a fairly long history in Zimbabwe. Around 1940 the sector was already responsible for 10 per cent of GDP and employed seven per cent of the formal sector labour force (Riddell 1990: 338). Since then it has expanded continuously. The federation period (1953–63) was favourable to growth as it established a large internal market. The major source of growth during this period was import substitution (Riddell 1990: 352).

Sanctions during the UDI period (1965–79) led to controls over foreign exchange and profit repatriation. These compensated for the loss of investment incentives and ensured the availability of capital for the production of import substitutes. The result was a shift away from dependence on tobacco exports towards a diversified export package including metal working and mining products. Commercial agriculture also provided new openings in food and cotton processing. Consequently the 1965–74 period showed a rapid expansion in manufacturing.

Domestic demand declined sharply during the 1974–9 war period, while inputs of skilled labour and capital were squeezed. Simultaneously, the first global oil crisis took its toll, further curtailing the import of manufacturing inputs. After 1983 the expansion of domestic demand, rather than 'an active policy of import substitution' (Riddell 1990: 341) or exports, accounted for the sector's growth. Since 1992 the domestic market has collapsed and manufactured exports have declined (ILO 1993: 71).

National income

Zimbabwe's per capita income stood at US$650 in 1989 but fell to about US$590 after the 40 per cent devaluation in 1991. The 1992 and 1993 devaluations lowered it even further. Immediately after Independence, the nominal GDP growth rate had been quite spectacular (21 per cent for 1980–82). This was due in part to one-off factors such as good rains, the removal of sanctions and the return to international legitimacy, but increasing confidence among investors and the growth in consumers' purchasing power also helped. However, GDP growth slowed dramatically from 1982 onwards. The 1983–4 drought, the fall in world mineral prices, foreign exchange shortages and the erosion of purchasing power all contributed to this. Despite these difficulties, Zimbabwe experienced an average annual growth rate during the 1980s of over four per cent, even reaching five per cent towards the end of the decade (Stoneman 1992: 94). This trend continued after 1990, but was reversed by the 1991–92 drought, the worst in recent history which resulted in a negative growth rate of 7.7 per cent in 1992. A modest positive growth rate of 1.6 per cent was projected for 1993 (EIU 1994: 3).

Sectoral composition
The sectoral composition of GDP shows that manufacturing is consolidating its leading position: its share increased from 27 per cent to over 30 per cent during the 1987–92 period. Although 1992 and 1993 were bad years for manufacturing, estimates for 1994 are optimistic (EIU 1994: 5).

Zimbabwe has a large commercial agricultural sector, dominated by some 4,000 white farmers who, together with 400 black commercial farmers, own more than half of all the agricultural land, all of it of the best quality in terms of fertility and rainfall. Agriculture's share in GDP rose from 14 per cent in 1987 to 22 per cent in 1992, with one-third being produced in the peasant sector.

Employment
During the first decade of independence, employment in the formal sector registered only a small increase of about 1.5 per cent, or some 18,000 jobs, per year. With 250,000 school-leavers entering the labour market annually in the late 1980s, un- and underemployment rose sharply. Despite the series of currency devaluations which increased the cost of capital, Muzulu (1994: 222) concludes that this has not led to a significant shift by labour to the manufacturing sector. This is corroborated by the ILO (1993: 36). In short, although the manufacturing sector increased its contribution to GDP, its capacity to generate new employment lagged behind.

A similar trend can be observed in commercial agriculture. Here, the introduction of minimum wages after Independence induced an increase in mechanization. Combined with the effects of several droughts and the restriction on retrenchments introduced by the Labour Relations Act (1985), this led to a decline in employment of some 63,000 jobs between 1980 and 1984. Since then, the total figure has increased again, reaching 304,200 in 1991. However, the share of formal agricultural employment in total formal employment has decreased steadily from 40 per cent in 1964 to 24 per cent in 1991. The impact of the 1992 drought is not yet reflected in the labour statistics but it will be substantial.

On a more structural note, recent years have seen a marked shift from permanent employment to a variety of non-permanent, casual employment contracts, since these are less protected by the Labour Relations Act. The ratio of casual employees on commercial farms rose to 42.2 per cent by 1993 (ILO 1993: 26; Loewenson 1992). This casualization of labour also extends to industry, where there is a particularly significant transfer from full-time to part-time employment among women (ILO 1993: 41).

Some sectors have registered a significant rise in employment. In education employment rose by 162 per cent between 1980 and 1991; over the same period, health services and public administration showed an increase of 74 per cent and 34 per cent respectively, while in the non-subsidized sector finance recorded an increase of 45 per cent (EIU 1993: 13). The organization of labour in these sectors, however, falls outside the scope of the trade unions. Public-sector workers, nurses and teachers are only allowed to form associations, not trade unions.

Whereas in absolute figures formal-sector employment remains fairly constant, when related to the total labour force it continues to register a decline. Its share dropped from 40 per cent of the labour force in 1980 to 31 per cent in 1992 (ILO 1993: 26). In a total population of 10.4 million, the labour force is 3.94 million. Of these, 1.2 million people are employed as wage earners in the formal sector.

Overall trade union density was 24 per cent in 1992 according to official figures (28 per cent when corrected for clear under-registration). This is an increase over the 20 per cent in 1984 calculated by Wood (1988). As already shown by Wood, great variations exist between sectors. For example, in 1984 he found densities as high as 85 per cent in Post and Telecommunications (PTC) and 80 per cent in Railways, but also as low as 7 per cent in agriculture, chemicals and petroleum, and domestic services, and 1 per cent in electricity and water (Wood 1988: 295). In 1992, agriculture had a density of 6.6 per cent, domestic service 3 per cent, and mining 69 per cent. Interestingly, the public-sector associations increased their ratios from 35 to 40 per cent over the period.

Massive retrenchments have swept the formal sector since 1991 as a result of the ESAP. Estimates of their magnitude vary widely. Official figures vary from 12,736 to 17,383 (ILO 1993: 141 and 142) between 1991 and early 1993. The employers' confederation puts the figure at 7,000 for 1992, while the ZCTU claims that 20,000 workers were laid off that year (ILO 1993: 44). One astute observer of the country's labour scene holds that in agriculture alone, some 40,000 jobs are feared lost as a combined result of the adjustment policies and the 1991–2 drought (Sachikonye 1992a: 91). Some 28,000 jobs are threatened in the public sector including the parastatals, while in the private sector commerce and industry are estimated to have retrenched 20,000 workers between 1991 and 1995 (Sachikonye 1992b: 24).

Wages

The introduction of the Minimum Wages Act in 1980 increased formal-sector wages but inflation soon eroded this gain. Only two sectors, agriculture and domestic services, recorded a small net increase in 1988. It should be noted, however, that these two sectors had extremely poor wages and working conditions in colonial times. Despite the initial small improvements, labour conditions on the commercial farms led the ILO to conclude that

> clearly the farm workers operate at the margin of bare survival, and their situation has worsened compared to a decade ago. ESAP, with its emphasis on wage restraint, subsidy reduction and decontrolled prices, spells further austerity for the farm workers. (ILO 1993: 58)

Real wages in other sectors eroded gradually after an initial increase immediately after Independence. The introduction of the ESAP in 1991 accelerated inflation. It reached an unprecedented 35 per cent in 1991 and 47 per cent in 1992. The prices of everything except the staple food of maizemeal and fresh milk were decontrolled early in 1991. However, the liberalization of agricultural prices affected low-income urban families disproportionally since over half of their budget is spent on food (ILO 1993: 39). The 1992 Consumer Price Index rose 60 per cent for low-income urban families, while the increase was only 40 per cent for high-income urban families (ILO 1993: 69).

Wage increases negotiated by collective bargaining in 1991 were, on average, only half of the inflation rate, while after the devaluation of September 1991 inflation increased to over 47 per cent. In addition, the ESAP introduced cost recovery measures which were equally hard-hitting: school fees were introduced in urban areas and a fee for health services was introduced for people earning more than Z$400 a month. Both these measures have led to a drop in the consumption of these services by the poorer strata in urban society, particularly women (Hanmer 1994).

McPherson (1991) notes that supplements to insufficient urban incomes have usually been sought in urban farming or home-based, small-scale manufacturing activities. Preliminary data show that wages now represent about 75 per cent of the household income, while the remainder primarily consists of transfers from the rural areas and entrepreneurial activities (ILO 1993: 120). The ZCTU has opened a special desk to assist would-be small-scale entrepreneurs with loan applications. Unfortunately, very few applications have been successful. The next section will deal in more detail with entrepreneurial activities in the small-scale, informal sector.

The informal sector and small enterprises

Numerous regulations and controls severely hampered the development of the informal sector before Independence:

- Africans were barred from apprenticeship training;
- Africans were not permitted to start their own businesses outside designated areas;
- movement to and in urban areas, and within these in white residential areas, was restricted to black Africans with legal residence and those who were formally employed.

These restrictions resulted in poor development of craft technology and poor access to markets before 1980. Since then, however, 'the conditions making for a large informal sector have been at least as powerful in Zimbabwe as elsewhere' (ILO 1993: 85). After Independence the government immediately announced in its policy document *Growth with Equity* that it would provide the sector with the necessary infrastructure and assistance to promote productive employment (Republic of Zimbabwe 1981).

Additional policy documents have further acknowledged the role of the sector. The Transitional Development Plan (1982–85) conceded that the formal sector was unable to absorb all new entrants to the labour market and proposed a large, urban and dynamic informal sector to provide additional incomes. Recourse to this sector for employment creation was again taken up by the government when it initiated its liberalization programme, and later its structural adjustment programme. The documents announcing these programmes (for example, Republic of Zimbabwe 1991) include encouraging paragraphs devoted to the possibilities of small investors in the informal sector. These announcements were not, however, followed by action, leading one observer to label them mere window-dressing meant to impress foreigners (Friedrich 1992: 178–9). Within the perspective of the desired advancement of black entrepreneurship, the discussion assumed a high public profile and an effective lobby group entered the scene with the formation of the Indigenous Business Development Centre in December 1990. However, the Confederation of Zimbabwe Industries, the lobby group for the large, often white-controlled industrial enterprises, dispelled any notion of strong linkages between the small-scale and large sectors when it ruled out subcontracting for Zimbabwe.

The historic legal constraints contributed to the existence of a strong rural component in the informal sector in Zimbabwe, while the urban informal sector developed in earnest only after 1980. The rapid growth of the smallholder sector helped to create a favourable environment for rural non-agricultural, informal activities (ILO 1993: 85). For historic reasons, the people working in the sector had low levels of formal education until approximately 1985 when secondary school-leavers unable to find other employment entered it (Ndoro 1990: 15). In view of the limited growth prospects in formal-sector employment, the ILO (1993: 13) has advised 'that more attention should be devoted to promoting more productive employment for educated youth in the rural and informal sectors'.

A country-wide survey has established that more than 845,000 enterprises, with an average size of 1.84 workers per enterprise including the owner, provide regular employment to 1.6 million people. Two-thirds of these enterprises are located in rural areas and the rest in urban areas (McPherson 1991: 7–13).

The sector comprises services, repair and maintenance, and production. Services include easy-entry activities such as street-hawking and car-guarding. In both rural and urban areas, the milling/grinding of maizemeal is important. Under repair and maintenance, one finds car repair (panel beating, spray painting, mending of punctures) as well as repairing of watches, shoes, radios and bicycles. The manufacturing sector is dominated by knitting and crocheting, with carpentry, upholstery and welding playing a lesser role.

Manufacturing activities predominate, accounting for almost 70 per cent of the enterprises while 23 per cent are engaged in trading activities. The majority of urban manufacturing enterprises are active in textiles and wearing apparel, in which the firms are the smallest (McPherson 1991: 11–13). A disturbing characteristic observed by Ndoro (1990: 16) is the low level of technology in all these activities and their lack of technological innovation.

Two-thirds of the small-scale enterprises are run by women, while 57 per cent of the total number of workers are female. Enterprises run by women are substantially smaller than those run by men, while the latter also have more male employees (McPherson 1991: 18–19). While women are involved mainly in petty trading, female proprietors of small enterprises are also found in textile, food and beverage, and tobacco production. Sectors dominated by male owners are wholesale trade, construction and metalwork (McPherson 1991: vii).

Few data are available on incomes in the sector. However, it is likely that incomes in easy-entry activities such as hawking, crocheting and services are under double pressure. On the one hand demand is declining; on the other, more and more people are forced to turn to these activities because of drops in real formal-sector wages and the ongoing retrenchments (Mhone 1994: 48). It is exactly in these activities that women are most active. The 1991 nationwide survey showed that the majority of the female-run small-scale enterprises contribute less than half of the family income, while almost 70 per cent of the enterprises run by men provide half or more of family income (McPherson 1991: 20).

Child labour can be found in commercial agriculture, peasant farming, domestic service, the small-scale industries of the informal sector, subcontractors to manufacturing, and in 'street' jobs (Loewenson 1991: 20). However, exact data on this are unavailable. In agriculture, the use of child labour peaks during the cotton harvest, both on commercial farms (Loewenson 1992: 53) and in the peasant sector (Reynolds 1991). Parents are often forced to send their children to work. Many children do not work in family enterprises but for an employer.

The number of street-children in urban areas has been growing. Loewenson reports that approximately 30 per cent of these children are girls involved in selling cooked food, collecting refuse and prostitution. Boys are active in car-guarding and cleaning, shoe-shining, recovering scrap metal and making toys out of it, and selling fruits and vegetables, sweets, cigarettes, matches and watches. One survey found that 60 per cent of the children had taken to the streets because of poverty. Another 20 per cent were influenced by their parents while the remainder cited, among other reasons, abuse at home and peer influence (Loewenson 1991: 26). Sachikonye (1989) notes that children are also involved in informal activities of a more productive nature such as carpentry, basket-making, welding and fence-making. Wages are low and some do not receive any wages because they are regarded as apprentices. With the implementation of the ESAP in full swing and without far-reaching plans to alleviate the accompanying social consequences, it has to be feared that the number of street-children will only increase.

It is against this political and socio-economic background that the development of trade unionism in Zimbabwe has to be seen.

The trade union movement

The trade union movement was divided and weak at the time of Independence, divided not only along racial lines, but also along skill lines. The existence of black trade unions was permitted only after 1959. Membership was drawn from unskilled labour. Operating in a hostile environment the unions were susceptible to the same rifts and factions that characterized the nationalist movement from the 1960s.

After Independence the new government favoured the creation of a new umbrella organization, and this led to the formation of the Zimbabwe Congress of Trade Unions in 1981. At its inaugural congress, the minister of labour personally ensured the election of a leadership loyal to the party. These officials were veteran trade unionists who had gained their experience in unions operating under duress, which, as Wood (1987, 1988) points out, had led to a clientèlist form of unionism. The lack of democratic structures in such unions was continued in the ZCTU, resulting in numerous instances of corruption, maladministration and unconstitutional actions. Mitchell (1987: 116) concludes:

> The first four years of the ZCTU's existence were nothing short of disastrous. The image presented to the public was that of individuals and cliques quarrelling among themselves, united only in their subservience to the Ministry of Labour.

It was finally realized both within trade union circles as well as in ZANU(PF) circles that such a situation was no longer tenable. After the intervention of the new minister of labour, which resulted in a short period during which the ZCTU was administered by officials from the ministry, a ZCTU congress was held in 1985 at which a new type of leadership emerged. Though these new leaders were younger and more energetic, they were unable to give the trade union movement an impeccable image. Throughout the 1985–89 period, the ZCTU stumbled from one financial or administrative scandal to another. Internally divided, the congress lacked the political will to formulate clear policy positions that could provide workers with alternatives to government policy. The situation was further compounded by the weak financial and organizational resources of the unions and the ZCTU.

All in all, it is impossible to escape the conclusion that up to that time the ZCTU was not able to attract a leadership strong and committed enough to be credible to trade union members throughout the country. The ZCTU president elected in 1985, Jeffrey Mutandare, was rather popular among workers for his straightforward manner and fearless comments on government policy, but he also presented the ZCTU as a junior partner of the government and was unable to resist the temptations of his office. Even after seven years, many workers did not accept the ZCTU as truly their organization. Workers related first to their own union and only then to the national centre.

After 1985 the relationship between the government and the ZCTU entered a new phase characterized by indifference. It seemed as if practically all the government's attention was directed towards the introduction of new labour legislation and its reception in the business community. The quasi-corporatist strategy of keeping organized labour in check by controlling or coopting its leadership having failed, the ruling party turned to legislation and the institutionalization of collective bargaining to achieve control. (For a detailed overview of this period, see Shadur 1994.)

The Labour Relations Act (1985) was a major tidemark in the development of industrial relations in Zimbabwe. The Act granted the right to form trade unions and laid down the procedures for collective bargaining at the national level. Furthermore, it defined the fundamental rights of workers and protected them from unfair labour practices and discrimination on any ground.

Trade unions criticized the Act for banning strikes in a large number of 'essential services' and providing lengthy and cumbersome arbitration procedures in other services. The provisions which allowed for workers' committees to be formed at the shopfloor level also caused bad blood, since these operated completely outside the trade union framework. Unions perceived the Act as an attempt to undermine them.

Collective bargaining started in earnest after the Act's introduction. In the beginning the government played an active part in the process. It determined the parameters, that is, it indicated the range of wage increases allowed. Moreover, the government's practice of annually announcing the increase in the minimum wage had two effects on unions: it reduced the strength of the trade unions because workers realized that their gains came from the government, and not as a result of organized collective action; and it encouraged employers to argue that the announced minimum wage was the maximum they had to pay. As such, the minimum wage announcement had much more influence on the wage determination process than did collective bargaining.

Hostility continued between the government and the ZCTU. The tensions heightened in the pre-election year of 1989, which also marked the beginning of a third phase in government–ZCTU relations. In 1988, following the election of Morgan Tsvangirai as its secretary-general, the ZCTU underwent a spring-cleaning. Tsvangirai reinstated sound administrative principles and a sense of professionalism in the head office and then moved to establish principles of democracy and accountability in the ZCTU.

He initiated a strategy to establish regional structures through which the organization would be more easily accessible to rank-and-file workers. In a speech to the ZCTU's 1990 congress, the organization's newly-elected president, Gibson Sibanda, reflected this new approach by arguing that political pluralism also had implications for the freedom of association. Nevertheless, the economic policies of the government called for a strong, united and democratic labour movement:

We need unity, not only within our ranks, and democratic policies within our organizations. The cry for democracy elsewhere will not spare us. (Loewenson 1990: 59)

In addition, the secretary-general personified the new forces within the movement that sought to broaden the basis of the ZCTU. At the organizational level, this was reflected in initiatives to open regional and district offices. Formal as well as solidarity alliances were sought with other groups and organizations in society such as the Organisation of Collective Cooperatives in Zimbabwe, human right groups and students.

From its public statements it also became apparent that the ZCTU no longer subscribed to a narrow view of the concerns of the labour movement. The ZCTU not only criticized wage freezes and price increases, but also urged a boycott to protest increases in municipal taxes and led the campaign against plans to build a Z$100 million civic centre in Harare. A major point of criticism of the ZCTU in 1989 was the government's new policy to attract foreign investment and subsequent initiatives to liberalize labour laws, in particular the law on dismissals. In addition, in 1989 the ZCTU challenged time and again the extension of the emergency powers which outlawed strikes in a wide range of essential services. Furthermore, the ZCTU resisted attempts by ZANU(PF) to bring it under the aegis of the party as a mass movement. Finally, it opposed the proposed transformation of Zimbabwe into a one-party state.

While the trade unions adopted an increasingly independent stance, a series of strikes occurred in 1989, 1990, 1992 and 1994 in which a variety of workers demanded higher wages and better working conditions. Some were wildcat strikes while others, like the railway workers' strike in 1992 and the PTC strike in 1994, received the full backing of their union. The 1994 action led ultimately to the official denouncement of management and a victory for the union. The way in which the union and the ZCTU operated during this strike earned them wide acclaim from workers.

Other walkouts occurred in the public sector, which was outside the organizational purview of the ZCTU. The government reacted to these protests by giving in to the demands of the higher-skilled workers but not to those of the lower skilled in an attempt to divide the labour movement. Whether this will have a long-term effect remains to be seen. The immediate short-run effect was that the associations of nurses and teachers were drawn more closely to the ZCTU and attempts to merge their organizations were accelerated. The same divide-and-rule tactics can be seen in the covert support which splinter unions received and the widespread media coverage given to some disgruntled ZCTU council members.

Another governmental strategy to deal with organized labour became clear with the introduction of the Labour Relations Amendment Act in 1992. The ZCTU was never meaningfully consulted about the Act and considers it an attempt to undermine the position of the unions through legal means. Two aspects of the Act that it finds especially disturbing are the fact that legal strikes have become virtually impossible, and that Works Councils now have the power to negotiate collective agreements with enterprises which can supersede national agreements between unions and employers' organizations. Public protests against the Bill met with a massive show of force by the riot police.

Summary

The 1980–94 period witnessed a confrontation between government and organized labour on several fronts. First, there was direct government intervention in the organization of labour. This intervention had dual motives. Some politicians still had the desire to bring the ZCTU under the aegis of the party, at least at the beginning of the period, while others wanted to control organized labour and ensure successful implementation of the ESAP. Amendments to the labour legislation played an important role in this attempt to check the influence of the trade unions. Possibilities for collective action were curtailed and collective bargaining was further undermined by handing more powers to shopfloor organizations than to trade unions.

Trade unions were initially convinced of the need to pursue free collective bargaining but gradually realized its limits. On the one hand rising inflation would dissipate whatever gains were made at the negotiating table; on the other, if collective bargaining were the only course of action it would exclude large groups of workers. Furthermore, it would do little to counterbalance managerial efforts to make workers more loyal to the company rather than to the unions. In bargaining, moreover, the leverage of the unions was increasingly undermined by the growing numbers of un(der)employed willing to accept any job, no matter how poorly paid or protected.

Consequently, the ZCTU changed from junior partner to the government to full-fledged player. In the wake of substantial retrenchments the trade union movement realized that it had to cater to a wider constituency; not only the waged workers in the formal sector, but also the retrenched workers, the unemployed and those working in the informal sector, as well as workers on the communal lands which again, as in colonial times, had become a dumping ground for those who could no longer afford to live in urban areas. If this could be labelled a widening of the constituency downwards, there was also a widening upwards towards the semi-professions. Therefore, the ZCTU widened its traditional constituency by reaching out to persons employed by the government, for example, nurses and teachers, and struck alliances with other groups, notably students, human rights organizations and the cooperative movement. All this was in defiance of the government's continuing attempts to divide and rule the labour movement.

Thus, the movement responded to the realization that in order to play a meaningful role in Zimbabwean society it could no longer lean against the big shoulder of ZANU(PF), but rather had to peg out an autonomous course. This it did. Time and again the ZCTU reiterated that it was not affiliated to any political party. It vigorously attacked ZANU(PF)'s economic adjustment policy, not just because of its effect on trade unions, but because it negatively affected the livelihood of millions of people. The ZCTU also attacked the political system for its exclusion of rural farm workers from the vote in the Rural Councils as they were not property owners. At the same time, the trade unions tried to strengthen their bases on the shopfloor by extending their organization to regional and district levels. Where possible, they also aimed at teaming up with workplace representative bodies in order to achieve concerted and strong empowerment of workers (Schiphorst forthcoming). In short, the ZCTU embarked on a serious attempt to represent the interests of workers and the community of which they are a part through collective bargaining and enterprise forms of worker representation, and by addressing issues at the district, regional and national levels.

References

Deve, T. and F. Gonçalves (1994) 'Whither the Opposition in Zimbabwe?', *Southern African Political and Economic Monthly* Vol. 7, No. 8: 9-11.
EIU (1993) *Country Profile 1993/94 Zimbabwe*. Economist Intelligence Unit, London.
—— (1994) *Country Report Zimbabwe* (2nd quarter). Economist Intelligence Unit, London.
Friedrich, H.J. (1992) 'Strukturanpassung in Simbabwe', *Afrika Spektrum* 27: 159–85.
Hanmer, L. (1994) *What Happens to Welfare When User Fees Finance Health Care? The Impact of Gender on Policy Outcomes–Theory and Evidence from Zimbabwe*. ISS Working Paper No. 180. Institute of Social Studies, The Hague.

ILO (1993) *Structural Change and Adjustment in Zimbabwe*. Interdepartmental Project on Structural Adjustment, Occasional Paper No. 16. ILO, Geneva.

Loewenson, R. (1990) 'ZCTU Watershed Congress', *Parade* November 1990: 25, 29, 55 and 59.

—— (1991) 'Child Labour in Zimbabwe and the Rights of the Child', *Journal of Social Development in Africa* Vol 6, No. 1: 19–31.

—— (1992) *Modern Plantation Agriculture: Corporate Wealth and Labour Squalor*. Zed Books, London.

Mandaza, I. and L. Sachikonye (eds) (1991) *The One Party State and Democracy: The Zimbabwe Debate*. SAPES Books, Harare.

McPherson, M.A. (1991) *Micro- and Small-Scale Enterprises in Zimbabwe: Results of a Country-Wide Survey*. Gemini Project, Washington DC.

Mhone, G.C.Z. (1994) 'Can ESAP Sustainably Transform the Non-Formal Sectors in Zimbabwe?' (parts 1 and 2), *Southern Africa Political and Economic Monthly* Vol. 7, No. 7: 47-9; Vol. 7, No. 8: 41-45.

Mitchell, B. (1987) 'The State and the Workers' Movement in Zimbabwe', *South African Labour Bulletin* Vol. 12, No. 6/7: 104–22.

Moyo, J.N. (1992) *Voting for Democracy: Electoral Politics in Zimbabwe*. University of Zimbabwe Publications, Harare.

Muzulu, J. (1994) 'The Impact of Currency Depreciation on Production Techniques in Zimbabwe's Manufacturing Sector', *Development Policy Review* Vol. 12, No. 2: 211–24.

Ndoro, H. (1990) 'The Informal Sector and Unemployment in Zimbabwe: A David Without a Sling Versus Goliath?' *Southern Africa Political and Economic Monthly* Vol. 3, No. 11: 15–16.

Republic of Zimbabwe (1981) *Growth with Equity: An Economic Policy Statement*. Government Printer, Harare.

—— (1991) *Zimbabwe: A Framework for Economic Reform*. Government Printer, Harare.

Reynolds, P. (1991) *Dance Civet Cat: Child Labour in the Zambezi Valley*. Zed Books, London.

Riddell, R. C. (1990) 'Zimbabwe', in R. Riddell (ed.) *Manufacturing Africa: Performance and Prospects of Seven Countries in Sub-Saharan Africa*, pp. 337–411. James Currey, London.

—— (1992) 'Manufacturing Sector Development in Zimbabwe and the Côte d'Ivoire', in F. Stewart, S. Lall and S. Wangwe (eds) *Alternative Development Strategies in Sub-Saharan Africa*, pp. 215–37. MacMillan, Basingstoke.

Sachikonye, L. (1989) 'Child Labour in Hazardous Employment in Zimbabwe', *ZIDS Consultancy Report* (for ILO). Zimbabwe Institute of Development Studies, Harare.

—— (1992a) 'Zimbabwe: Drought, Food and Adjustment', *Review of African Political Economy* No. 53: 88–94.

—— (1992b) 'Structural Adjustment, State and Organised Labour in Zimbabwe', Mimeo. Zimbabwe Institute of Development Studies, Harare.

Schiphorst, F. (forthcoming) 'Worker Representation in Zimbabwe', Ph.D. Thesis. University of Leiden.

Shadur, M.A. (1994) *Labour Relations in a Developing Country: A Case Study on Zimbabwe*. Avebury, Aldershot.

Stoneman, C. (1992) 'The World Bank Demands its Pound of Zimbabwe's Flesh', *Review of African Political Economy* No. 53: 94–6.

Wood, B. (1987) 'Roots of Trade Union Weakness in Post-Independence Zimbabwe', *South African Labour Bulletin* Vol. 12, No. 6/7: 47–92.

———— (1988) 'Trade Union-Organization and the Working Class', in C. Stoneman (ed.) *Zimbabwe's Prospects: Issues of Race, Class, State, and Capital in Southern Africa*, pp. 284-308. MacMillan, Basingstoke.

Part Four: Concluding Observations

11. Challenges Facing Trade Unions

Henk Thomas

The six case studies in this book have shown the precarious situation in which trade unions find themselves in Asia, Latin America and Africa. The case studies are presented against the background of broad, interdisciplinary continental overviews which provide an analytical framework within which the predicaments facing trade unions in most of the Third World can be better understood. The finding that stands out is the loss of power, in economic, social, and political terms, of the trade union movement during the last decades. In particular, broad societal problems of access to, and quality of, employment pose challenges which the trade unions generally have not been able to address.

The challenges faced by the trade union movement in many parts of the world call for new approaches that may imply institutional renovations, new tasks, and even new ways of cooperation with other societal institutions.

New roles for the trade union movement are naturally related to the old traditions of protecting workers and better equipping people for work, and of struggling for wider emancipation and democratization. However, given the fast and dramatic structural changes taking place in national and international labour markets, it appears that so far the trade union movement has been unable to assert itself with respect to both employment conditions and worsening power relations.

While it is almost self-evident that trade unions should be a key actor in the search for a new role, the findings of the preceding studies do not hold out much hope for a speedy breakthrough in such a direction. Even allowing for the numerous problems experienced by trade union movements, including those of leadership and internal democratic functioning, it is clear that the overriding causes of their weakness lie in the changes that have occurred in the broader political and economic environment.

The three continental overviews cannot but leave the reader with the perplexing impression that the trade union movement in these continents is not only in crisis as a national actor, but also in large parts of the world has already stopped playing a prominent role as a national institution or is being prevented from developing in such a direction. The specifics of this situation vary in different parts of the world. This chapter reviews the findings in each of the three continents and then presents some thoughts on four crucial issues which call for research, dialogue and action from the perspective of labour organization.

Asia

The most disturbing finding is probably that in *East And Southeast Asia* rapid industrialization and economic development have been successfully pursued and partially achieved by governments, economic institutions, owners of capital and management of enterprises, while allowing only a heavily controlled, if not severely oppressed, trade union movement.

Labour and work formed, and still form, strategic variables as inputs in the various economic sectors. The cheapness of labour was of strategic importance in the early stages; at the present stage its human capital formation calls for close state monitoring. The rights of workers and the level of their earnings are strictly dictated by macro-economic policy making in which there is little scope for organized labour but to play a ceremonial role at the national level. At the enterprise level, management–labour relations are tightly defined by the dictates of competitiveness rather than direct social concern and responsibility for equity and workers' rights. At best, this is an unstable situation politically in the long run.

The Malaysian case study not only reflects all these tendencies, but adds further problems because of particular national characteristics related to deep ethnic divisions, and the prominent role played by the electronics sector, with its large female workforce.

In South Asia, the trade union movement has been formed as part of a largely colonial heritage of industrial relations legislation. Given the relative lack of economic success in this part of the world, and the abundant labour-markets, the trade union movement has a weak presence in enterprises as well as outdated institutions at the national level. In the absence of new strategies, dismal labour market conditions and gradual exclusion from national political involvement compel the trade union movement to cling to past achievements. Thus the unions tend to defend their tenured membership in enterprises that increasingly also hire workers on temporary arrangements; to oppose privatization of public enterprises since they cannot provide a safety-net arrangement for those who will lose their jobs as a result; and ignore child labour other than by opposing the low wages paid to children since those undercut even further the weak bargaining position of the unions.

Tragically, such situations offer hardly any scope for the institutional overhaul needed so badly by the trade union movement. The bridging of gaps between national trade union institutions and workers' organization at shopfloor and enterprise levels especially calls for urgent attention.

The Pakistan case, with its very weak labour market, feeble political system and deep ethnic divisions, typically represents adversities for which a trade union movement that is to function within precisely defined industrial relations systems is simply not equipped. Support structures such as can be provided by institutions that are independent of but sympathetically linked with the trade union movement and above all the appearance of a new generation of trade union leaders provide, in the words of the author of the Pakistan study, a silver lining; the international labour movement may have to take on the heavy responsibility of co-designing new strategies and even participating in their implementation.

Latin America

Here long-term political and economic trends, and waves of history, have had deep impacts which are traceable in almost all countries. Undoubtedly, the history of the trade union movement forms an important part of political and economic developments in Latin America since the early part of this century, and so has been part of these long-term processes.

During the first decades of this century, the numerous links with labour movements in European countries ensured that the issues and debates of those movements were taken up in Latin America. The import substitution strategy (ISI) that was implemented in relatively large markets allowed trade unions to achieve major gains. As long as macro-economic balances could be sustained, this model was sufficiently flexible to permit transition from easy to dynamic import substitution and transformations in the labour market, such as the substitution of higher skill levels for unskilled work in strategic economic branches. Most importantly, relatively high wages ensured strong consumer demand in national protected markets.

The trade union movement was judged to be sufficiently important to be a partner in corporatist nation-state development or to form a strategic component in populist alliances. In this way, it became a partner in creating the well-known dualism that forms one of the central aspects of Latin American social development.

However, in the economic as well as political and ideological senses, the trade union movement gradually acquired a prominence which was no longer tolerated by the dominant societal groups. This explains the violent anti-democratic developments in the 1960s and 1970s during which human and labour rights were violated on a large scale and many leaders lost their lives.

The manifestation of the debt crisis in the early 1980s dramatically exposed the vulnerability of the industrialization and development strategy that had been implemented for so many decades. The resulting changes in the economic and social fields confronted the trade union movement with developments for which it was ill prepared even though it had been deeply involved in alliances with all groups that aimed at restoring democracy.

Abrupt changes from import substitution to liberalization of markets, the introduction of new technologies and new, flexible labour-relations practices put the entire trade union movement conceptually on the defence. The more so since large categories of work in small and micro enterprises, and in home work, were emerging to which the trade union movement had no attachment; on the contrary, grass-root movements, NGOs and even new ideologies of the type advocated by de Soto[1] seemed to have no place for a trade union movement.

The Chilean trade union movement suffered most dramatically under the military regime, yet with great courage it has played one of the leading roles in the struggle for democracy up to the present. However, now, in the process of regaining its old national status through agreements of concertation, it is discovering that economic conditions have changed. Informalization of the labour market with social dualities, and new management patterns in open international competition, leave no scope to gain any benefits for its members at the macro level. The state is preoccupied with gradual, controlled but steady reduction of poverty at the price of wage restraints and in no way intends to reinstitute its old role of prime interlocutor for the labour movement. At the same time, the business community does not lose any opportunity to weaken the labour movement and develop direct enterprise–worker loyalties.

The Venezuelan case is an example of extreme and corrupting incorporation from which the dominant trade union movement failed to recover when economic realities changed completely during the 1980s. Although the trade union movement had not suffered major setbacks in the political domain as had been the case in most of Latin America, it had no answer to the dramatic social dualities and erosion of the political and economic system that took place in the 1980s. As a result, grass-roots movements and alternative organizations appear to be the only institutions with which the poor classes can identify.

These two cases are clear illustrations of the overall Latin American political, economic and social history. Although recent political events were different in the two countries, the developments in labour markets and business attitudes indicate that the strength of the trade union movement can never be reconstituted merely through a new political and more independent role. It is hard to see how a long-term future can be secured without a complete redesigning of objectives, institutions, membership and capabilities founded in these new economic and social realities. Yet a base of historical strength survives to take on these new challenges.

Africa

An inflated image of the role that can be played by trade unions in the continent has been conveyed by recent events such as the destruction of apartheid in South Africa and the struggle for democracy in Nigeria. While much credit goes to trade unions in a small number of countries for their autonomous struggle to democratize the political process, regrettably in most countries authoritarian regimes have the upper hand. Their heavy control of the trade unions is due mostly to the absence of successful industrialization as well as to the heavy concentration of trade union membership in the public sector.

The long-standing lack of recognition in the political field has now been supplemented with more devastating trends in labour markets. There is no part of the world where labour markets offer a gloomier outlook to those seeking work and incomes. Dramatic falls in earnings, sharper even for wage earners than the average national reductions in income, massive retrenchment in public-sector employment and the absence of job creation in medium- and large-scale enterprises have destroyed any possibility of the trade union movement's acting as a stable institution in labour-market development and transformation.

The migratory flows of various kinds and enormous expansion of informal-sector activities are clear symptoms of structural economic weaknesses that need to be overcome. A complete overhaul of economic strategies is called for, with human resources development and promotion of technological innovations in small and micro-enterprises, in particular, figuring prominently. All these developments are heavily at odds with the experience, membership and institutional frameworks of the trade union movement. A new concept of strategic unionism has been coined to indicate possible new directions; but also to indicate that alliances with other social partners should be built and strengthened in order to ensure some effectiveness.

The case of Zambia shows an historically strong labour movement with a relatively sound economic base, the copper mines. For many years it succeeded in opposing attempts by the authoritarian regime to incorporate it. Indeed, it was a leading actor in bringing down the Kaunda regime and establishing a democratically elected government. The challenge then was to adjust to this new political situation. Here one observes a typical example of a movement in search of its mission under a changed environment.

The developments in Zimbabwe provide grounds for more optimism. Here a young trade movement has gradually succeeded in loosening the controls of the corporatist state machinery. The economic base, while shaken by structural adjustment, is still in good enough shape to ensure some stability in trade union membership. Also, programmes of international cooperation have been designed to further enhance institution building. Again it should be noted, however, that labour-market developments such as the growing prominence of small and informal production and the complex situation of women workers pose many fundamental challenges.

Issues and challenges

This review has raised four themes that pose new challenges to the trade union movement: reconstitution of labour markets, informalization of labour relations, women and the trade union movement, and a reformulation of the content of trade unionism.

Local, national and regional labour markets
An approach towards trade union studies, or for that matter employment and labour studies, which takes wide geographical regions

as a point of departure, offers some major advantages over alternative methods. Aspects of labour, work and employment should be defined in larger contexts than those that are defined by national borders, given the globalization of economic forces, of patterns of industrialization and technological developments, and of capital-market developments. In spite of this, however, national definition continues to be the common approach towards trade union studies and labour relations patterns.

The inherent limited mobility of people and the ingrained tendency of power coalitions to create labour-market segmentation and fragmentation imply that local, national and regional, rather than global, labour markets should form the bases for organization of all kinds of workers in trade unions.

Three areas where action is needed have been identified in this study:

- Labour relations need to be defined more precisely in individual firms and enterprises. The century-old traditions of adversarial strategies will become less and less effective as trade unions are increasingly confronted with new patterns of Japanese industrial organization that make use of sophisticated systems of networking with small-scale production; such networks extend geographically as well as sectorally.
- At national level trade unions will need to address issues of macro-economic policy formulation if they wish to exercise any decisive influence on the functioning of labour markets, creation of employment and distribution of earnings and incomes.
- At a regional level there is a need for institutions that address issues such as regional industrialization and technology development, and their impact on migratory patterns and regional labour-market consequences.

It looks, therefore, as if trade union studies, and for that matter research into employment, labour and working conditions, should focus on three areas: enterprise and sectoral dimensions, national-level issues and regional developments.

Informalization of labour relations

Extensive informalization of labour relations, whether in formal or informal sectors, has become a major characteristic of the labour and work situation in many countries. This process has not yet crystallized into predictable patterns. In East Asia, for instance, the informal sector has been much reduced and yet new informal work patterns are being initiated through casualization of work. In parts of Africa, the structural shocks of macro-economic management have been so deep that, for example, it will be some years before new balances emerge between urban and rural labour markets and new mobility patterns become apparent. In Latin America it remains to be seen how the conditions of sizeable urban masses whose earnings do not allow a crossing of minimum survival lines can be improved.

These processes have been analysed in depth for more than a decade. An important finding in some cases has been that fluctuations in one part of the informal economy coincide with fluctuations in the macro economy, whereas another part displays exactly countercyclical behaviour.

Also, the differentiation between dynamic small enterprises, surviving micro-enterprises and household work undertaken under conditions of direst poverty hold important implications for patterns of labour relations and policy interventions. Again, major differences have been observed between countries and regions.[2]

Relevant informal-sector phenomena such as labour organization, working conditions and access to employment, many of which are poverty related, have not been given a high policy priority so far by the trade union movement.

If the trade union movements, especially the national ones, do not change course and take up informal-sector work as their key policy concern, it is hard to see how they can continue to exist as more than skeleton institutions which lack social legitimacy.

It will take much institutional energy to become familiar with the enormous complexities of social relations of production in these spheres, namely enterprises, households, multiple jobs, mobility patterns and social-security systems, yet it is hard to see how this challenge can be avoided.

Women and trade unions

The discrimination against women in labour markets and the pro-male bias in development policies have been analysed extensively in recent years. For instance, the strategic role that women as a low-cost production factor have played in Free Production Zones as part of a Third World industrialization strategy is well documented. Also, more generally, discrimination in earnings and working conditions – in our study the evidence from East Asian labour markets is telling – constitutes an issue that has received much attention. Furthermore, the over-representation of women in vulnerable working conditions in the informal sector forms a central theme in numerous gender-oriented studies.[3]

The issue of multiple identities of women in the context of trade unions deserves more attention than it has received so far. These identities relate to family, community, workplace and state (Chhacchi and Pittin forthcoming).

The ambivalence of the traditional trade union movement towards these issues and female labour leadership is well known. Unless women are allowed and assume leadership and articulate the interests of their constituencies, the trade union movement will continue to be seen as defending narrow, male interests only. Debates and research over the past decade have shown that fundamental issues are at stake.

A central theme concerns autonomy, whether in the sense of separate organizations or separate departments within existing trade union structures. Thus, should women strive after feminization of the existing trade union movement or should they organize independently and associate closely with extensive networks of new social movements? One example of the latter strategy has been the Self-Employed Women's Association (SEWA) in India which has received widespread attention. Whether this can be duplicated in South Asia and other parts of the world is as yet unclear.[4]

Another articulation of autonomy is the promotion of women's departments in trade union organizational systems. The union movement all over the world has allocated such institutional space for women's issues of work and employment, yet it seems obvious that much more needs to be done before women workers and female leadership will view the trade union as representing their interests. To put it more bluntly, it is often observed that women's departments form isolated units which are placed outside the mainstream of trade union activities.[5]

It should be noted, however, that because the gaps in culture, analysis and approach towards women's work between trade unions and women's movements and organizations are very wide, these strategies will probably have major impacts only in the long run. In the short and medium terms, the most feasible strategy is to extend wide the dialogue and cooperation on an equal footing between women's social movements and trade unions.

Trade unionism and employment

With the onslaught of the global debt crisis it has become extremely difficult for the trade union movement to define its role beyond, or as a replacement for, well-established patterns such as of collective bargaining and adversarial behaviour towards management.

However, given the enormous problems faced by workers – inequalities of power, violation of working rights, and vulnerabilities of different kinds – which are made more complex by global aspects of environmental sustainability, one wonders whether the time has not come to design totally new goals and action programmes that would address these issues and give new meaning and ideals to trade unionism. The fundamental points of departure for this would be the creation of productive employment and the nature of working conditions in local, national and regional labour markets.

Partial approaches cannot give hope of access to work and decent income for men and women in widely differing labour markets. Multipronged strategies will be required which will call for a high degree of political determination.

In the wake of more than a decade during which the international stage was dominated by structural adjustment, balance of payments problems and debt burdens, with neglect of social issues and worsening of employment opportunities, it has been encouraging to note that the 1995 UNDP Global Social Summit adopted the global employment situation as one of its lead themes, along with poverty and social disintegration. This gives the trade union movement an opportunity to participate in defining the problems and searching for solutions.

Apparently concern has arisen that most serious imbalances prevail in gaining access to productive employment for unacceptably high numbers of people in large parts of the world. In another 20 years' time the global labour force will have risen by another billion people to a total of three billion, a low estimate if we assume that many more women would join if opportunities were available.[6]

Phenomena such as national and international migration, child labour, social clauses – whether or not attached to international trade agreements – vulnerable and exploitative conditions of work in the informal sector and absence of safety nets provide only the beginning of any serious agenda to overcome huge problems which men, women and, too often, also children experience in the daily struggle to survive.

A list of policies would minimally include attention to appropriate macro-economic measures, human resource development, technology enhancement in informal production systems, labour-market initiatives and a strengthening of male and female entrepreneurship in small and micro enterprises.

Regrettably it took a long time for the labour relations dimensions of structural adjustment to be analysed. While it would be unfair to blame only the trade union movement for this, it is legitimate to expect from it a solidly professional approach in the search for solutions. The forming of networks with NGOs, relevant experts and interested research groups may well provide a feasible road to address these complex new challenges.

Somewhat ambitiously one might call such strategy the beginning of a new approach towards economic democracy. Only time will tell whether or not there will be scope to provide a viable new orientation to concepts such as industrial democracy and participatory work relations. Trade unions in development are confronted with challenges as great as, if not greater than, the labour movement has faced since the early days of the industrial revolution.

Notes

1. De Soto has become known globally for his thesis that the legal institutions which are associated with the formal sector of medium- and large-scale enterprises should be broken down. Such a policy supposedly will free the full potential which is available in the informal economy as it places the small enterprises in that sector on an equal competitive footing with larger firms.

2. For extensive literature on small-scale and informal production and labour relations, see the bibliographical information in Chapters 1,2,5 and 8.

3. See, for example, Elson (1991); Chhacchi and Pittin (forthcoming), and Psacharopoulos and Tzannatos (1992).

4. For recent sources on women's mobilization and information on SEWA in particular, see Rowbotham and Mitter (1994) and Rose (1992). A classic source on these themes is the Report on Self Employed Women and Women in the Informal Sector in India (National Commission 1988).

5. A recent programme evaluation report on the development of women's departments in a number of Southeast Asian countries yields very interesting information (Kurian, Aurland and Kamalan 1994).

6. Aspects of employment have been extensively discussed in the 'continental overviews' in Chapters 2, 5 and 8. For a recent statement on global developments, see Turnham (1994) and Khan (1994). Lipton (1994) provides a much-needed analysis of the relationship between poverty and labour issues.

References

Chhacchi, A. and R. Pittin (eds) (forthcoming) *Confronting State, Capital and Patriarchy: Women Organising in the Process of Industrialisation*. MacMillan.

de Soto, H. (1989) *The Other Path (The Invisible Revolution in the Third World)*. Harper & Row Publishers, New York.

Elson, D. (ed.) (1991) *Male Bias in Macro-Economics; the Case of Structural Adjustment*. Manchester University Press, Manchester.

Khan, A.R. (1994) 'A Global Agenda for the Expansion of Productive Employment', Discussion Paper. UNDP Stockholm Roundtable. Stockholm.

Kurian, R., E. Aurland and P. Kamalan (1994) 'South East Asia: Integration of Women into Trade Union Organisation', Evaluation Report. ICFTU, Brussels.

Lipton, M. (1994) 'Growing Points in Poverty Research: Labour Issues', Discussion Paper. International Institute of Labour Studies, Geneva.

National Commission on Self-Employed Women and Women in the Informal Sector (1988) 'Report of the Commission'. New Delhi.

Psacharopoulos, G. and Z. Tzannatos (1992) *Women's Employment and Pay in Latin America (Overview and Methodology)*. World Bank, Washington DC.

Rees, T. (1992) *Women and the Labour Market.* Routledge, London.
Rose, K. (1992) *Where Women Are Leaders (The SEWA Movement in India).* Zed Books, London.
Rowbotham, S. and S. Mitter (eds) (1994) *Dignity and Daily Bread (New Forms of Economic Organising Among Poor Women in the Third World and the First).* Routledge, London.
Turnham, D. (1994) 'Employment Creation and Development', Discussion Paper. UNDP Stockholm Roundtable, Stockholm.

Statistical Appendix: Selected Socio-economic Indicators

Table 1. Asia

	A: Basic indicators					B: Labour indicators									C: Social indicators					
	GNP per capita 1992	GNP growth rate 1980–92	Total population 1992	Population growth rate 1992–2000	Urban growth rate 1992–2000	Total labour force 1990–92	Gender composition labour force 1990–92		Sectoral composition labour force 1990–92			Sectoral composition GDP 1992			Life expectancy at birth 1992		Adult literacy Rate 1992		Human Development Index	
							Male	Fem.	Agr.	Ind.	Serv.	Agr.	Ind.	Serv.	Male	Fem.	Male	Fem.	1960	1992
units	US$	%	mln	%	%	mln	%	%	%	%	%	%	%	%	Yrs	Yrs	%	%		
Bangladesh	220	1.8	119.5	2.4	6.2	56.2	59	41	59	13	28	34	17	49	55	56	49	23	0.166	0.309
India	310	3.1	880.1	1.8	3.9	334.4	71	29	62	11	27	32	27	40	61	62	64	35	0.206	0.382
Pakistan	420	3.1	124.9	2.7	4.6	35.0	86	14	47	20	33	27	27	46	59	59	49	22	0.183	0.393
Sri Lanka	540	2.6	17.7	1.2	2.5	7.3	67	33	49	21	30	26	25	49	70	74	94	85	0.475	0.665
Indonesia	670	4.0	191.2	1.7	4.4	82.2	60	40	56	14	30	19	40	40	59	62	91	77	0.223	0.586
Philippines	770	-1.0	65.2	2.0	3.6	36.5	63	37	45	16	39	22	33	45	63	67	90	90	0.419	0.621
Thailand	1,840	6.0	56.1	1.1	4.0	31.4	53	47	67	11	22	12	39	49	67	72	96	92	0.373	0.798
Malaysia	2,790	3.2	18.8	2.1	3.9	7.1	64	36	26	28	46	na	na	na	69	73	89	72	0.330	0.794
Korea	6,790	8.5	44.1	0.8	2.1	26.9	60	40	17	36	47	8	45	47	67	75	99	95	0.398	0.859
Hong Kong	15,360	5.5	5.8	0.7	1.0	2.9	63	37	1	35	64	0	23	77	75	81	na	na	0.561	0.875
Singapore	15,730	5.3	2.8	0.9	1.0	1.8	60	40	0	35	65	0	38	62	72	77	na	na	0.519	0.836
Japan	28,190	3.6	124.5	0.4	0.5	64.7	59	41	7	34	59	2	42	56	76	82	na	na	0.686	0.929

Note: Growth rates are average annual rates.

* The Human Development Index (HDI) was first published by the UNDP in the Human Development Report (1990). The HDI of a country is an unweighted average of the relative distances measured in longevity, education and resources of the population, based on proximate variables such as life expectancy, literacy and income per capita. The UNDP defines a HDI between 0.000 and 0.499 as low human development, 0.500–0.799 as medium human development and 0.800–0.999 as high human development.

Sources: Adapted from UNDP (1994) *Human Development Report 1994.* UNDP, Oxford University Press, Oxford; and World Bank (1994) *World Development Report.* Oxford University Press, Oxford.

Table 2. Latin America

	A: Basic indicators						B: Labour indicators								C: Social indicators					
	GNP per capita 1992	GNP growth rate 1980–92	Total population 1992	Population growth rate 1992–2000	Urban growth rate 1992–2000	Total labour force 1990–92	Gender composition labour force 1990–92		Sectoral composition labour force 1990–92			Sectoral composition GDP 1992			Life expectancy at birth 1992		Adult literacy rate 1992		Human Development Index	
							Male	Fem.	Agr.	Ind.	Serv.	Agr.	Ind.	Serv.	Male	Fem.	Male	Fem.	1960	1992
units	US$	%	mln	%	%	mln	%	%	%	%	%	%	%	%	Yrs	Yrs	%	%		
Bolivia	680	-1.5	7.5	2.3	4.2	2.9	59	41	47	19	34	na	na	na	58	62	86	72	0.308	0.530
Peru	950	-2.8	22.5	2.0	2.7	9.0	61	39	35	12	53	na	na	na	63	67	93	80	0.420	0.642
Ecuador	1,070	-0.3	11.1	2.1	3.7	3.9	74	26	33	19	48	13	39	48	65	69	89	85	0.422	0.718
Colombia	1,330	1.4	33.4	1.6	2.5	15.0	57	43	10	24	66	16	35	49	66	72	88	86	0.469	0.813
Paraguay	1,380	-0.7	4.5	2.6	4.0	1.9	59	41	48	21	31	24	23	52	65	70	93	89	0.474	0.679
Chile	2,730	3.7	13.5	1.5	1.8	5.1	68	32	19	26	55	na	na	na	69	76	95	94	0.584	0.848
Brazil	2,770	0.4	154.0	1.5	2.5	67.8	64	36	25	25	47	11	37	52	64	69	84	81	0.394	0.756
Venezuela	2,910	-0.8	20.2	2.0	2.6	7.5	68	32	13	25	62	5	41	53	67	73	88	91	0.600	0.820
Uruguay	3,340	-1.0	3.1	0.6	0.8	1.4	59	41	5	22	73	11	29	61	69	76	98	97	0.737	0.859
Mexico	3,470	-0.2	88.2	1.9	2.6	33.5	69	31	23	29	48	8	28	63	67	74	91	86	0.517	0.804
Argentina	6,050	-0.9	33.1	1.1	1.4	12.6	72	28	13	34	53	6	31	63	68	75	97	96	0.667	0.853

Notes: Growth rates are average annual rates.

Sources: Adapted from UNDP (1994) *Human Development Report 1994*. UNDP, Oxford University Press, Oxford; and World Bank (1994) *World Development Report*. Oxford University Press, Oxford..

Table 3. Africa

units	GNP per capita 1992 (US$)	GNP growth rate 1980-92 (%)	Total population 1992 (mln)	Population growth rate 1992-2000 (%)	Urban growth rate 1992-2000 (%)	Total labour force 1990-92 (mln)	Gender composition labour force 1990-92 Male (%)	Gender composition labour force 1990-92 Fem. (%)	Sectoral composition labour force 1990-92 Agr. (%)	Sectoral composition labour force 1990-92 Ind. (%)	Sectoral composition labour force 1990-92 Serv. (%)	Sectoral composition GDP 1992 Agr. (%)	Sectoral composition GDP 1992 Ind. (%)	Sectoral composition GDP 1992 Serv. (%)	Life expectancy at birth 1992 Male (Yrs)	Life expectancy at birth 1992 Fem. (Yrs)	Adult literacy rate 1992 Male (%)	Adult literacy rate 1992 Fem. (%)	Human Development Index 1960	Human Development Index 1992
Tanzania	110	0.0	27.9	3.2	7.5	13.1	52	48	85	5	10	61	12	26	49	52	na	na	0.162	0.306
Zaire	220*	na	40.0	3.1	5.0	14.8	64	36	71	13	16	30*	33*	36*	50*	54*	86	63	0.179	0.341
Kenya	310	0.2	25.3	3.3	7.0	10.1	60	40	81	7	12	27	19	54	57	61	82	60	0.192	0.434
Nigeria	320	-0.4	115.9	5.1	5.4	35.9	67	33	48	7	45	37	38	25	50	54	63	41	0.184	0.348
Zambia	420*	na	8.6	2.7	5.5	2.8	71	29	38	8	54	16	47	37	46	49	83	67	0.258	0.352
Ghana	450	-0.1	16.0	2.9	4.6	6.1	60	40	59	11	30	49	16	35	54	58	74	54	0.233	0.382
Zimbabwe	570	-0.9	10.6	2.8	5.4	4.3	52	48	71	8	21	22	35	43	58	61	76	61	0.284	0.474
Senegal	780	0.1	7.8	2.7	4.4	2.7	74	26	81	6	13	19	19	62	48	50	55	26	0.146	0.322
Cameroon	820	-1.5	12.2	2.8	5.7	4.8	70	30	79	7	14	22	30	48	54	58	70	45	0.191	0.447
South Africa	2,670	0.1	39.9	2.3	3.2	15.2	61	39	13	25	62	4	42	54	60	66	na	na	0.464	0.650
Botswana	2,790	6.1	1.3	2.9	7.9	0.4	62	38	28	11	61	5	52	43	66	70	85	66	0.207	0.670

Notes: Growth rates are average annual rates.
* 1990 figures.

Sources: Adapted from UNDP (1994) *Human Development Report 1994*. UNDP, Oxford University Press, Oxford; and World Bank (1994) *World Development Report*. Oxford University Press, Oxford.

Contributors

Charles Amjad-Ali is the Director of the Christian Study Centre in Rawalpindi, Pakistan. He is a member of the Board of the Pakistan Institute for Labour Education and Research (PILER) in Karachi, for which he has conducted several research projects on labour issues. At present he is working on a study on 'Trade Unions and Democracy in Pakistan' for the Friedrich Ebert Stiftung (FES) and PILER.

Amrita Chhacchi is Lecturer in Women and Development Studies at the Institute of Social Studies (ISS) in The Hague. Her research focuses on women workers in industry, and the relationship between labour laws and family laws in India. She is currently director of a project on women workers and organizational strategies in India.

Patricio Frías is a sociologist who has specialized in trade union research. He is senior researcher of the Programa de Economia del Trabajo (PET) institute in Santiago, Chile. He is author of various books on these themes, including *El Movimiento Sindical Chileno en la Lucha por la Democracia 1973–1988*.

Michel Hendriks has been research associate for the preparation of this book and provided editorial assistance. A development economist, he is currently working on aspects of social accounting in a project in Islamabad, Pakistan.

Syed Hussein Ali has retired as Professor of Anthropology and Sociology from the Universiti Malaya in Kuala Lumpur. His books include *Poverty and Landlessness in Kelantan* and (ed.) *Ethnicity, Class and Development in Malaysia*. For several decades he has been a close observer of and researcher into the Malaysian trade union movement.

Kees Koonings studied Anthropology and Comparative Sociology at Utrecht University. His research focuses upon industrialization, development and the state, especially in Brazil. His publications include readers, articles and two books on development, regional industrialization, militarism, technocrats and ethnicity. At present he is acting vice-director of the Centre for Latin American and Caribbean Studies at Utrecht University.

Dirk Kruijt is Professor of Development Studies at Utrecht University. He has published books on the labour movement in transnational mining enclaves, on labour self-management, on the informal economy and society, and on civil war and Latin American armies. From 1988-92 he acted as a policy advisor on Central America, with regard to the informal sector and poverty, to the Netherlands government.

Domingo Mendez-Rivero is presently teaching Macro-economics and Political Theory at the Division of Economic Graduate studies at La Universidad del Zulia (Luz), Venezuela. He has extensive working experience as an advisor on social policies to NGOs and the Department of Labour of the Venezuelan government.

Paschal B.Mihyo is Senior Lecturer in Labour Studies at the ISS in The Hague. He is the author of articles on labour relations and labour law in Africa. His books include *Industrial Conflict and Change in Tanzania* and *Non-Market Controls and the Accountability of Public Enterprises in Tanzania*. Currently he is also Dean of Studies at the ISS in The Hague.

E.A. Ramaswamy has taught at the Delhi School of Economics and the Administrative Staff College of India in Hyderabad. Currently he is visiting professor at the ISS in The Hague. His major recent publications include *Worker Consciousness and Trade Union Response* and *The Rayon Spinners: The Strategic Management of Industrial Relations*.

Jaime Ruiz-Tagle, a sociologist, is executive director of the Programa de Economia del Trabajo (PET) institute in Santiago, Chile. He is the author of various books on trade union movements in Chile and Latin America, and editor of the journal *Economía y Trabajo*.

Freek Schiphorst is Lecturer in Labour Relations in the Employment and Labour Studies Programme at the ISS in The Hague. He is participating in a cooperation project with the Zimbabwe Congress of Trade Unions (ZCTU) for the African Workers' Participation Development Programme at the ISS. Currently he is carrying out a research project on worker representation in Zimbabwe.

Henk Thomas is Professor of Employment and Labour Studies at the ISS in The Hague. His research has covered industrial cooperatives (particularly the Mondragon system), the economics of education, and labour relations in small and informal production. His recent books are (co-edited) *The Other Policy* and (co-edited) *Small-Scale Production*.

Frits Wils is Associate Professor of Sociology at the ISS in The Hague. Currently he is working on problems of income and employment creation, especially in the informal sector. He has undertaken extensive advisory work on and for NGOs, especially in Asia and Latin America.

Index